T0271300

Granularity Theory with Applications to Finance and Insurance

The recent financial crisis has heightened the need for appropriate methodologies for managing and monitoring complex risks in financial markets. The measurement, management, and regulation of risks in portfolios composed of credits, credit derivatives, or life insurance contracts is difficult because of the nonlinearities of risk models, dependencies between individual risks, and the number of contracts in large portfolios. Granularity principle was introduced in the Basel regulations for credit risk to solve these difficulties in computing capital reserves. In this book, authors Patrick Gagliardini and Christian Gouriéroux provide the first comprehensive overview of the granularity theory and illustrate its usefulness for a variety of problems related to risk analysis, statistical estimation, and derivative pricing in finance and insurance. They show how the granularity principle leads to analytical formulas for risk analysis that are simple to implement and accurate even when the portfolio size is large.

Patrick Gagliardini is a full professor of econometrics at Università della Svizzera Italiana, Lugano, Switzerland. He graduated from the ETH in Zürich with a degree in physics in 1998 and received his PhD in economics from the University of Lugano in 2003. He has also served as an assistant professor at the University of St. Gallen. His research interests lie in econometrics and financial econometrics and focus on large-scale factor models, credit risk, asset pricing, and semi- and nonparametric methods. He is the coauthor of research articles published in *Econometrica*, the *Review of Financial Studies*, the *Journal of Econometrics*, and *Econometric Theory*.

Christian Gouriéroux is director of the Laboratory of Finance and Insurance at the Center for Research in Economics and Statistics (CREST) in Paris and a professor at the University of Toronto. He has published numerous papers on both theoretical and applied econometrics, with a special emphasis on credit, finance, insurance, and systemic risk. He is the coauthor of *Statistics and Econometric Models* and *Time Series and Dynamic Models* (Cambridge University Press) and of *Financial Econometrics* and *Econometrics of Individual Risks*. He has also received the Tjalling C. Koopmans Econometric Theory Prize. Gouriéroux was scientific advisor for credit scoring and implementation of the Basel regulations at BNP Paribas. He is a member of the scientific committees of the French Financial Market Authority and the Prudential Supervision and Resolution Authority.

Themes in Modern Econometrics

GRANULARITY THEORY WITH APPLICATIONS TO FINANCE AND INSURANCE

PATRICK GAGLIARDINI
Università della Svizzera Italiana, Switzerland

CHRISTIAN GOURIÉROUX
CREST (Paris) and University of Toronto

CAMBRIDGE UNIVERSITY PRESS

CAMBRIDGE
UNIVERSITY PRESS

University Printing House, Cambridge CB2 8BS, United Kingdom

One Liberty Plaza, 20th Floor, New York, NY 10006, USA

477 Williamstown Road, Port Melbourne, VIC 3207, Australia

314-321, 3rd Floor, Plot 3, Splendor Forum, Jasola District Centre, New Delhi - 110025, India

79 Anson Road, #06-04/06, Singapore 079906

Cambridge University Press is part of the University of Cambridge.

It furthers the University's mission by disseminating knowledge in the pursuit of education, learning and research at the highest international levels of excellence.

www.cambridge.org
Information on this title: www.cambridge.org/9781107662889

First published 2014

A catalogue record for this publication is available from the British Library

Library of Congress Cataloging in Publication data
Gagliardini, Patrick, 1974–
Granularity theory with applications to finance and insurance / Patrick Gagliardini, Christian Gouriéroux.
   pages cm. – (Themes in modern econometrics)
Includes bibliographical references and index.
ISBN 978-1-107-07083-7 (hardback) – ISBN 978-1-107-66288-9 (paperback)
1. Finance – Mathematical models.   2. Insurance – Mathematical models.
I. Gouriéroux, Christian, 1949–   II. Title.
HG106.G34   2015
332.01′51–dc23   2014006682

ISBN 978-1-107-07083-7 Hardback
ISBN 978-1-107-66288-9 Paperback

Contents

Preface

This book provides the first comprehensive overview of granularity theory and illustrates its potential for risk analysis in finance and insurance.

The Granularity Principle

The recent financial crisis has heightened the need for appropriate methodologies to control and regulate risks in financial markets. The balance sheets of banks and insurance companies contain large portfolios of individual risks that correspond to financial securities, such as stocks and corporate or sovereign bonds, as well as individual contracts, such as corporate loans, household mortgages, and life insurance contracts. Risk analysis in such large portfolios is made difficult by the nonlinearities of the risk models, the dependencies between the individual risks, and the large sizes of the portfolios, which can include several thousand assets and contracts. The nonlinearities are induced, for instance, by the qualitative nature of the risks associated with default, rating migration, and prepayment for credit portfolios, or with mortality and lapse for life insurance portfolios. The dependencies between the individual securities and contracts are caused by systematic risk factors that affect the random payoffs of the individual assets. Systematic risks cannot be diversified even when the size of the portfolio becomes infinitely large. The consequence of these difficulties is that standard portfolio risk measures, such as the Value-at-Risk (VaR), cannot be computed analytically for realistic risk models. The portfolio VaR corresponds to the quantile of the portfolio loss distribution at a given percentile level; that is, the loss that is exceeded only with a given small probability. The VaR is currently the basis for the computation of the required capital, and hence of the reserves. Similar difficulties in analytical tractability are encountered when estimating the unknown parameters in risk models and when pricing derivative assets written on large portfolios of individual risks, such as basket default swaps. A basket default swap (BDS) pays off \$1 at maturity, if the percentage of defaults in a large portfolio of loans is larger than a given threshold.

Efficient simulation-based techniques for computing risk measures, estimating model parameters, and pricing basket derivatives have been developed in the literature. However, these techniques can be very time consuming and can be insufficient, for instance, when fast intraday computations of the reserves are required or when investigating the effects on portfolio risk from stress scenarios of model parameters and risk factors. For these tasks, analytical (i.e., closed-form) approximations of the risk quantities of interest provide a valuable input. In this book, we focus on the class of analytical approximations that are derived from the so-called granularity principle.

The granularity principle was introduced in the Basel 2 regulation for credit risk for the purpose of facilitating the internal computation of the reserves by financial institutions. The granularity principle proceeds according to three steps.

1. First, the modeling step considers a risk factor model (RFM) that relates the payoffs/losses of the individual assets in the portfolio to systematic risk factors and unsystematic (i.e., idiosyncratic) risks. Systematic risk factors represent the undiversifiable sources of uncertainty that are common to all individual assets in the portfolio and that introduce dependencies between the individual risks.

2. Second, the RFM is applied to a virtual portfolio of infinite size, which represents the ideal limit of a very large portfolio. In this asymptotic risk factor model (ARFM), all idiosyncratic risks are perfectly diversified, and the only remaining uncertainty governing the individual risks is through systematic risk factors. In general this simplification allows the derivation of explicit formulas for the portfolio risk measures (standardized per unit of contracts in the portfolio) and thus for the required capital. The value of a risk measure for a portfolio of infinite size is called the cross-sectional asymptotic (CSA) risk measure.

3. Third, for the real portfolio with a finite but large size, closed-form approximations of the risk measures are derived by an asymptotic expansion around the ARFM. These approximations are given by the CSA risk measure plus an adjustment term, called the granularity adjustment (GA). The GA is of order $1/n$, where n denotes the number of individual contracts in the portfolio. The GA accounts for the remaining idiosyncratic risks and for their interaction with the systematic risks in a portfolio of finite size.

Very often in practice the third step is omitted in the computation of the reserves. This omission can lead to a significant underestimation of the required capital. In fact, as we see in the illustrations in the book, the GA can contribute to adjustments of several percentage points in the risk measure even for portfolios with thousands of assets, especially in a dynamic multifactor framework.

Although granularity theory was originally motivated by the problem of computing risk measures for large portfolios, the same principle can be followed to address a variety of different but related issues. For instance, it can be applied to estimate the unknown parameters in the RFM using a large panel of individual risk histories, for filtering the unobservable values of systematic risk factors, or for pricing basket derivatives written on large portfolios. For these tasks, the basic concept of performing an asymptotic expansion around a large cross-sectional limit is applied to different objects of interests: a likelihood function, a filtering distribution, and a derivative price. Thus, granularity theory provides a tractable framework for risk analysis of large portfolios that integrates the effects of systematic risks, idiosyncratic risks, uncertainty on the model parameters, and unobservability of the states.

The Terminology

The granularity terminology was introduced by Gordy[1] by analogy with the terminology used in physics or in photography. A system is infinitely fine grained, or granular, if it can be broken down into small parts, or grains, of similar size, such that no grain has a significant effect on the entire system. In the application to credit, the system is a loan portfolio, and the grains are the individual loans. Then, the portfolio is infinitely granular if the loans have similar exposures and there exists no loan carrying a systemic risk. In a probabilistic setting, the individual risks associated with the grains are not necessarily independent. More precisely, in an infinitely fine-grained system the dependencies and heterogeneities across the grains are such that, conditionally on some systematic risk factor, the grains are independent and identically distributed (i.i.d.). This conditional i.i.d. property is more general than what might appear initially because the factor can be dynamic and multidimensional (even infinite-dimensional), and it is compatible with random individual effects. The conditional i.i.d. property allows application of the standard stochastic limit theorems, such as the Law of Large Numbers (LLN) and the Central Limit Theorem (CLT), conditionally on the realization of the systematic risk factors. This property is the key to deriving the asymptotic expansions underlying the granularity principle.

Topics Covered by This Book

This book covers the computation of risk measures, the estimation of model parameters, the prediction of unobservable factors, and the pricing of basket derivatives for a large population of individual risks by means of granularity

[1] Gordy, M. (2003). "A Risk-Factor Model Foundation for Ratings-Based Bank Capital Rules," *Journal of Financial Intermediation*, 12, 199–232.

theory. In each chapter, selected numerical and empirical applications in finance and insurance illustrate the theoretical results. The organization of the material reflects our attempt to present the results in a unifying framework that highlights the methodological similarities among apparently different problems. We also favor a pedagogical exposition – building the theory from the simpler to the more sophisticated setting. These principles explain why the sequence of the topics treated in the various chapters does not reflect the historical development of granularity theory, for instance, the chapter on risk measures is the last one.

Chapter 1 introduces the general modeling framework used throughout this book, namely that of a large homogeneous panel of histories of individual risks. These individual risks correspond to the assets and contracts in a portfolio. We explain the standard stochastic limit theorems – the LLN and the CLT – and why they cannot be applied directly when the individual histories feature dependencies caused by systematic risk factors. However, the infinitely granular nature of a homogeneous population allows us to apply the limit theorems conditionally on the realization of the systematic risk factors. Chapters 2 and 3 consider static RFM (i.e., the systematic and unsystematic risks are i.i.d. across time). Specifically, Chapter 2 introduces the linear static RFM and presents the granularity adjustments for parameter estimation and portfolio management. Chapter 3 considers nonlinear static RFM for qualitative individual risks. An important specification in this class is the single risk factor (SRF) model for default that is based on a multifirm version of the Merton structural model. The individual risk variables correspond to default indicators of the firms, and a systematic risk factor drives the probability of default (PD) of any single firm. We present several empirical illustrations, including the estimation of a factor model for corporate default in the United States, and of a stochastic intensity model for longevity risk on French mortality data.

In Chapters 4–6 we move to dynamic (nonlinear) RFM. We distinguish between the microdynamic – the dependence of the individual risks on their own lagged values conditionally on the factor path – and the macrodynamic, namely the serial persistence of the common factor. Specifically, Chapter 4 focuses on the estimation of the RFM parameters based on a large panel with T time observations for n individuals. Maximum likelihood (ML) estimation in such a nonlinear state space model is complicated because the likelihood function involves a large-dimensional integral with respect to the factor path. We show how the granularity theory leads to asymptotic closed-form approximations of the likelihood function for large cross-sectional dimension n. By maximizing the approximate likelihood function we get easy-to-compute estimators that are asymptotically efficient in a large n and T asymptotics. We illustrate the methodology with an application to estimation of a stochastic migration model for corporate rating using S&P data. In this model, rating migration correlation across firms is introduced by systematic unobservable factors that drive the stochastic transition matrices.

Chapter 5 concerns the prediction and filtering of the unobservable value of the systematic risk factors given the available individual risk histories. The predictive and filtering distributions of the unobservable common factor in a nonlinear state space model are analytically intractable. However, in our framework granularity theory can be used to derive closed-form Gaussian approximations of these distributions for large cross-sectional size. Although the value of the common factor becomes ex-post observable from well-chosen cross-sectional aggregates in the limit of an infinite portfolio size, the granularity adjustment describes the bias and uncertainty on the factor value for finite but large n. This result finds applications for basket derivative pricing. Indeed, the payoff of a basket derivative such as a BDS is written on the portfolio default frequency, which is a proxy of (a transformation of) the systematic risk factor, namely the default probability. We show in Chapter 5 that the pricing of basket derivatives such as BDS can be reduced to the pricing of (fictitious) derivatives written on the value of the systematic risk factor. The approximate pricing of the latter derivatives can be performed under the Gaussian predictive and filtering distributions of the factor.

Chapter 6 focuses on the granularity adjustment for risk measures. We first show that the GA for the VaR is the input to derive the GA for a broad class of risk measures, known as distortion risk measures (DRM), that include, for instance, the expected shortfall (ES). The ES is a coherent risk measure that provides the average loss amount when a loss above the level of VaR occurs. We then derive the GA for the VaR in both the static and dynamic RFM with single or multiple risk factors. In a dynamic RFM, the VaR is a quantile of the conditional portfolio loss distribution given past individual risk histories. The GA consists of two components. The first GA component is an adjustment for the idiosyncratic risk (which is not completely diversified in a portfolio with a large but finite size) and for its interaction with systematic risk. The second GA component accounts for the filtering of the unobservable systematic risk factor from the individual risk histories. We illustrate the patterns and dynamics of the GA with an application to a dynamic model with stochastic default and recovery. This example shows that the GA VaR is larger and features a smoother pattern across time than the CSA VaR. Thus, accounting for GA leads to a larger and more stable level of reserves.

The book is intended for graduate students, researchers, and professionals working in the areas of risk control and regulation. We tried to reach a balance between emphasis on the financial applications motivating this book and on the theoretical tools in probability and econometrics necessary for a sufficiently rigorous presentation of the results. A minimal background in statistics and finance is required at the level of introductory master courses in these subjects. However, two review chapters help the reader reach this level. These chapters cover basic material in econometrics (such as linear panel models, principal component analysis [PCA], and the Kalman filter) and finance theory (such as portfolio management, arbitrage theory, and risk measures).

Instructors who use this book might find it difficult or unnecessary to cover all included material. Selecting certain chapters is possible depending on one's specific purposes. For instance, an introduction to granularity theory at a basic level can be limited to static RFM (Chapters 1–3 and Sections 6.1–6.3). A short course focusing on the granularity adjustment for risk measures can be based on Chapters 1 and 6 and Section 5.1.

Acknowledgments

We thank our colleagues J. Jasiak, A. Monfort, O. Scaillet, and J. M. Zakoian for their joint work on papers related to the topics of this book. We have greatly enjoyed our time spent together on research. We are grateful to M. Gordy for many stimulating discussions on the draft of our book. We thank two referees for very useful comments and suggestions that have improved our work. Finally, we are grateful to our families for their love and support.

List of Acronyms

AAO   absence of arbitrage opportunities
APT   arbitrage pricing theory
ARFM   asymptotic risk factor model
BCBS   Basel Committee on Banking Supervision
BDS   basket default swap
c.d.f.   cumulative distribution function
CDO   collateralized debt obligation
CDS   credit default swap
CLT   Central Limit Theorem
CSA   cross-sectional asymptotic
DRM   distortion risk measure
ELGD   expected loss given default
ES   expected shortfall
GA   granularity adjustment
i.i.d.   independent identically distributed
L&P   loss and profit
LGD   loss given default
LLN   Law of Large Numbers
LSRF   linear single risk factor
ML   maximum likelihood
MLS   mortality linked securities
OLS   ordinary least squares
P&L   profit and loss
PaR   population at risk
PCA   principal component analysis
PD   probability of default
p.d.f.   probability distribution function
RFM   risk factor model
SDF   stochastic discount factor

SRF   single risk factor
SVD   singular value decomposition
VaR   value at risk
VAR   vector autoregression
VGA   variance granularity adjusted

1 The Standard Asymptotic Theorems and Their Limitations

Granularity theory is important because the standard asymptotic theorems, such as the Law of Large Numbers (LLN) and the Central Limit Theorem (CLT), lack robustness in the presence of a common factor. The granularity theory leads to asymptotic approximations that can be applied in such a case. We briefly review in Section 1.1 the standard asymptotic theorems along with their underlying regularity assumptions. In Section 1.2, we modify the standard regularity assumptions by introducing a common unobservable stochastic factor, and we discuss the asymptotic behavior of the sample mean of the observations in a simple example. Finally, in Section 1.3, we extend our analysis and present the general modeling framework in which the granularity theory is applied throughout this book. This framework is characterized by a large homogeneous panel of individual risk histories that are linked through the unobservable common factors representing systematic risk.

1.1 The Basic Asymptotic Theorems

In the basic framework, the asymptotic theorems are presented under a simple set of regularity conditions.

Assumption A.1. *The observations Y_i, $i = 1, \ldots, n$, are independent, identically distributed, with finite second-order moments.*

The observations Y_i can be multidimensional, say with dimension K. The mean of Y_i is a $(K, 1)$ vector denoted by $m = E(Y_i)$, whose components are the expectations of the components of Y_i. The variance-covariance matrix of Y_i is a (K, K) symmetric matrix denoted by $\Sigma = V(Y_i)$. The diagonal elements of matrix Σ are the variances of the components of Y_i, whereas the out-of-diagonal elements of Σ are the covariances between pairs of components of Y_i.

Then, we have the following two theorems [see, e.g., Feller (1968)]:

Theorem 1.1: Law of Large Numbers (LLN). *Under Assumption A.1, the sample mean* $\bar{Y}_n = \frac{1}{n}\sum_{i=1}^{n} Y_i$ *converges almost surely to the theoretical mean* m; *that is,* $\bar{Y}_n \overset{a.s.}{\to} m$, *as* $n \to \infty$.

Theorem 1.2: Central Limit Theorem (CLT). *Under Assumption A.1, the sample mean is asymptotically (multivariate) Gaussian; that is,* $\sqrt{n}(\bar{Y}_n - m) \overset{d}{\to} N(0, \Sigma)$, *where* $\overset{d}{\to}$ *denotes the convergence in distribution as* $n \to \infty$.

Thus, the first term in the asymptotic expansion of the sample mean $\bar{Y}_n$ is deterministic equal to m (by the LLN), whereas the second term is stochastic of order $1/\sqrt{n}$ (by the CLT).

The LLN and CLT are used in statistics and econometrics to prove the consistency and asymptotic normality of maximum likelihood and moment-based estimators under standard regularity assumptions. They can also be used to derive core results in economics and finance theory. As an illustration, let us consider n risky assets $i = 1, \ldots, n$, with a unitary price at date t and returns $Y_{i,t+1}, i = 1, \ldots, n$ over period $(t, t + 1)$. Let us assume that the risky returns satisfy Assumption A.1 with mean m_t and variance Σ_t, and denote $r_{f,t}$ the risk-free return over the same period.

A portfolio including $1/n$ shares of each risky asset has a unitary price at date t and a return over period $(t, t + 1)$ equal to the cross-sectional average return $\bar{Y}_{n,t+1} = \frac{1}{n}\sum_{i=1}^{n} Y_{i,t+1}$. By applying the LLN, we see that $\bar{Y}_{n,t+1}$ tends to m_t. Equivalently, in financial terms, the following proposition holds:

Proposition 1.1. *Under Assumption A.1, the risk is totally eliminated by diversification for a large-sized portfolio.*

Because the (asymptotic) portfolio is risk-free, we deduce by no-arbitrage that $m_t = r_{f,t}$ (see Review B.2 for the definition of no-arbitrage).

Proposition 1.2. *Under Assumption A.1 and no-arbitrage, the (conditional) expected return of the individual assets is equal to the risk-free rate.*

Thus, in an economy satisfying Assumption A.1, the individual assets cannot generate a conditional expected return strictly larger than the risk-free rate. Equivalently, they necessarily pay a zero risk premium.

1.2 A Lack of Robustness to Cross-Sectional Dependence

The LLN and CLT can be extended to sequences of variables satisfying weaker conditions than Assumption A.1; for instance, they can be extended to stationary time series or to variables with heterogeneous distributions. However, the limit theorems can be strongly modified as a result of other changes in the basic assumptions, in particular, those concerning the dependence structure of the observations.

To illustrate the effects of dependence, let us assume that the observations are scalar such that

$$Y_i = F + u_i, \quad i = 1, \ldots, n, \tag{1.1}$$

where $F, u_1, \ldots, u_n$, are independent random variables, $u_1, \ldots, u_n$ have the same distribution with zero-mean and variance σ^2, and F is a random variable with mean μ, variance η^2, and probability density function (pdf) g. The variables Y_i, $i = 1, \ldots, n$ have identical marginal distributions with mean $E(Y_i) = \mu$ and variance $V(Y_i) = \sigma^2 + \eta^2$. However, these variables are dependent because of the common factor F. For instance, the correlation between two observations is $Corr(Y_i, Y_j) = \frac{\eta^2}{\eta^2 + \sigma^2}$, for $i \neq j$. We get a model with equicorrelation, because this correlation does not depend on the selected pair i and j of individuals.

Let us consider the sample mean. We have

$$\bar{Y}_n = \frac{1}{n} \sum_{i=1}^{n} Y_i = F + \frac{1}{n} \sum_{i=1}^{n} u_i.$$

By applying the LLN to the average of the idiosyncratic terms u_i, we deduce the following asymptotic behavior:

Proposition 1.3. *Under factor model (1.1), the sample mean tends to the factor value. In particular this limit is stochastic and different from the common mean* $E(Y_i) = \mu$.

In financial terms, the "idiosyncratic risks" $u_i, i = 1, \ldots, n$ can be diversified, but not the common risk F, which is often called **systematic** or **systemic** risk in the finance literature. Thus, diversification cannot totally eliminate the risk.

Let us now consider the asymptotic distribution of the sample mean of variables Y_i.

(1) If the cross-sectional dimension n is infinite, we have $\lim_{n \to \infty} \bar{Y}_n = F$, and the asymptotic distribution of the sample mean is simply the distribution of the factor F. This analysis with a virtual sample of infinite size corresponds to the **cross-sectional asymptotic** (CSA) analysis.

(2) If n is large but finite, we obtain a more accurate approximation of the distribution of the sample mean by applying the CLT to the variables

$u_1, \ldots, u_n$, conditional on factor F. Conditional on factor F, we have approximately

$$\bar{Y}_n | F \overset{d}{\sim} N(F, \sigma^2/n).$$

Then, we can integrate out the unobservable factor to get the approximate pdf of $\bar{Y}_n$ as

$$h_n(y) = \int \frac{1}{\sqrt{2\pi \sigma^2/n}} \exp\left[-\frac{n(y-f)^2}{2\sigma^2}\right] g(f)df,$$

that is, a mixture of Gaussian distributions with different means and the same variance σ^2/n. By changing the variable from f to $z = \sqrt{n}(y-f)/\sigma$, applying a second-order Taylor expansion, and using the symmetry of the Gaussian distribution, we obtain

$$h_n(y) = \int \frac{1}{\sqrt{2\pi}} \exp\left(-\frac{1}{2}z^2\right) g(y - \sigma z/\sqrt{n})dz$$

$$= g(y) + \frac{\sigma^2}{2n}g''(y) + o(1/n). \tag{1.2}$$

When $n \to \infty$, the density h_n tends to g, which corresponds to limiting case (1). For finite n, the leading term in the difference $h_n(y) - g(y)$ is of order $1/n$ and is given by $\frac{\sigma^2}{2n}g''(y)$. It involves the idiosyncratic volatility and the second-order derivative of the density of the common factor. This term is the **granularity adjustment** (GA) and accounts for the residual fluctuations in the sample mean caused by the idiosyncratic disturbances with finite cross-sectional dimension n.

To illustrate the magnitude and pattern of the granularity adjustment, we display in Figure 1.1 the pdf of the sample mean $\bar{Y}_n$ in model (1.1) where the systematic risk factor F admits a standard Gaussian $N(0, 1)$ distribution and the idiosyncratic shocks u_i have a Student t_3 distribution. We consider cross-sectional dimensions $n = 5$, $n = 20$, and $n = 100$.[1]

As expected, the pdf becomes more concentrated as n increases, because the idiosyncratic risks are diversifiable. Even for large n, the sample mean $\bar{Y}_n$ remains stochastic, and its distribution approaches the standard Gaussian distribution of the systematic factor. The granularity adjustment is positive (resp. negative) in the domain of convexity (resp. concavity) of the standard Gaussian pdf, as suggested by the formula in equation (1.2).

These derivations in the linear factor model (1.1) rely on the application of the standard LLN and CLT conditional on factor F. When the conditional

---

[1] The pdf is computed by kernel estimation on a simulated sample of $\bar{Y}_n$ with sample size $S = 10,000$.

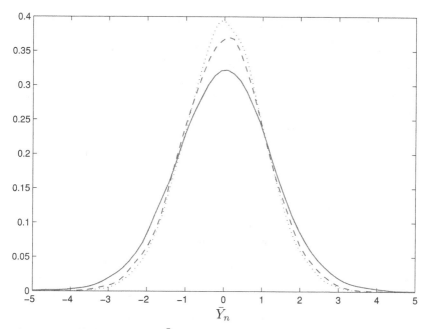

Figure 1.1. Pdf of Sample Mean $\bar{Y}_n$ in a Linear Single-Factor Model. The figure displays the pdf of the sample mean $\bar{Y}_n$ in the linear single-factor model (1.1), where $F \sim N(0, 1)$ and $u_i \sim t_3$. The solid, dashed, and dotted lines correspond to cross-sectional sizes $n = 5$, $n = 20$, and $n = 100$, respectively.

application of the asymptotic theorems is possible, the model is said to be **infinitely granular** or **infinitely fine grained**. The granularity terminology was introduced by Gordy (2003) by analogy with the terminology used in physics, or photography; see also Wilde (2001) and Martin and Wilde (2002). A system is fine grained if it can be broken down into small parts, or grains, of similar size, such that no grain has a significant effect on the entire system. In the linear factor (1.1), model, similar conditions are satisfied by the set of individual risks represented by the variables Y_i. Indeed, these variables are symmetric, and each contributes with weight $1/n$ to the sample mean. As we see in the next section, this symmetry between individuals, called exchangeability, is sufficient to allow for the conditional application of the limit theorems.[2]

---

[2] The term "granularity hypothesis" was introduced recently in a paper by Gabaix (2011) to analyze the fluctuations of the GDP. This granular hypothesis is satisfied if an idiosyncratic shock to a large firm (grain) has the potential to generate fluctuations at the macro level. It is also satisfied if there is a large heterogeneity in the sizes of the grains; that is, if the system is not infinitely fine grained. In the standard Basel terminology, such heterogeneous grains create the concentration risk.

1.3 Panel Data Models with Systematic Risk Factors

In this section, we extend the analysis in the previous example to a general framework where the observations are the histories of n individual risks. The key notion in this framework is that of a homogeneous population. We relate this notion to the possibility of representing the observations by a panel data model with a common risk factor. Then, we describe the associated dynamics either in a nonlinear state space framework or by means of the transition densities (see Appendix 1.5).

1.3.1 Homogeneous Population

The difference between model (1.1) and the i.i.d. Assumption A.1 is the dependence between observations, which is the same across any pair. This leads to the definition of an exchangeable, or homogeneous, set of variables.

Definition 1.1. *A set of variables* Y_i, $i = 1, \ldots, n$ *is **exchangeable** (or **homogeneous**) if and only if the distribution of* $Y_1, \ldots, Y_n$ *is the same as the distribution of* $Y_{\sigma(1)}, \ldots, Y_{\sigma(n)}$, *for any permutation* $\sigma(\cdot)$ *of the set of indexes.*

The notion of exchangeability is also valid for a set of individual histories $Y_i = (y_{i,1}, \ldots, y_{i,t}, \ldots)$, $i = 1, \ldots, n$. The history Y_i gathers the observations for individual i over a period of time. Thus, the observations $y_{i,t}$ are doubly indexed by individual i and date t. This kind of data is called panel data (see the review Appendix A.3).

Loosely speaking, the exchangeability condition requires that all the individuals are equivalent. This condition is satisfied for an i.i.d. sequence of variables, but it is also compatible with a specific form of dependence (called **equidependence**) between the variables, as seen in model (1.1).

A representation theorem for an exchangeable (homogeneous) set of variables was first derived by de Finetti (1931) and extended by Hewitt and Savage (1955). We provide next the version of this theorem appropriate for panel data models.

Theorem 1.3: Factor Representation of an Infinite Set of Exchangeable Histories ($n = \infty$). *The infinite set of histories* $Y_i = (y_{i,t}, t \in I\!N)$, $i = 1, 2, \ldots$, *is exchangeable if and only if there exists an underlying factor process* $F = (F_t, t \in I\!N)$ *such that the individual processes* $Y_1, \ldots, Y_n$, *are i.i.d. conditional on process* F, *for any natural number* n.

The underlying factor process is generally multidimensional. Theorem 1.3 implies that a homogeneous (exchangeable) set of histories is such that the standard LLN and CLT can generally be applied, but are conditional on the factor path (F_t). Thus, this set is infinitely fine grained according to the terminology introduced in Section 1.2.

1.3.2 Homogenous Dynamic Panel Data Models

In the rest of the book, we generally consider a homogeneous set of individual histories with **state space dynamics**. In terms of autoregressive equations of order 1, these models can be written as follows:[3]

$$\text{State equation: } F_t = a(F_{t-1}, \eta_t), \tag{1.3}$$

$$\text{Measurement equations: } y_{i,t} = c(y_{i,t-1}, F_t, \varepsilon_{i,t}), \quad i = 1, \ldots, n, \tag{1.4}$$

where η_t, $t \in I\!N$ and $\varepsilon_{i,t}$, $i = 1, \ldots, n$, $t \in I\!N$ are i.i.d standard Gaussian vectors. Thus, the dynamics of the individual histories $(y_{i,t})$, $i = 1, \ldots, n$ are defined in two steps. First, for a fixed factor path, there is an individual dynamic, or **microdynamic**, defined by autoregression (1.4). This microdynamic is driven by the idiosyncratic disturbances $\varepsilon_{i,t}$ and features serial persistence by means of the lagged individual observation. Then, the common factor also influences the individual histories and introduces cross-sectional dependency. In the second step, the dynamic of the common factor, or **macro-dynamic**, is defined by the autoregression (1.3).

Functions a and c can be nonlinear, which will induce complicated serial dependence and codependence between the variables. However, model (1.3)–(1.4) is tractable, because the joint process $(F_t, y_{1,t}, \ldots, y_{n,t})$ depends on the past by lagged values of order 1 only, which is the Markov assumption on this joint process.

In finance and insurance applications, the individual risk histories correspond, for instance, to the returns of the stocks in an equity portfolio, the default and prepayment histories in a credit portfolio of corporate loans, or the individual mortality and lapse histories in a portfolio of life insurance contracts. Depending on the type of data, special cases of model (1.3)–(1.4) are considered. For instance, the "standard approach" of Basel 2 regulation [4] suggests a **static model**; that is a model without micro- or macro-dynamics and with a Gaussian factor, such as

$$\text{State equation: } F_t = \eta_t, \tag{1.5}$$

$$\text{Measurement equations: } y_{i,t} = c(F_t, \varepsilon_{i,t}), \quad i = 1, \ldots, n. \tag{1.6}$$

For this static framework, we introduce in Chapters 2 and 3 linear and nonlinear specifications of the measurement equations that are appropriate to describe

---

[3] They can equivalently be written in terms of transition distributions (see Appendix 1.5). In the following chapters, we use either one or the other representation.

[4] The Basel 2 regulation allows for a choice between a basic risk analysis, called the **standard approach**, and more sophisticated ones, called the **advanced approach**. Ceteris paribus, the required capital is higher under the standard approach. In our framework, an advanced approach may consider dynamic multiple factors, for instance.

8   Granularity Theory with Applications to Finance and Insurance

stock returns and corporate default histories, respectively. In a dynamic framework, the standard **Gaussian linear state space model**, which underlies the
implementation of the linear Kalman filter, assumes the following:

$$\text{State equation: } F_t = \Phi F_{t-1} + \eta_t, \tag{1.7}$$

$$\text{Measurement equations: } y_{i,t} = \alpha + \beta' F_t + \varepsilon_{i,t}, \quad i = 1, \ldots, n. \tag{1.8}$$

In the Gaussian linear state space model, the entire dynamic passes through the
common factor, and this dynamic corresponds to a Gaussian **vector autoregressive** (VAR) model. Relevant specifications of linear and nonlinear dynamic
panel factor models are introduced in Chapters 4–6.

Throughout this book, the focus is on how to measure and analyze the
risks on homogeneous classes of assets by means of granularity theory. This
means that exchangeable dynamic panel data models with common factors are
applied on homogeneous subportfolios, after an appropriate segmentation of the
original portfolio has been performed. Explaining how to best construct these
homogeneous subpopulations is beyond the scope of our book. Nevertheless,
let us briefly discuss the basic Basel 2 regulation for corporate risks. The
number of companies available in the internal databases of a bank can be very
large, up to several hundred thousand. Of course, these companies differ in
several ways, and so the regulator asks that the population be segmented into
more homogeneous classes defined by crossing at least domicile country ×
industrial sector × rating category. After this segmentation, the sizes of the
more homogeneous subpopulations will range from several dozen to several
thousand. Thus, it will be important to examine the accuracy of the asymptotic
approximations given by granularity theory for this range of subpopulation size.
The degree of accuracy will depend on the problem of interest, the available
data, and the selected model.

1.4 Summary

In a homogeneous population, the joint dynamics of the individual histories
can always be represented by means of unobservable dynamic factors. When
the dynamic of the full vector of common factor and individual observations
$(F_t, y_{i,t}, i = 1, \ldots, n)$ admits an autoregressive state space representation, the
model is easy to simulate, and the cross-sectional asymptotic analysis is easy
to interpret, as seen in the following chapters. Moreover, the standard limit
theorems (LLN and CLT) can still be applied by conditioning on the factor
path.

1.5 Appendix: Autoregression and Transition Density

In this appendix, we explain how the nonlinear state space representation of a panel data model with common factor (Section 1.3) can be equivalently written in terms of transition densities of the individual processes and the common factor.

1.5.1 One-Dimensional Continuously Valued Process

Let us consider a one-dimensional Markov process (F_t) with continuous distribution, and denote by $H(f_t|f_{t-1}) = P[F_t \leq f_t|F_{t-1} = f_{t-1}]$ its transition **cumulative distribution function** (c.d.f.). We have the following lemma (see also Appendix A, Review A.1):

Lemma 1.1. *The variable $\eta_t^* = H(F_t|F_{t-1})$ is independent of F_{t-1} and follows a uniform distribution on $(0, 1)$.*

Proof. We have

$$P[\eta_t^* \leq u|F_{t-1} = f_{t-1}] = P[H(F_t|F_{t-1}) \leq u|F_{t-1} = f_{t-1}]$$

$$= P[F_t \leq H^{-1}(u|f_{t-1})|F_{t-1} = f_{t-1}]$$

$$= H[H^{-1}(u|f_{t-1})|f_{t-1}] = u, \quad \forall u \in (0, 1),$$

where $H^{-1}(u|f_{t-1})$ denotes the inverse of $H(f|f_{t-1})$ with respect to f. The result follows, because $G(u) = u$ is the c.d.f. of the uniform distribution on $(0, 1)$.

QED

Thus, $\eta_t = \Phi^{-1}(\eta_t^*)$, where Φ is the c.d.f. of a standard Gaussian distribution, is also independent of F_{t-1} and is $N(0, 1)$ distributed. We have $\eta_t = \Phi^{-1}[H(F_t|F_{t-1})]$. We deduce the autoregressive representation:

$$F_t = H^{-1}[\Phi(\eta_t)|F_{t-1}] = a(F_{t-1}, \eta_t), \quad \text{(say)},$$

with Gaussian innovation. This type of result can be extended not only to multivariate processes but also to discrete or qualitative processes [see, e.g., Gouriéroux and Monfort (1996), Section 1.4, and the references therein].

1.5.2 The Exchangeable Dynamics in Terms of Distributions

Let us introduce the information available at time $t - 1$:

$$J_{t-1} = (F_{t-1}, y_{1,t-1}, \ldots, y_{n,t-1}, F_{t-2}, y_{1,t-2}, \ldots, y_{n,t-2}, \ldots).$$

By applying Lemma 1.1, we see that the following conditions are equivalent to equations (1.3)–(1.4):

- *State equation:* The conditional distribution of F_t given J_{t-1} depends on the past by means of lagged factor value F_{t-1} only. The transition density of the factor is denoted by $g(f_t|f_{t-1})$.
- *Measurement equations:* Conditional on (J_{t-1}, F_t), the variables $y_{1,t}, \ldots, y_{n,t}$ are independent. The conditional distribution of $y_{i,t}$ given (J_{t-1}, F_t) depends on $(y_{i,t-1}, F_t)$ only, and this dependence is identical for all individuals. The conditional pdf is denoted by $h(y_{i,t}|y_{i,t-1}, f_t)$, with function h independent of individual i.

1.5.3 The Joint Distribution of the Individual Histories

We deduce the joint density of $(F_t, y_{1,t}, \ldots, y_{n,t}, t = 1, \ldots, T)$ given the initial values $f_0, y_{1,0}, \ldots, y_{n,0}$. It is given by

$$\prod_{t=1}^{T} \left\{ \left(\prod_{i=1}^{n} h(y_{i,t}|y_{i,t-1}, f_t) \right) g(f_t|f_{t-1}) \right\}.$$

Then, by integrating out the unobservable factor path, we get the joint density of the individual histories only (given J_0) as

$$\int \cdots \int \prod_{t=1}^{T} \left\{ \left(\prod_{i=1}^{n} h(y_{i,t}|y_{i,t-1}, f_t) \right) g(f_t|f_{t-1}) \right\} \prod_{t=1}^{T} df_t.$$

This joint density involves an integral of a very large dimension (i.e., a dimension equal to the number of dates multiplied by the number of common factors), which explains the need for tractable approximations of this density. This is a latent variables problem that is commonly encountered in finance, for instance in models with stochastic volatility. In Chapter 4, we present asymptotic closed-form approximations of the log-likelihood function based on expansions for large cross-sectional dimension n.

References

de Finetti, B. (1931). "Funzione Caratteristica di un Fenomeno Aleotorio," *Atti della R. Accademia dei Lincei, 6, Memorie, Classe di Scienze Fisiche, Mathematiche e Naturali*, 4, 251–299.
Feller, W. (1968). *An Introduction to Probability Theory and Its Applications*, Wiley.
Gabaix, X. (2011). "The Granular Origins of Aggregate Fluctuations," *Econometrica*, 79, 733–772.
Gordy, M. (2003). "A Risk-Factor Model Foundation for Ratings-Based Bank Capital Rules," *Journal of Financial Intermediation*, 12, 199–232.

Gouriéroux, C., and A. Monfort (1996). *Simulation Based Econometric Methods*, Oxford University Press.

Hewitt, E., and L. Savage (1955). "Symmetric Measures on Cartesian Products," *Transactions of the American Mathematical Society*, 80, 470–501.

Martin, R., and T. Wilde (2002). "Unsystematic Credit Risk," *Risk*, November, 123–128.

Wilde, T. (2001). "Probing Granularity," *Risk*, 14, 103–106.

2 Gaussian Static Factor Models

The linear static factor model with Gaussian errors is a benchmark in panel data econometrics [see, e.g., Rao (1971); Harville (1977)], portfolio management [Markowitz (1952); Lintner (1968)], and arbitrage pricing theory [APT; Ross (1976, 1982); Chamberlain and Rothschild (1983)]. This type of panel data model is analyzed in this chapter. In Section 2.1, we discuss the model and its structure. Then we make explicit the granularity adjustment for the estimation of micro- and macro-parameters in Section 2.2. Granularity adjustment for portfolio management is considered in Section 2.3. For both applications to estimation and portfolio management, we discuss the introduction of individual heterogeneity in the basic exchangeable model.

2.1 The Model

The panel data model considered in this section is known in the literature as the **variance-component**, or **random effects**, model.[1] Its simplest version allows for a closed-form expression of the maximum likelihood estimator, which is easy to interpret and analyze [see, e.g., Searle (1971)].

2.1.1 The Regressions

Let us first introduce the state and measurement equations [see equations (1.3)–(1.4)]. We assume scalar observations $y_{i,t}$ and factor F_t, and impose a linear static structure. Then, the state equation is

$$F_t = u_t, \tag{2.1}$$

---

[1] In the panel literature, random effects refer to either individual-specific or period-specific stochastic components in the error term of a regression model [see, e.g., Baltagi (1995) and Appendix A, Review Appendix A.3]. It is the second type of random effects, namely time effects, that we consider in this chapter.

whereas the measurement equations are

$$y_{i,t} = F_t + \varepsilon_{i,t}, \quad i = 1, \ldots, n, \tag{2.2}$$

where (u_t) and $(\varepsilon_{i,t})$ are i.i.d. Gaussian variables, $u_t \sim N(\mu, \eta^2)$ and $\varepsilon_{i,t} \sim N(0, \sigma^2)$, mutually independent. Note that the errors in both the state and measurement equations have not been standardized and that the error in the state equation is not zero-mean.

The model (2.1)–(2.2) is called the Gaussian **linear single risk factor** (LSRF) model. It involves two types of parameters: μ and η^2 are macro-parameters associated with the common factor, whereas σ^2 is a micro-parameter summarizing the individual (or idiosyncratic) risk. We discuss later the micro- or macro-interpretations of these parameters. The model (2.1)–(2.2) was used early in the literature on risky individual contracts. Indeed, this is the Buhlmann model considered in actuarial science, which is the basis for **credibility theory** [Buhlmann (1967); Buhlmann and Straub (1970)].

2.1.2 First- and Second-Order Moments

Let us denote by $\tilde{y}_t = (y_{1,t}, \ldots, y_{n,t})'$ the vector of individual observations at date t. The random vector $\tilde{y}_t$ is Gaussian, with mean

$$E(\tilde{y}_t) = \mu e, \tag{2.3}$$

where e is the $(n, 1)$ vector with unitary components $e = (1, \ldots, 1)'$. The variance-covariance matrix of $\tilde{y}_t$ is

$$V(\tilde{y}_t) = \sigma^2 Id + \eta^2 ee' = \Omega, \text{ say,} \tag{2.4}$$

whereas the random vectors $\tilde{y}_t$ and $\tilde{y}_{t'}$ corresponding to two different dates t and t' are independent. The dependence between individual observations at the same date (i.e., the cross-dependence) is captured by the term $\eta^2 ee'$ in the variance-covariance matrix, which makes Ω nondiagonal.

It is interesting to analyze more deeply the structure of the variance-covariance matrix Ω. The matrix $M_1 = ee'/n$ (resp. $M_2 = Id - ee'/n$) is the orthogonal projector on the one-dimensional linear space generated by vector e [resp. on the $(n-1)$-dimensional linear space orthogonal to the space generated by vector e]. Recall that a matrix M is an orthogonal projector if and only if it is symmetric and idempotent; that is, $M' = M$ and $M^2 = M$. The variance-covariance matrix can be decomposed in terms of orthogonal projectors as follows:

$$\Omega = \sigma^2 \left(Id - \frac{ee'}{n} \right) + \lambda^2 \frac{ee'}{n}, \tag{2.5}$$

with

$$\lambda^2 = \sigma^2 + n\eta^2. \tag{2.6}$$

The decomposition (2.5) can be used to derive the **spectral decomposition**[2] and the inverse of matrix Ω (see Appendix 2.5).

Proposition 2.1. (i) *The matrix Ω admits as eigenvalues σ^2, with multiplicity order $n - 1$, and λ^2 with multiplicity order 1. The eigenspace associated with λ^2 is the space $\mathcal{E}$ generated by the vector e. The eigenspace associated with σ^2 is the vector space $\mathcal{E}^\perp$ orthogonal to $\mathcal{E}$. In particular, $\det \Omega = (\sigma^2)^{n-1}\lambda^2$.*
(ii) *The inverse of Ω is*

$$\Omega^{-1} = \frac{1}{\sigma^2}(Id - \frac{ee'}{n}) + \frac{1}{\lambda^2}\frac{ee'}{n}.$$

2.1.3 The Cross-Sectional Distribution of the Observations

In terms of the transition and measurement pdf's [see Appendix 1.5.2], model (2.1)–(2.2) can be specified as

$$g(f_t; \mu, \eta^2) = \frac{1}{\sqrt{2\pi\eta^2}} \exp\left\{-\frac{(f_t - \mu)^2}{2\eta^2}\right\} \tag{2.7}$$

and

$$h(y_{it}|f_t; \sigma^2) = \frac{1}{\sqrt{2\pi\sigma^2}} \exp\left\{-\frac{(y_{i,t} - f_t)^2}{2\sigma^2}\right\}. \tag{2.8}$$

Thus, the density of $\tilde{y}_t$ is [see Appendix 1.5.3]

$$l(\tilde{y}_t; \sigma^2, \mu, \eta^2)$$

$$= \int \prod_{i=1}^{n} h(y_{i,t}|f_t; \sigma^2) g(f_t; \mu, \eta^2) df_t$$

$$= \int \frac{1}{(2\pi\sigma^2)^{n/2}} \exp\left\{-\frac{1}{2\sigma^2}\sum_{i=1}^{n}(y_{i,t} - f_t)^2\right\}$$

$$\times \frac{1}{\sqrt{2\pi\eta^2}} \exp\left\{-\frac{1}{2\eta^2}(f_t - \mu)^2\right\} df_t. \tag{2.9}$$

This joint pdf has a simplified expression, which can be derived directly by noting that the vector $\tilde{y}_t$ is Gaussian $\tilde{y}_t \sim N(\mu e, \Omega)$ [see Section 2.1.2]. We deduce that

$$l(\tilde{y}_t; \sigma^2, \mu, \eta^2) = \frac{1}{(2\pi)^{n/2}(\det\Omega)^{1/2}} \exp\left\{-\frac{1}{2}(\tilde{y}_t - \mu e)'\Omega^{-1}(\tilde{y}_t - \mu e)\right\}.$$

---

[2] The spectral decomposition of a matrix is the set of its eigenvalues and associated eigenvectors.

By Proposition 2.1, we know that

$$\det \Omega = (\sigma^2)^{n-1}\lambda^2, \qquad \Omega^{-1} = \frac{1}{\sigma^2}(Id - \frac{ee'}{n}) + \frac{1}{\lambda^2}\frac{ee'}{n}.$$

We deduce

$$l(\tilde{y}_t; \sigma^2, \mu, \lambda^2)$$

$$= \frac{1}{(2\pi)^{n/2}(\sigma^2)^{\frac{n-1}{2}}(\lambda^2)^{1/2}} \exp\left\{-\frac{1}{2\sigma^2}(\tilde{y}_t - \mu e)'(Id - \frac{ee'}{n})(\tilde{y}_t - \mu e)\right.$$

$$\left. - \frac{1}{2\lambda^2}(\tilde{y}_t - \mu e)'\frac{ee'}{n}(\tilde{y}_t - \mu e)\right\}.$$

This likelihood is written in terms of the new parameter λ^2, which involves the number n of cross-sectional observations [see equation (2.6)]. Because $(Id - \frac{ee'}{n})e = 0$, we obtain

$$l(\tilde{y}_t; \sigma^2, \mu, \lambda^2) = \frac{1}{(2\pi)^{n/2}(\sigma^2)^{\frac{n-1}{2}}(\lambda^2)^{1/2}} \exp\left\{-\frac{1}{2\sigma^2}\tilde{y}_t'(Id - \frac{ee'}{n})\tilde{y}_t\right.$$

$$\left. - \frac{1}{2\lambda^2}\frac{1}{n}[e'(\tilde{y}_t - \mu e)]^2\right\}.$$

Let us now introduce the following cross-sectional summary statistics of the panel data:

$$\bar{y}_t = \frac{1}{n}\sum_{i=1}^{n} y_{i,t} \tag{2.10}$$

is the cross-sectional sample mean of the individual data, and

$$\sigma_t^2 = \frac{1}{n}\sum_{i=1}^{n}(y_{i,t} - \bar{y}_t)^2 \tag{2.11}$$

is its cross-sectional variance. It is easily checked that

$$e'(\tilde{y}_t - \mu e) = n(\bar{y}_t - \mu), \tag{2.12}$$

$$\tilde{y}_t'(Id - \frac{ee'}{n})\tilde{y}_t = n\sigma_t^2. \tag{2.13}$$

By substituting in the expression of the pdf, we get

$$l(\tilde{y}_t; \sigma^2, \mu, \lambda^2)$$

$$= \frac{1}{(2\pi)^{n/2}(\sigma^2)^{(n-1)/2}(\lambda^2)^{1/2}} \exp\left\{-\frac{n}{2\sigma^2}\sigma_t^2 - \frac{n}{2\lambda^2}(\bar{y}_t - \mu)^2\right\}. \tag{2.14}$$

We come to the central result of this subsection: the pair $(\bar{y}_t, \sigma_t^2)$ defined in (2.10)–(2.11) is a sufficient statistic to capture all the information contained in the observations of date t.

2.2 Estimation and Prediction

2.2.1 Maximum Likelihood (ML) Estimators

From the simplified expression (2.14) of the cross-sectional pdf, we deduce the log-likelihood function:

$$\mathcal{L}_{n,T}(\sigma^2, \mu, \lambda^2) = \sum_{t=1}^{T} \log l(\bar{y}_t; \sigma^2, \mu, \lambda^2)$$

$$= -\frac{nT}{2}\log(2\pi) - \frac{T(n-1)}{2}\log\sigma^2 - \frac{T}{2}\log\lambda^2$$

$$- \frac{n}{2\sigma^2}\sum_{t=1}^{T}\sigma_t^2 - \frac{n}{2\lambda^2}\sum_{t=1}^{T}(\bar{y}_t - \mu)^2. \qquad (2.15)$$

The maximum likelihood (ML) estimators are obtained by maximizing this log-likelihood function with respect to the parameters. The maximization can be first performed with respect to the mean parameter μ. The first-order condition is

$$\frac{\partial \mathcal{L}_{n,T}}{\partial \mu}(\sigma^2, \mu, \lambda^2) = 0$$

$$\Longleftrightarrow \sum_{t=1}^{T}(\bar{y}_t - \mu) = 0$$

$$\Longleftrightarrow \mu = \frac{1}{T}\sum_{t=1}^{T}\bar{y}_t. \qquad (2.16)$$

Let us now introduce the following additional summary statistics of the observations:

$$\bar{\bar{y}} = \frac{1}{nT}\sum_{t=1}^{T}\sum_{i=1}^{n} y_{i,t} \qquad (2.17)$$

is the sample average over all observations;

$$B(y) = \frac{1}{T}\sum_{t=1}^{T}(\bar{y}_t - \bar{\bar{y}})^2 \qquad (2.18)$$

is the variance **between** the cross-sectional averages of different dates; and

$$W(y) = \frac{1}{T}\sum_{t=1}^{T}\sigma_t^2 \qquad (2.19)$$

is the sample average of the variances **within** dates.

From equation (2.16), the ML estimator of the mean parameter is

$$\hat{\mu}_{n,T} = \bar{\bar{y}}. \qquad (2.20)$$

Then, the log-likelihood can be concentrated with respect to parameter μ. The concentrated log-likelihood – that is, the log-likelihood preliminarily optimized with respect to μ – is

$$\mathcal{L}_{n,T}^c(\sigma^2,\lambda^2) = -\frac{nT}{2}\log(2\pi) - \frac{T(n-1)}{2}\log\sigma^2 - \frac{T}{2}\log\lambda^2$$
$$- \frac{nT}{2\sigma^2}W(y) - \frac{nT}{2\lambda^2}B(y). \qquad (2.21)$$

This concentrated log-likelihood is the sum of a function of σ^2 and a function of λ^2. Therefore, the optimizations with respect to these parameters can be performed separately. We get

$$\hat{\sigma}_{n,T}^2 = \frac{n}{n-1}W(y), \qquad (2.22)$$

$$\hat{\lambda}_{n,T}^2 = nB(y). \qquad (2.23)$$

The ML estimator of η^2 is deduced by using its definition given in equation (2.6).

These results are summarized in the following proposition:

Proposition 2.2. *The maximum likelihood estimators of the parameters are*

$$\hat{\mu}_{n,T} = \bar{\bar{y}}, \qquad \hat{\sigma}_{n,T}^2 = \frac{n}{n-1}W(y), \qquad \hat{\eta}_{n,T}^2 = B(y) - \frac{W(y)}{n-1}.$$

Thus, the ML estimators of the parameters have closed-form expressions in the basic variance component model. They are functions of the full sample empirical mean and of the within and between variances. Their properties are deduced from the properties of these three summary statistics.

2.2.2 Asymptotic Behavior and Granularity Adjustment

As usual in panel data models, there exist different settings for asymptotic analysis, because we can have either n large, T large, or both n and T large. The appropriate asymptotic setting depends on the application and the available data. In the applications in which we are interested, the individual observations typically concern financial assets, contracts, or companies, and the number n can be of the order of several thousands. The order of the time dimension T is related to the frequency of the observations. The number of dates can be about 20–50 with yearly data (e.g., for corporate rating histories) or of the order of several hundreds with monthly data (e.g., for households mortgages).

Let us assume that the time and cross-sectional dimensions T and n are both large, and let us focus on the effect of n to analyze the granularity adjustment.

(*) The ML estimator of μ can be decomposed as

$$\hat{\mu}_{n,T} = \frac{1}{nT}\sum_{t=1}^{T}\sum_{i=1}^{n}(F_t + \varepsilon_{it}) = \frac{1}{T}\sum_{t=1}^{T}F_t + \frac{1}{nT}\sum_{t=1}^{T}\sum_{i=1}^{n}\varepsilon_{it}. \quad (2.24)$$

Thus,

$$\hat{\mu}_{n,T} - \mu = \frac{1}{T}\sum_{t=1}^{T}(F_t - \mu) + \frac{1}{nT}\sum_{t=1}^{T}\sum_{i=1}^{n}\varepsilon_{i,t}. \quad (2.25)$$

The first term in decomposition (2.25) is Gaussian, zero-mean, with order $1/\sqrt{T}$, whereas the second term is Gaussian, zero-mean, with order $1/\sqrt{nT}$. Moreover, the two terms are independent. We have

$$V(\hat{\mu}_{n,T}) = \frac{\eta^2}{T} + \frac{\sigma^2}{nT}. \quad (2.26)$$

When $n = \infty$, only the first term matters, and the speed of convergence of the estimator of μ corresponds to the number of observation dates T, which is compatible with the interpretation of μ as a macro-parameter. In fact, in the limit case of an infinite cross-sectional size n, from equation (2.24) we see that the estimator $\hat{\mu}_{n,T}$ corresponds to the empirical average of the factor values. When n is large but finite, the second term in the decomposition (2.26) provides the necessary adjustment for the cross-sectional effect; that is, the granularity adjustment for the variance of the estimator.

(**) The ML estimator of σ^2 can be written as

$$\hat{\sigma}_{n,T}^2 = \frac{n}{n-1}\frac{1}{T}\sum_{t=1}^{T}\left[\frac{1}{n}\sum_{i=1}^{n}(y_{i,t} - \bar{y}_t)^2\right]$$

$$= \frac{n}{n-1}\frac{1}{T}\sum_{t=1}^{T}\left[\frac{1}{n}\sum_{i=1}^{n}(\varepsilon_{i,t} - \bar{\varepsilon}_t)^2\right]$$

$$= \frac{n}{n-1}W(\varepsilon).$$

Because the idiosyncratic errors are i.i.d. Gaussian, the variables $\sum_{i=1}^{n}(\varepsilon_{i,t} - \bar{\varepsilon}_t)^2/\sigma^2$, t varying, are independent, with chi-square distribution $\chi^2(n-1)$. Then, by the CLT we deduce that $\hat{\sigma}_{n,T}^2$ tends to σ^2 at speed $1/\sqrt{nT}$. This speed involves the total number of observations nT, which corresponds to the interpretation of the idiosyncratic variance as a micro-parameter. In the limiting case $n = \infty$, the estimator coincides with the true parameter value σ^2. Thus, the order of the granularity adjustment is equal to the order of $\frac{n}{n-1}W(\varepsilon) - \sigma^2$; that is, to the order $1/\sqrt{nT}$.

(***) Let us finally consider the behavior of the estimator of η^2 for infinite cross-sectional size. For $n = \infty$, we get

$$\hat{\eta}_{n,T}^2 = B(y) = \frac{1}{T}\sum_{t=1}^{T}(F_t + \bar{\varepsilon}_t - \bar{F} - \bar{\bar{\varepsilon}})^2$$

$$= \frac{1}{T}\sum_{t=1}^{T}(F_t - \bar{F})^2,$$

because $\bar{\varepsilon}_t = \bar{\bar{\varepsilon}} = 0$, by the LLN. Thus, when $n = \infty$, the estimator $\hat{\eta}_{n,T}^2$ is equal to the empirical variance of the factor. It tends to η^2 at speed $1/\sqrt{T}$, corresponding to the interpretation of η^2 as a macro-parameter.

These results are summarized in the following proposition:

Proposition 2.3. (i) *If $n = \infty$, the estimator of σ^2 is constant and equal to the unknown true parameter value. The estimators of μ and η^2 are stochastic; they tend to the true value of the associated parameters when T tends to infinity, at the macro-speed $1/\sqrt{T}$.*

(ii) *If both n and T tend to infinity, the different estimators are consistent, with different speeds of adjustment: the micro-speed $1/\sqrt{nT}$ for parameter σ^2, and the macro-speed $1/\sqrt{T}$ for parameters μ and η^2.*

The difference between cases (i) and (ii) in Proposition 2.3 provides the granularity adjustments for the distributions of the maximum likelihood estimators of the micro- and macro-parameters.

2.2.3 Finite Sample Behavior

Let us now investigate the finite sample behaviors of estimators $\hat{\mu}_{n,T}$, $\hat{\sigma}_{n,T}^2$, and $\hat{\eta}_{n,T}^2$. Figures 2.1, 2.2, and 2.3 display, respectively, the pdfs of these estimators for different combinations of cross-sectional and time sample sizes: $(n = 20, T = 24), (n = 20, T = 120), (n = 100, T = 24)$, and $(n = 100, T = 120)$. The time sample sizes $T = 24$ and $T = 120$ correspond to 2 and 10

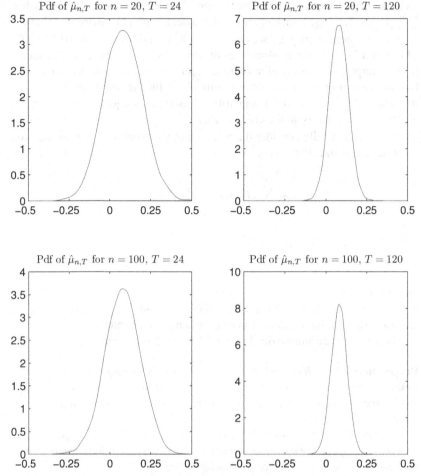

Figure 2.1. Pdf of Estimator $\hat{\mu}_{n,T}$. The figure displays the pdf of estimator $\hat{\mu}_{n,T}$ for different sample sizes: $n = 20$, $T = 24$ in the upper left panel; $n = 20$, $T = 120$ in the upper right panel; $n = 100$, $T = 24$ in the lower left panel; and $n = 100$, $T = 120$ in the lower right panel. The true values of the parameters are $\mu = 0.08$, $\eta^2 = 0.15^2 = 0.0225$, and $\sigma^2 = 0.30^2 = 0.09$ (annualized units).

years of monthly observations, respectively. We select the cross-sectional sample sizes $n = 20$ and $n = 100$ to investigate the quality of the asymptotic approximations for relatively small homogeneous subportfolios obtained after segmentation. The true values of the parameters are selected to be representative for monthly stock returns data. In annualized units, they are $\mu = 0.08$, $\eta^2 = 0.15^2 = 0.0225$, and $\sigma^2 = 0.30^2 = 0.09$. The pdfs in Figures 2.1–2.3 are

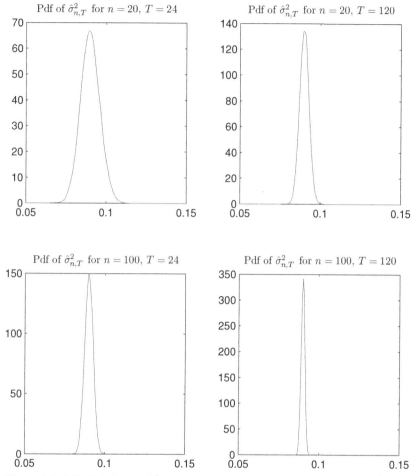

Figure 2.2. Pdf of Estimator $\hat{\sigma}_{n,T}^2$. The figure displays the pdf of estimator $\hat{\sigma}_{n,T}^2$ for different sample sizes: $n = 20$, $T = 24$ in the upper left panel; $n = 20$, $T = 120$ in the upper right panel; $n = 100$, $T = 24$ in the lower left panel; and $n = 100$, $T = 120$ in the lower right panel. The true values of the parameters are $\mu = 0.08$, $\eta^2 = 0.15^2 = 0.0225$, and $\sigma^2 = 0.30^2 = 0.09$ (annualized units).

obtained by simulating $10,000$ independent samples; computing the estimates of μ, σ^2, and η^2 for each sample in annualized units; and then computing the kernel density of the estimates.

In Figure 2.1 the pdf of the estimator of μ is centered around the true value of the parameter. The pdf becomes more concentrated when the time dimension T of the sample increases (compare the left and right panels), but is rather

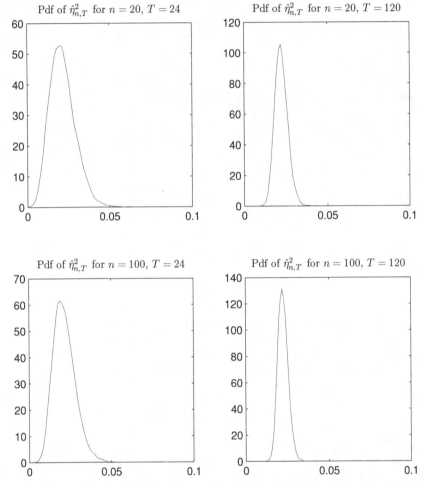

Figure 2.3. Pdf of Estimator $\hat{\eta}^2_{n,T}$. The figure displays the pdf of estimator $\hat{\eta}^2_{n,T}$ for different sample sizes: $n = 20$, $T = 24$ in the upper left panel; $n = 20$, $T = 120$ in the upper right panel; $n = 100$, $T = 24$ in the lower left panel; and $n = 100$, $T = 120$ in the lower right panel. The true values of the parameters are $\mu = 0.08$, $\eta^2 = 0.15^2 = 0.0225$, and $\sigma^2 = 0.30^2 = 0.09$ (annualized units).

insensitive to the cross-sectional dimension n (compare the upper and lower panels). This finding is compatible with the asymptotic analysis in the previous section and the macro-speed $1/\sqrt{T}$ of parameter μ. The pdf of estimator $\hat{\mu}_{n,T}$ is Gaussian for all sample sizes, because the estimator is a linear transformation of the Gaussian data.

Figure 2.2 shows that the variance of the estimator of σ^2 decreases when either the time dimension T or the cross-sectional dimension n increases.

This confirms the interpretation of σ^2 as a micro-parameter with a rate of convergence $1/\sqrt{nT}$. The pdf of $\hat{\sigma}^2_{n,T}$ appears close to a Gaussian distribution for the considered sample sizes. In fact, from (2.27) the finite sample distribution of $\hat{\sigma}^2_{n,T}$ is $\sigma^2 \chi^2[(n-1)T]/[(n-1)T]$.

Finally, in Figure 2.3 the distribution of the estimator of parameter η^2 becomes more concentrated around the true value when the time dimension increases, but not when the cross-sectional dimension alone increases. Indeed, as seen in the previous section, parameter η^2 admits a macro-interpretation, and its estimator features a $1/\sqrt{T}$ rate of convergence. For sample size $T = 24$, the distribution of estimator $\hat{\eta}^2_{n,T}$ is far from Gaussian, even for $n = 100$. However, the distribution is close to Gaussian for $T = 120$.

2.2.4 Choice of the State-Space Representation

There exist different state space representations of the same dynamic system with an unobservable factor because the notion of the factor is not defined in a unique way. For instance system (2.1)–(2.2) can be equivalently written as

System (1):

State equation: $F_t = \mu + \eta u_t, \quad u_t \sim IIN(0, 1),$

Measurement equations: $y_{i,t} = F_t + \sigma \varepsilon_{i,t}, \quad \varepsilon_{i,t} \sim IIN(0, 1).$

System (2):

State equation: $F_t = \eta u_t, \quad u_t \sim IIN(0, 1),$

Measurement equations: $y_{i,t} = \mu + F_t + \sigma \varepsilon_{i,t}, \quad \varepsilon_{i,t} \sim IIN(0, 1).$

System (3):

State equation: $F_t = u_t, \quad u_t \sim IIN(0, 1),$

Measurement equations: $y_{i,t} = \mu + \eta F_t + \sigma \varepsilon_{i,t}, \quad \varepsilon_{i,t} \sim IIN(0, 1).$

For a relevant economic interpretation, it is preferable to select a representation that includes the micro-parameters in the measurement equations and the macro-parameters in the state equation. We deduce ex post from the analysis of the asymptotic properties of the estimators (see Proposition 2.3) that the appropriate state space representation is System (1); that is, the initial representation (2.1)–(2.2).

2.2.5 Model with Observed Heterogeneity

The results derived for exchangeable panel data models can be extended to models including **observed heterogeneity**. To highlight this point, let us consider the following extension of model (2.1)–(2.2):

> *State equation:* $F_t = u_t, \quad u_t \sim IIN(\mu, \eta^2),$
>
> *Measurement equations:* $y_{i,t} = \beta_i F_t + \varepsilon_{i,t}, \quad \varepsilon_{i,t} \sim IIN(0, \sigma^2),$

where $\beta_i, i = 1, \ldots, n$, are known scalars.

The parameter β_i represents the sensitivity of observation $y_{i,t}$ to factor F_t. In this extension of model (2.1)–(2.2), the sensitivities can differ across individuals. The sensitivities are usually called betas in the finance literature, which justifies our notation. This type of linear factor model and its multivariate extensions underlie, for instance, the **arbitrage pricing theory** (APT) of security returns [Ross (1976, 1982); Chamberlain and Rothschild (1983)]. Thus, the model of Section 2.1 can also be seen as a special case of the linear factor model with homogeneous betas. Moreover, if the betas are i.i.d. draws from some distribution and are independent of the factor path, the individual histories $y_i = (y_{i,t})$ are exchangeable. Thus, the model with observed heterogeneity is compatible with Theorem 1.3 in Chapter 1.[3]

By following an approach similar to the method used for the model without heterogeneity, we get the log-likelihood function (see Appendix 2.5)

$$\mathcal{L}_{n,T}(\sigma^2, \mu, \lambda^2) = -\frac{nT}{2}\log(2\pi) - \frac{T(n-1)}{2}\log\sigma^2 - \frac{T}{2}\log\lambda^2$$

$$-\frac{1}{2\sigma^2}\sum_{t=1}^{T}\tilde{y}_t'(Id - \beta\beta'/\beta'\beta)\tilde{y}_t - \frac{1}{2\lambda^2}\sum_{t=1}^{T}\frac{[\beta'(\tilde{y}_t - \mu\beta)]^2}{\beta'\beta},$$

where the new parameter λ^2 is equal to $\lambda^2 = \sigma^2 + \eta^2\beta'\beta$, and $\beta = (\beta_1, \ldots, \beta_n)'$.

Let us focus on the estimation of the factor mean μ. By writing the first-order condition with respect to μ, we get

$$\hat{\mu}_{n,T}(\beta) = \frac{1}{T}\sum_{t=1}^{T}\frac{\beta'\tilde{y}_t}{\beta'\beta}. \tag{2.27}$$

This estimator admits a two-step interpretation. Let us consider the model for given date t, i.e,

$$y_{i,t} = \beta_i F_t + \varepsilon_{i,t}, \quad i = 1, \ldots, n, \quad \varepsilon_{i,t} \sim IIN(0, \sigma^2).$$

This cross-sectional equation could be considered as a regression model, with unknown regression parameter F_t. In this case, F_t would be approximated by

---

[3] When the beta coefficients $\beta_i, i = 1, \ldots, n$, are unknown, they have to be included among the parameters to estimate. The Gaussian ML estimator cannot be written in closed form. We do not consider this case in this book and refer to Lawley and Maxwell (1971) and Anderson (2003).

the cross-sectional **ordinary least squares** (OLS) estimator:

$$\hat{F}_{n,t} = \beta' \tilde{y}_t / \beta' \beta. \tag{2.28}$$

Intuitively, the common factor expectation $\mu = E(F_t)$ is accurately approximated by

$$\mu \sim \frac{1}{T} \sum_{t=1}^{T} F_t \sim \frac{1}{T} \sum_{t=1}^{T} \hat{F}_{n,t},$$

which is exactly formula (2.27).

Let us now derive the decomposition of the estimator $\hat{\mu}_{n,T}(\beta)$. We get

$$\hat{\mu}_{n,T}(\beta) - \mu = \frac{1}{T} \sum_{t=1}^{T} (F_t - \mu) + \frac{1}{T} \sum_{t=1}^{T} \frac{\beta' \tilde{\varepsilon}_t}{\beta' \beta},$$

where $\tilde{\varepsilon}_t = (\varepsilon_{1,t}, \ldots, \varepsilon_{n,t})'$. The finite sample distribution of this difference is Gaussian with zero-mean and variance

$$\frac{\eta^2}{T} + \frac{\sigma^2}{T} \frac{1}{\sum_{i=1}^{n} \beta_i^2} = \frac{\eta^2}{T} + \frac{\sigma^2}{nT} \frac{1}{(\bar{\beta}_n)^2 + \sigma_{\beta,n}^2},$$

where $\bar{\beta}_n = \frac{1}{n} \sum_{i=1}^{n} \beta_i$ and $\sigma_{\beta,n}^2 = \frac{1}{n} \sum_{i=1}^{n} (\beta_i - \bar{\beta})^2$ are the empirical mean and variance of the sensitivity coefficients, respectively.

Let us assume that the individual heterogeneity is well distributed across individuals in the sense that the limits

$$\bar{\beta}_\infty = \lim_{n \to \infty} \bar{\beta}_n, \qquad \sigma_{\beta,\infty}^2 = \lim_{n \to \infty} \sigma_{\beta,n}^2 \tag{2.29}$$

exist. It is always possible to assume $\bar{\beta}_\infty = 1$, possibly by changing the definition of parameters μ, η^2. Thus, for n large, the distribution of $\hat{\mu}_{n,T}(\beta) - \mu$ is approximately Gaussian with variance $\frac{\eta^2}{T} + \frac{\sigma^2}{nT} \frac{1}{1+\sigma_{\beta,\infty}^2}$. We get the following proposition:

Proposition 2.4. *In a Gaussian static factor model with observed beta heterogeneity, the distribution of the ML estimator of μ for $n = \infty$ does not depend on the individual heterogeneity and has a variance proportional to $1/T$. The granularity adjustment (i.e., the term of order $1/(nT)$ in the variance) depends on the individual heterogeneity[4] by means of the variance of the sensitivity coefficients.*

The estimator is the least accurate when $\sigma_{\beta,\infty}^2 = 0$; that is, when the distribution of the betas is the most concentrated. Indeed, the variability of the betas

---

[4] Also called **concentration** [Lutkebohmert (2008)].

across assets increases the precision of the cross-sectional OLS estimator of the factor values in (2.28).

2.2.6 Granularity Adjustment for Factor Prediction

Let us still consider the static factor model with observed heterogeneity. The theoretical prediction of F_t given all observations $\underline{y_T} = (y_{i,t}, i = 1, \ldots, n, t = 1, \ldots, T)$ – that is, the **smoothed value** of F_t – is

$$E(F_t | \underline{y_T}) = E(F_t | \tilde{y}_t)$$

$$= E(F_t) + Cov\ (F_t, \tilde{y}_t) V(\tilde{y}_t)^{-1}(\tilde{y}_t - E(\tilde{y}_t)),$$

by using standard results for Gaussian random vectors (see Appendix A, Review A.5). We have

$$E(F_t) = \mu, \quad E(\tilde{y}_t) = \mu\beta,$$

$$Cov(F_t, \tilde{y}_t) = Cov(F_t, \beta F_t) = \eta^2 \beta',$$

$$V(\tilde{y}_t) = \Omega = \sigma^2 Id + \eta^2 \beta\beta'.$$

By using the results in Appendix 2.5, we obtain

$$E(F_t | \underline{y_T}) = \mu + \eta^2 \beta' \left[\frac{1}{\sigma^2}(Id - \frac{\beta\beta'}{\beta'\beta}) + \frac{1}{\lambda^2} \frac{\beta\beta'}{\beta'\beta} \right] (\tilde{y}_t - \mu\beta),$$

that is,

$$E(F_t | \underline{y_T}) = \mu + \frac{\eta^2 \beta'\beta}{\lambda^2}(\hat{F}_{n,t} - \mu)$$

$$= \hat{F}_{n,t} - \frac{\sigma^2}{\sigma^2 + \eta^2 \beta'\beta}(\hat{F}_{n,t} - \mu)$$

$$\sim \hat{F}_{n,t} - \frac{\sigma^2}{\sigma^2 + n\eta^2(1 + \sigma_{\beta,\infty}^2)}(\hat{F}_{n,t} - \mu)$$

$$\sim \hat{F}_{n,t} - \frac{\sigma^2}{n\eta^2(1 + \sigma_{\beta,\infty}^2)}(\hat{F}_{n,t} - \mu) \tag{2.30}$$

when n is large. We deduce the following:

(*) The cross-sectional OLS estimator $\hat{F}_{n,t}$ of F_t is an accurate approximation of the smoothed factor value if $n = \infty$. In other words, $\hat{F}_{n,t}$ is the CSA optimal predictor of F_t.

(**) The cross-sectional OLS estimator has to be corrected for a large but finite sample size n. The granularity adjustment for prediction is equivalent to

$$-\frac{\hat{\sigma}_{n,T}^2}{n\hat{\eta}_{n,T}^2 \left(1 + \sigma_{\beta,n}^2\right)} \left(\hat{F}_{n,t} - \frac{1}{T}\sum_{s=1}^{T} \hat{F}_{n,s}\right)$$

after consistent estimates are substituted for the parameters. The GA is negative when the factor estimate is above the sample average.

2.3 Granularity Adjustment in Portfolio Management

In this section, we consider a static linear factor model for asset excess returns and analyze the standard mean-variance portfolio management. Assets can be, for instance, a homogeneous class of stocks. We distinguish the effects of the systematic risk factor and idiosyncratic errors on the efficient allocation and Sharpe performance, respectively.

We assume that the asset excess returns over period $(t-1, t)$, which are the differences between the risky and risk-free returns, satisfy the model with heterogeneity of Section 2.2.5 namely,

$$y_{i,t} = \beta_i F_t + \varepsilon_{i,t}, \quad i = 1, \ldots, n,$$

where $F_t \sim IIN(\mu, \eta^2)$ and $\varepsilon_{i,t} \sim IIN(0, \sigma^2)$. Thus, the expected excess returns are $E(y_{i,t}) = \beta_i \mu$, and the idiosyncratic risk is measured by $V(\varepsilon_{i,t}) = \sigma^2$. There exists a systematic source of risk through the common factor. This creates not only an additional individual risk equal to $\beta_i^2 \eta^2$ but also a dependence between the excess returns of two different risky assets, because the correlations

$$corr\,(y_{i,t}, y_{j,t}) = \frac{\beta_i \beta_j \eta^2}{(\beta_i^2 \eta^2 + \sigma^2)^{1/2}(\beta_j^2 \eta^2 + \sigma^2)^{1/2}}$$

are nonzero for $i \neq j$.

2.3.1 The Mean-Variance Efficient Allocation

Let us consider a mean-variance efficient allocation based on the n risky assets and the risk-free asset, held at time t for a one-period horizon. The vector of efficient allocations in the n risky assets is proportional to[5] [Markowitz (1952) and Appendix B, Review B.1]

$$a_{n,t} = V_t(\tilde{y}_{t+1})^{-1} E_t(\tilde{y}_{t+1}),$$

where E_t and V_t denote the conditional expectation and variance, respectively, given the information at date t. Due to the static assumption, the conditional

---

[5] With a scale depending on the absolute risk aversion of the investor.

and unconditional moments coincide, and the efficient allocations vector is time independent, given by

$$a_n = V(\tilde{y}_{t+1})^{-1} E(\tilde{y}_{t+1})$$

$$= \Omega^{-1} \mu \beta$$

$$= \left[\frac{1}{\sigma^2}(Id - \frac{\beta\beta'}{\beta'\beta}) + \frac{1}{\lambda^2}\frac{\beta\beta'}{\beta'\beta} \right] \mu \beta,$$

that is,

$$a_n = \frac{\mu}{\sigma^2 + \eta^2 \beta'\beta} \beta. \tag{2.31}$$

The associated **Sharpe performance** – that is, the square of the marginal expected return adjusted for risk of the n risky assets [Sharpe (1966) and Appendix B, Review B.1] – is

$$S_n = E(\tilde{y}_{t+1})' V(\tilde{y}_{t+1})^{-1} E(\tilde{y}_{t+1})$$

$$= \mu^2 \beta' \left[\frac{1}{\sigma^2}(Id - \frac{\beta\beta'}{\beta'\beta}) + \frac{1}{\lambda^2}\frac{\beta\beta'}{\beta'\beta} \right] \beta$$

$$= \frac{\mu^2}{\lambda^2} \beta'\beta$$

$$= \frac{\mu^2 \beta'\beta}{\sigma^2 + \eta^2 \beta'\beta}. \tag{2.32}$$

We get the following result.

Proposition 2.5. (i) *The efficient allocation in the LSRF model with hetero-geneity is*

$$a_n = \frac{\mu}{\sigma^2 + \eta^2 \beta'\beta} \beta.$$

(ii) *The associated Sharpe performance is*

$$S_n = \frac{\mu^2 \beta'\beta}{\sigma^2 + \eta^2 \beta'\beta} = \frac{\mu^2}{\eta^2} - \frac{\sigma^2}{\eta^2} \frac{\mu^2}{\sigma^2 + \eta^2 \beta'\beta}.$$

As usual in such a factor model, the vector of efficient allocations is proportional to the vector of betas. The Sharpe performance depends on the betas by means of $\beta'\beta$ and is an increasing function of this quantity.

2.3.2 Large Portfolio Analysis

Proposition 2.5 provides the explicit expressions of the efficient allocation and Sharpe performance. Let us now study their behaviors for large portfolio size;

that is, for large n. From (2.29) with $\bar{\beta}_\infty = 1$ we have

$$\beta'\beta \sim n(1 + \sigma_{\beta,\infty}^2).$$

We deduce the following corollary.

Corollary 2.1. *We have* $\lim_{n\to\infty} a_{n,j} = 0$ *for any portfolio component* j; $S_\infty = \lim_{n\to\infty} S_n = \mu^2/\eta^2$.

To understand the result in Corollary 2.1, let us consider the excess return of the entire portfolio. Indeed, even if the allocation in each single asset tends to zero, the entire risky portfolio return does not necessarily vanish because of the increase in the number n of assets. More precisely, we have

$$
\begin{aligned}
a_n'\tilde{y}_t &= \frac{\mu\beta'}{\sigma^2 + \eta^2\beta'\beta}(\beta F_t + \tilde{\varepsilon}_t) \\
&= \frac{\mu\beta'\beta}{\sigma^2 + \eta^2\beta'\beta}F_t + \frac{\mu\beta'\tilde{\varepsilon}_t}{\sigma^2 + \eta^2\beta'\beta}.
\end{aligned}
\tag{2.33}
$$

Since $\beta'\tilde{\varepsilon}_t \sim N(0, \sigma^2\beta'\beta)$ is of order $\sqrt{n}$, we deduce that

$$a_n'\tilde{y}_t \sim \frac{\mu}{\eta^2}F_t, \tag{2.34}$$

does not vanish asymptotically. The results are summarized in the following proposition.

Proposition 2.6. *For an infinitely large portfolio, the efficient risky allocation is constructed to perfectly hedge the common factor. In particular, the Sharpe performance of the n assets tends to the Sharpe performance of the common factor, namely* $\frac{[E(F_t)]^2}{V(F_t)} = \frac{\mu^2}{\eta^2} = S_\infty$.

From a financial point of view, the common factor does not correspond a priori to the return of a tradable asset. Nevertheless, the efficient portfolio a_n defines a new asset, which is tradable and mimics perfectly factor F_t when $n = \infty$. It is called the asymptotic **mimicking portfolio**. This portfolio diversifies the idiosyncratic risks to capture the relevant common risk.

2.3.3 Granularity Adjustment

In practice the set of assets available to an investor is large, but not "asymptotically large." The portfolio performance is therefore influenced by a residual of undiversified idiosyncratic risks. To account for this residual risk, we can consider the next terms in the expansion with respect to n of the Sharpe performance. For this purpose, let us assume that the square of the betas are also well diversified across individuals in the sense that

$$\frac{1}{\sqrt{n}} \sum_{i=1}^{n} [\beta_i^2 - (1 + \sigma_{\beta,\infty}^2)] = \Delta_n \xrightarrow{d} N(0, \Delta), \text{ say,}$$

when the betas are treated as random effects. We have

$$S_n = \frac{\mu^2}{\eta^2} \left(1 + \frac{\sigma^2}{\eta^2 \beta'\beta}\right)^{-1}$$

$$= \frac{\mu^2}{\eta^2} \left[1 - \frac{\sigma^2}{\eta^2 \beta'\beta} + O(1/n^2)\right]$$

$$= \frac{\mu^2}{\eta^2} \left[1 - \frac{\sigma^2}{\eta^2} \frac{1}{n(1+\sigma_{\beta,\infty}^2)} \frac{1}{1 + \dfrac{\Delta_n}{\sqrt{n}(1+\sigma_{\beta,\infty}^2)}} + O(1/n^2)\right]$$

$$= \frac{\mu^2}{\eta^2} - \frac{1}{n}\frac{\mu^2\sigma^2}{\eta^4}\frac{1}{1+\sigma_{\beta,\infty}^2} + \frac{1}{n\sqrt{n}}\frac{\mu^2\sigma^2}{\eta^4}\frac{\Delta_n}{(1+\sigma_{\beta,\infty}^2)^2} + O(1/n^2).$$

We deduce the following proposition.

Proposition 2.7. (i) *The second term (or granularity adjustment) in the expansion of the Sharpe performance is deterministic, of order $1/n$. It involves the Sharpe performance of the factor, the ratio of the idiosyncratic and factor risks, and a measure of heterogeneity (concentration).*
(ii) *The third term in the expansion is of order $1/(n\sqrt{n})$ and is stochastic. It captures the uncertainty of the squared betas distribution.*

The GA of the Sharpe performance is negative as an effect of the idiosyncratic risks. We quantify the magnitude of the limit Sharpe ratio and the granularity adjustment when the mean and variance of the systematic factor, and the idiosyncratic volatility admit the values used for the Monte Carlo analysis in Section 2.2.3; namely, $\mu = 0.08$, $\eta^2 = 0.0225$, and $\sigma^2 = 0.09$ in annualized units. Further, let us set the cross-sectional variance of the betas equal to $\sigma_{\beta,\infty}^2 = 1$. Then, in annualized units the Sharpe ratio of the factor is $\mu^2/\eta^2 = 0.284$, and the granularity adjustment for $n = 100$ is $-\mu^2\sigma^2/[n\eta^4(1+\sigma_{\beta,\infty}^2)] = -0.006$.

Similar expansions can be performed for the efficient allocation or for the net portfolio return [see Gouriéroux and Monfort (2013), which also considers the extension to portfolio management under short-sell restrictions].

2.4 Summary

The Gaussian linear single risk factor model is often used because it is easy to understand and to implement. In particular it provides closed-form expressions for the maximum likelihood estimators, the predictions of the latent factor, the mean-variance efficient allocation, and the associated Sharpe performance. These closed-form expressions can be used to disentangle the CSA and granularity adjustment components of the object of interest and to analyze the magnitude of the granularity adjustment.

2.5 Appendix: Structure of the Variance-Covariance Matrix

Let us consider a variance-covariance matrix of the type

$$\Omega = \sigma^2 Id + \eta^2 \beta\beta',$$

where σ^2, η^2 are two positive scalars and β is a vector of dimension n. By introducing the orthogonal projectors $\beta\beta'/\beta'\beta$ and $Id - \beta\beta'/\beta'\beta$, we can write

$$\Omega = \sigma^2(Id - \beta\beta'/\beta'\beta) + (\sigma^2 + \eta^2\beta'\beta)(\beta\beta'/\beta'\beta). \qquad (2.35)$$

This equation provides the spectral decomposition of matrix Ω. Its eigenvalues are

- σ^2, with multiplicity order $n - 1$, and the associated eigenspace is the orthogonal of the linear space generated by vector β;
- $\lambda^2 = \sigma^2 + \eta^2\beta'\beta$, with multiplicity order 1, and the eigenspace is the linear space generated by β.

In particular,

$$\det \Omega = (\sigma^2)^{n-1}\lambda^2,$$

because the determinant is equal to the product of the eigenvalues taking into account their multiplicity orders, and

$$\Omega^{-1} = \frac{1}{\sigma^2}(Id - \beta\beta'/\beta'\beta) + \frac{1}{\lambda^2}(\beta\beta'/\beta'\beta),$$

as easily checked by computing the product of this latter matrix with matrix Ω.

References

Anderson, T. (2003). *An Introduction to Multivariate Statistical Analysis*, 3rd edition, Wiley.

Baltagi, B. (1995). *Econometric Analysis of Panel Data*, Wiley.

Buhlmann, H. (1967). "Experience Rating and Credibility," *ASTIN Bulletin*, 4, 199–207.

Buhlmann, H., and L. Straub (1970). "Credibility for Loss Ratios," Mitteilungen der Vereinigung Schweizerischer Versicherungsmathematiker, 70, 111–133.

Chamberlain, G., and M. Rothschild (1983). "Arbitrage, Factor Structure and Mean-Variance Analysis in Large Asset Markets," Econometrica, 51, 1281–1304.

Gouriéroux, C., and A. Monfort (2013). "Granularity Adjustment for Efficient Portfolio," Econometric Reviews, 32, 449–468.

Harville, D. (1977). "ML Approaches to Variance Components Estimation and Related Problems," Journal of the American Statistical Association, 72, 320–340.

Lawley, D., and A., Maxwell (1971). Factor Analysis as a Statistical Method, 2nd edition, Elsevier.

Lintner, J. (1965). "The Valuation of Risky Assets and the Selection of Risky Investments in Stock Portfolio and Capital Budgets," Review of Economic and Statistics, 47, 13–37.

Lutkebohmert, E. (2008). Concentration Risk in Credit Portfolio, Springer-Verlag.

Markowitz, H. (1952). "Portfolio Selection," Journal of Finance, 7, 77–91.

Rao, C. (1971). "Estimation of Variance and Covariance Components: MINQUE Theory," Journal of Multivariate Analysis, 1, 257–275.

Ross, S. (1976). "The Arbitrage Theory of Capital Asset Pricing," Journal of Economic Theory, 13, 341–360.

Ross, S. (1982). "On the General Validity of the Mean-Variance Approach in Large Markets," in Financial Economics: Essays in Honor of Paul Cootner, ed., by W. Sharpe and C. Cootner, Prentice-Hall.

Searle, S. (1971). Linear Models, Wiley.

Sharpe, W. (1966). "Mutual Fund Performance," Journal of Business, 36, 119–138.

3 Static Qualitative Factor Model

This chapter proposes a unified setting for static factor models applied to panel data of qualitative observations. We first describe in Section 3.1 the **single risk factor** (SRF) model suggested in the Basel 2 regulation for the analysis of default correlation [see the Basel Committee on Banking Supervision (BCBS, 2001)]. This model is a probit model with a common Gaussian factor. In Section 3.2, we consider a general qualitative model with Gaussian factors and macro-parameters only. Then, we explain how to obtain the CSA maximum likelihood estimator and the GA estimator with adjustment for the variance, and to derive their asymptotic properties. In some special cases the estimators and their asymptotic variances have closed-form expressions. These models are discussed in Section 3.3. Finally, the results are applied to more complicated settings, such as a stochastic intensity factor model (Section 3.4) or factor analysis of dependence between qualitative variables (Section 3.5). Proofs are gathered in Appendix 3.7.

3.1 The Single Risk Factor Model for Default

The model was initially introduced by Vasicek (1991) and is based on Merton's structural model [Merton (1974)].

3.1.1 The Structural Model

The structural model defines the default of a corporation from a (crude) analysis of its balance sheet. Let us denote by i, for $i = 1, \ldots, n$, the corporation assumed to be alive at the beginning of period $(t, t + 1)$. The amount of debt to be reimbursed at the end of the period is known at date t and denoted $L_{i,t}$ (L for **liability**). The future **asset value** $A_{i,t+1}$ is uncertain. Then, the corporation defaults at date $t + 1$ if, and only if, the amount of its assets is not sufficient to pay the debt; that is, if $A_{i,t+1} < L_{i,t}$. Thus, the default indicator is

$$Y_{i,t+1} = 1, \quad \text{if } A_{i,t+1} < L_{i,t},$$

$$Y_{i,t+1} = 0, \quad \text{otherwise,}$$

or equivalently

$$Y_{i,t+1} = \mathbf{1}_{\log A_{i,t+1} < \log L_{i,t}}, \tag{3.1}$$

where **1** denotes the indicator function.

If the log-asset value is Gaussian with mean $m_{A,i,t}$ and variance $\sigma^2_{A,i,t}$, conditional on the information available at time t, the conditional distribution of the default indicator is a Bernoulli distribution with parameter

$$P_t[Y_{i,t+1} = 1] = \Phi \left(\frac{\log L_{i,t} - m_{A,i,t}}{\sigma_{A,i,t}} \right). \tag{3.2}$$

The probability of default depends on the debt amount and on the expected log-asset value and the log-asset volatility.

3.1.2 The Single Risk Factor (SRF) Model

Merton's structural model is the basis for the specification proposed by Vasicek (1991), which concerns jointly n firms and allows for default correlation. In the original model, it is assumed that the n firms are identical. We describe an extension in which the set of companies can be partitioned into K homogeneous subpopulations, or cohorts, indexed by $k = 1, \ldots, K$.

We characterize by a double index (i, k) the corporation i in cohort k, for $i = 1, \ldots, n_k$ and $k = 1, \ldots, K$. In cohort k, the latent model for the log asset/liability ratio is

$$\log A_{i,k,t+1} - \log L_{i,k,t} = a_k + b_k F_t + u_{i,k,t}, \tag{3.3}$$

where the variables F_t and $u_{i,k,t}$, with i, k, t varying, are independent, such that $F_t \sim N(0, 1)$ and $u_{i,k,t} \sim N(0, \sigma_k^2)$. The variable F_t is a common factor representing systematic risk, whereas the errors $u_{i,k,t}$ correspond to idiosyncratic (or unsystematic) risks. The parameters a_k, b_k, and σ_k are equal for all firms within cohort k, but may differ across cohorts. Thus, the log asset/liability ratios in a cohort follow the Gaussian LSRF model introduced in Chapter 2. From (3.3) we deduce that the individual default indicators are independent conditional on the factor path, with conditional default probability:

$$PD_{k,t} = P[Y_{i,k,t+1} = 1 | F_t] = \Phi \left(-\frac{a_k + b_k F_t}{\sigma_k} \right). \tag{3.4}$$

The conditional default probability is stochastic and driven by the systematic factor F_t.

As usual in a dichotomous qualitative model, the parameters are identifiable up to a positive scaling factor. Equivalently, identifiable functions of the structural parameters[1] are $\alpha_k = -a_k/\sigma_k$ and $\beta_k = -b_k/\sigma_k$, say. Then the model becomes

$$P[Y_{i,k,t+1} = 1|F_t] = \Phi(\alpha_k + \beta_k F_t). \tag{3.5}$$

Remark 3.1. An alternative parameterization is proposed in the documents of the Basel Committee [see BCBS (2001, 2003)]. Because the unconditional distribution of the log asset-to-liability ratio $\log(A_{i,k,t+1}/L_{i,k,t})$ is Gaussian with mean a_k and variance $\sigma_k^2 + b_k^2$, the unconditional **probability of default** (*PD*) in cohort k is[2]

$$PD_k = P[Y_{i,k,t} = 1] = \Phi\left(-\frac{a_k}{\sqrt{\sigma_k^2 + b_k^2}}\right).$$

Moreover, the correlation between the log(asset/liability) of two firms in a same cohort, called **asset correlation**, is[3]

$$Corr[\log(A_{i,k,t+1}/L_{i,k,t}), \log(A_{j,k,t+1}/L_{j,k,t})] = b_k^2/(b_k^2 + \sigma_k^2) = \rho_k > 0, \text{ say.}$$

Thus, we get

$$P[Y_{i,k,t+1} = 1|F_t] = \Phi\left(-\frac{a_k}{\sigma_k} - \frac{b_k}{\sigma_k}F_t\right)$$

$$= \Phi\left(\frac{\Phi^{-1}(PD_k)}{\sigma_k/\sqrt{\sigma_k^2 + b_k^2}} - \frac{b_k}{\sigma_k}F_t\right)$$

$$= \Phi\left(\frac{\Phi^{-1}(PD_k) - \sqrt{\rho_k}F_t}{\sqrt{1-\rho_k}}\right). \tag{3.6}$$

This new parameterization through the unconditional probability of default PD_k and asset correlation ρ_k provides insights for financial interpretation, although it is less convenient than the initial parameterization (3.5) for estimation purposes. Formula (3.6) shows how the conditional probability of default stochastically varies across time around its historical mean equal to PD_k. This is illustrated in Figure 3.1 for a simulated path of the factor F_t in a cohort of firms with unconditional default probability $PD = 0.05$. We consider two different values of asset correlation: $\rho = 0.10$ and $\rho = 0.30$. The conditional default probability peaks at dates with large negative shocks on the factor. The

---

[1] Up to the sign for β_k.
[2] The unconditional default probability PD_k is different from the conditional default probability equal to $PD_{k,t} = \Phi(\alpha_k + \beta_k F_t)$ (see also Figure 3.1).
[3] In the Basel documents, the asset correlation is denoted ρ_k^2 instead of ρ_k.

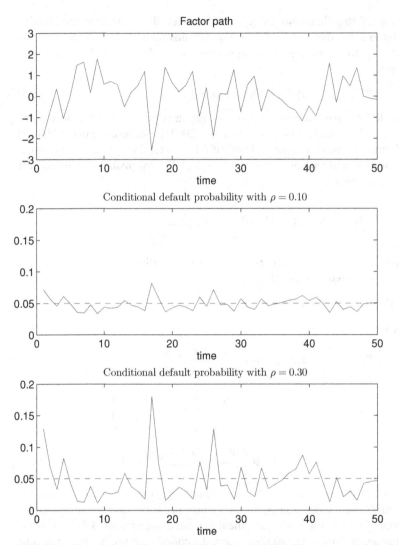

Figure 3.1. Time-Varying Conditional Default Probability. The upper panel displays a simulated path of the factor $F_t \sim IIN(0, 1)$ of time length of 50 periods. The middle panel displays the corresponding path of conditional default probability (solid line) in a cohort of firms with unconditional default probability $PD = 0.05$ (dashed horizontal line) and asset correlation $\rho = 0.10$. The lower panel displays the pattern of conditional default probability with asset correlation $\rho = 0.30$.

time variability of the conditional default probability is more pronounced for larger values of the asset correlation.

Specification (3.5) can be written in a hierarchical way as

$$P_t[Y_{i,k,t+1} = 1] = \Phi(a_{k,t}), \text{ with } a_{k,t} = \alpha_k + \beta_k F_t, \quad F_t \sim IIN(0,1)$$

or equivalently as

$$
\begin{cases}
P_t(Y_{i,k,t+1} = 1) = \Phi(a_{k,t}), \\
\text{where vectors } a_t = (a_{1,t}, \ldots, a_{K,t})', \ t \text{ varying, are independent,} \qquad (3.7) \\
\text{with distribution } N(\alpha, \beta\beta'), \ \alpha = (\alpha_1, \ldots, \alpha_K)', \beta = (\beta_1, \ldots, \beta_K)'.
\end{cases}
$$

System (3.7) defines the **canonical factors** a_t and introduces restrictions on their distribution. These restrictions correspond to an exact factor structure for the components of vector a_t induced by the **reduced factor** F_t.

In the next two subsections we introduce simple estimation methodologies for parameters α and β.

3.1.3 The CSA Estimator

Because of the homogeneity within cohorts, the individual observations can be summarized by the default frequencies:

$$\bar{Y}_{k,t+1} = \frac{1}{n_k} \sum_{i=1}^{n_k} Y_{i,k,t+1}. \qquad (3.8)$$

To understand the intuition for the CSA estimator, let us consider for a moment the (virtual) limiting case where the cohorts have infinite size; that is, $n_k = \infty$, for all $k = 1, \ldots, K$. Then, by applying the LLN conditionally on the factor path (see Chapter 1), the cross-sectional default frequencies are equal to the conditional probabilities of default,

$$\bar{Y}_{k,t+1} = E_t(Y_{i,k,t+1}) = PD_{k,t} = \Phi(a_{k,t}),$$

and the values of the canonical factors are known and equal to

$$a_{k,t} = \hat{a}_{k,t} = \Phi^{-1}(\bar{Y}_{k,t+1}). \qquad (3.9)$$

We have to distinguish between the case with a single cohort, namely $K = 1$, which corresponds to the original Vasicek (1991) model, and the extension with $K \geq 2$ cohorts. In the first case, from (3.7) the canonical factor is such that

$$a_t \sim IIN(\alpha, \beta^2). \qquad (3.10)$$

Then (3.9) and (3.10) suggest that the scalar parameters α and β can be estimated by ML applied to the time series of estimated canonical factors $\hat{a}_t$, to get

$$\hat{\alpha} = \bar{a}_T = \frac{1}{T} \sum_{t=1}^{T} \hat{a}_t = \frac{1}{T} \sum_{t=1}^{T} \Phi^{-1}(\bar{Y}_{k,t+1}),$$

$$\hat{\beta}^2 = \frac{1}{T} \sum_{t=1}^{T} (\hat{a}_t - \bar{a}_T)^2 = \frac{1}{T} \sum_{t=1}^{T} \left(\Phi^{-1}(\bar{Y}_{k,t+1}) - \frac{1}{T} \sum_{t=1}^{T} \Phi^{-1}(\bar{Y}_{k,t+1}) \right)^2.$$

These estimators are called CSA estimators. Although the CSA estimators have been motivated by the limiting argument of infinite cohort sizes, they can be computed with finite cohort sizes and are expected to yield accurate estimates when the cohort sizes are sufficiently large. The large sample properties of the CSA estimators are discussed in Section 3.2.3 for the general model.

When we have more than one cohort ($K \geq 2$), we cannot follow a similar approach because the distribution of the canonical factors in (3.7) is degenerate with a singular variance-covariance matrix. This is because there is a linear deterministic relationship between the canonical factors. Indeed, in the limiting case of infinite cohort sizes, we could deduce without error the values of parameter vectors α, β and factor values F_t, $t = 1, \ldots, T$ by solving the system of KT equations,

$$a_{k,t} = \alpha_k + \beta_k F_t, \quad k = 1, \ldots, K, \ t = 1, \ldots, T,$$

in the $2K + T$ unknown quantities. When we take into account the estimation error for the canonical factors, a nondegenerate log-likelihood function is recovered, as seen in the next subsection. However, with more than one cohort, it is natural to include cohort-specific effects in the canonical factors. Then, the distribution of the canonical factors becomes nonsingular, and a well-defined CSA estimator can be derived [see Section 3.3.2 and in particular the discussion in Remark 3.3 for the financial relevance of including cohort-specific effects].

3.1.4 Variance Granularity Adjusted (VGA) Estimators

Because in reality the cohort sizes are large but finite, we may expect that the CSA approach can be improved by taking into account the estimation error on the canonical factors. By applying the CLT by date and cohort, we see that the default frequencies $\bar{Y}_{k,t+1}$ are asymptotically independent, with mean $PD_{k,t} = \Phi(a_{k,t})$ and variance $\frac{PD_{k,t}(1-PD_{k,t})}{n_k} = \frac{\Phi(a_{k,t})[1-\Phi(a_{k,t})]}{n_k}$.

By applying the delta method and noting that the derivative of function $\Phi^{-1}(.)$ is $1/\phi[\Phi^{-1}(.)]$, where ϕ denotes the pdf of the standard normal distribution, we deduce that the approximations of the canonical factors are also independent and asymptotically Gaussian:

$$\hat{a}_{k,t} = \Phi^{-1}(\bar{Y}_{k,t+1}) \simeq N\left(a_{k,t}, \frac{\Phi(a_{k,t})[1-\Phi(a_{k,t})]}{n_k\phi(a_{k,t})^2}\right).$$

Equivalently,

$$\hat{a}_{k,t} \simeq a_{k,t} + \left(\frac{\Phi(a_{k,t})[1-\Phi(a_{k,t})]}{n_k\phi(a_{k,t})^2}\right)^{1/2} v_{k,t}$$

$$\simeq \alpha_k + \beta_k F_t + \left(\frac{\Phi(\hat{a}_{k,t})[1-\Phi(\hat{a}_{k,t})]}{n_k\phi(\hat{a}_{k,t})^2}\right)^{1/2} v_{k,t},$$

where F_t and $v_{k,t}$, for k, t varying, are independent, standard Gaussian variables. Let us denote by Δ_t the $K \times K$ diagonal matrix with elements $\Phi(\hat{a}_{k,t})[1 - \Phi(\hat{a}_{k,t})]/[n_k\phi(\hat{a}_{k,t})^2]$, $k = 1,\ldots,K$. The parameters α and β are estimated by optimizing the VGA log-likelihood function:

$$\mathcal{L}^{VGA}(\alpha,\beta) = \sum_{t=1}^{T}\left\{-\frac{K}{2}\log(2\pi) - \frac{1}{2}\log\det(\beta\beta' + \Delta_t)\right.$$

$$\left. - \frac{1}{2}(\hat{a}_t - \alpha)'(\beta\beta' + \Delta_t)^{-1}(\hat{a}_t - \alpha)\right\}. \qquad (3.11)$$

These estimators are called **variance granularity adjusted (VGA) maximum likelihood** estimators. To take into account the finite cross-sectional size, we introduce an adjustment of the variance of the error term, which explains the terminology.

Remark 3.2. The VGA maximum likelihood method has to be compared with the finite sample ML method. The true log-likelihood function is

$$\mathcal{L}(\alpha,\beta) = \sum_{t=1}^{T}\log\left[\int\prod_{k=1}^{K}\left\{\Phi(\alpha_k + \beta_k f)^{n_{k,t}}[1 - \Phi(\alpha_k + \beta_k f)]^{n_k - n_{k,t}}\right\}\right.$$

$$\left. \cdot \frac{1}{\sqrt{2\pi}}\exp(-f^2/2)df\right], \qquad (3.12)$$

where $n_{k,t} = \sum_{i=1}^{n_k} Y_{i,k,t} = n_k\bar{Y}_{k,t}$ is the number of defaults in cohort k for period $(t - 1, t)$. When the true log-likelihood is maximized, the integrals in (3.12) are often approximated by simulation, leading to simulated maximum likelihood estimators [see, e.g., Gouriéroux and Monfort (1996)]. The approximation (3.11) circumvents the computation of the T integrals involved in (3.12). We see in Chapter 4 that the function $\mathcal{L}^{VGA}(\alpha,\beta)$ can be derived from an asymptotic expansion of $\mathcal{L}(\alpha,\beta)$ when the cohort sizes n_k are large, and the estimators obtained by maximizing $\mathcal{L}^{VGA}(\alpha,\beta)$ are asymptotically equivalent to the ML estimator. Moreover, we see that it can be appropriate to introduce a granularity adjustment for the mean as well.

3.2 The General Model and Its Estimation

The approaches described for the single risk factor (SRF) model can be extended to more general static qualitative factor models.

3.2.1 The Model

As in the SRF model for default, let us consider a set of cohorts and individual observations of a qualitative variable $Y_{i,k,t}$, for $i = 1, \ldots, n_k$, $k = 1, \ldots, K$, $t = 1, \ldots, T$. The qualitative variable is polytomous with J alternatives.[4]

The model is defined in two steps. We first explain how the distribution of the observations depends on underlying canonical factors; then, we introduce restrictions on the canonical factor distribution.

(*) Distribution of the Observations Given the Canonical Factors. The individual observations are assumed independent, conditionally on canonical factors $a_{k,t}$, $k = 1, \ldots, K$, $t = 1, \ldots, T$,

$$P[Y_{i,k,t} = j | a_t] = p(j; a_{k,t}), \tag{3.13}$$

where $p(j; .)$ denotes the elementary probability of alternative j, for $j = 1, \ldots, J$. The distribution can depend on cohort and time by means of the canonical factor, but does not depend on the individual within the cohort. The canonical factor can be multidimensional, with dimension $\dim(a_{k,t}) = S$, say, and we assume that it can take any value in $I\!R^S$.

(**) Joint Distribution of the Canonical Factors. The model is completed by specifying the distribution of the canonical factors. Let us introduce the KS-dimensional vector of canonical factor values at date t, denoted by $a_t = (a'_{1,t}, \ldots, a'_{K,t})'$. We assume that the random vectors a_t, $t = 1, \ldots, T$, are independent with identical Gaussian distributions,

$$a_t \sim IIN[\mu(\theta), \Omega(\theta)], \tag{3.14}$$

where θ is a p-dimensional unknown parameter and matrix $\Omega(\theta)$ is invertible. The model is static because of the assumption of serial independence of the factors.

---

[4] Recall that a one-dimensional polytomous variable with J alternatives can be equivalently represented as a J-dimensional vector of dichotomous qualitative components. The components are the indicators of the J different alternatives and sum up to one.

The likelihood function of model (3.13)–(3.14) is obtained by integrating out the unobservable canonical factor path,

$$l(\underline{y_T}; \theta) = \prod_{t=1}^{T} \int \cdots \int \prod_{k=1}^{K} \prod_{i=1}^{n_k} p(y_{i,k,t}; a_{k,t})$$

$$\frac{1}{(2\pi)^{SK/2}[\det \Omega(\theta)]^{1/2}} \exp\left\{ -\frac{1}{2}[a_t - \mu(\theta)]'\Omega(\theta)^{-1}[a_t - \mu(\theta)] \right\} da_t,$$

(3.15)

where $\underline{y_T}$ denotes the individual histories $y_{i,1}, \ldots, y_{i,T}$ for $i = 1, \ldots, n$. The likelihood function depends on macro-parameter θ and involves multidimensional integrals with dimension KS. Because the cohorts are homogeneous, the likelihood function can be simplified. Let us denote by $n_{j,k,t}$ the number of observations taking alternative j, in cohort k, at time t. We obtain

$$l(\underline{y_T}; \theta) = \prod_{t=1}^{T} \int \cdots \int \prod_{k=1}^{K} \prod_{j=1}^{J} p(j; a_{k,t})^{n_{j,k,t}}$$

$$\frac{1}{(2\pi)^{SK/2}[\det \Omega(\theta)]^{1/2}} \exp\left\{ -\frac{1}{2}[a_t - \mu(\theta)]'\Omega(\theta)^{-1}[a_t - \mu(\theta)] \right\} da_t.$$

(3.16)

Thus, without loss of information, the cross-sectional observations for cohort k can be summarized by the J cross-sectional aggregates $n_{j,k,t}$, $j = 1, \ldots, J$.

The likelihood function (3.16) is complicated because of the T numerical integrals of dimension KS. We consider in the next subsection estimators of θ that are computationally simpler than the maximum likelihood (ML) estimator.

3.2.2 The Fixed Effect Maximum Likelihood Estimator

By analogy with the discussion of the SFR model in Section 3.1, let us consider the cross-sectional observations for a given date t, and treat a_t as an unknown parameter. Approximate factor values are the **fixed effects ML estimators** defined by

$$\hat{a}_{k,t} = \arg\max_{a_{k,t}} \sum_{i=1}^{n_k} \log p(y_{i,k,t}; a_{k,t}) \tag{3.17}$$

$$= \arg\max_{a_{k,t}} \sum_{j=1}^{J} n_{j,k,t} \log p(j; a_{k,t}), \tag{3.18}$$

where the arg max operator provides the argument $a_{k,t}$ that maximizes the objective function.

Identification assumptions have to be introduced to ensure a unique solution to this cross-sectional optimization. Intuitively, we must have fewer "parameters" than (linearly independent) aggregate observations; that is, the order condition

$$S \leq J - 1. \tag{3.19}$$

When $S = J - 1$, the canonical factors are just-identified; they are overidentified if $S < J - 1$.

The LLN and CLT can be applied conditionally on the canonical factor values if n_k is large for any $k = 1, \ldots, K$ (see Section 1.3 in Chapter 1). Hence, the standard asymptotic results for the maximum likelihood estimators are valid. More precisely, the fixed effects ML estimators $\hat{a}_{k,t}$, for $k = 1, \ldots, K$, $t = 1, \ldots, T$ are asymptotically independent, with

$$\sqrt{n_k}(\hat{a}_{k,t} - a_{k,t}) \xrightarrow{d} N(0, \Sigma_{k,t}), \tag{3.20}$$

where

$$\Sigma_{k,t} = \left\{ E \left[-\frac{\partial^2 \log p(Y_{i,k,t}; a_{k,t})}{\partial a \partial a'} |a_{k,t} \right] \right\}^{-1}. \tag{3.21}$$

The asymptotic variance of $\hat{a}_{k,t}$ is the inverse of an information matrix computed as if $a_{k,t}$ were a (multidimensional) parameter. The derivatives are taken with respect to $a_{k,t}$, and the computation of the expectation is performed conditional on $a_{k,t}$; that is, as if $a_{k,t}$ were a vector of constants.

3.2.3 The CSA Maximum Likelihood Estimator

The motivation for the CSA estimator is best understood if we consider for a moment the limiting (virtual) case where the cohort sizes are infinite; that is, $n_k = \infty$ for $k = 1, \ldots, K$. Then, the fixed effects ML estimators would coincide with the unknown canonical factor values by the LLN. The log-likelihood function would become

$$\mathcal{L}^{CSA}(\theta) \propto -\frac{T}{2} \log \det \Omega(\theta) - \frac{1}{2} \sum_{t=1}^{T} [\hat{a}_t - \mu(\theta)]' \Omega(\theta)^{-1} [\hat{a}_t - \mu(\theta)]. \tag{3.22}$$

This argument suggests that we consider the CSA maximum likelihood estimator of θ defined by

$$\hat{\theta}^{CSA} = \arg \max_{\theta} \mathcal{L}^{CSA}(\theta). \tag{3.23}$$

Let us now discuss the asymptotic distribution of the CSA estimator when both the cross-sectional dimension and the time dimension of the panel are large. More precisely, let us assume that the cohort sizes are such that $n_k = c_k n$ for some constants $c_k > \infty$, and $n, T \to \infty$ such that $T/n \to 0$. Thus, the cohort sizes increase at the same speed, which is faster than the speed of increase in the time size. Then, the large sample distribution of estimator $\hat{\theta}^{CSA}$ is the same as if the canonical factors were observable $a_t = \hat{a}_t$, and we can apply the standard asymptotic theory with respect to the time dimension ($T \to \infty$) for the log-likelihood function (3.22) (see references in Chapter 4 for the regularity conditions). We deduce that the CSA estimator is consistent, at speed $1/\sqrt{T}$, with asymptotic distribution:

$$\sqrt{T}(\hat{\theta}^{CSA} - \theta) \xrightarrow{d} N\left(0, \left[\plim_{T \to \infty} -\frac{1}{T}\frac{\partial^2 \mathcal{L}^{CSA}(\theta)}{\partial \theta \partial \theta'}\right]^{-1}\right). \quad (3.24)$$

In particular, the CSA estimator $\hat{\theta}^{CSA}$ is asymptotically equivalent to the true ML estimator of θ that maximizes the likelihood (3.16). For the SRF model with $K = 1$ cohort [see Section 3.1.3], the asymptotic variances of the CSA estimators are $As Var(\hat{\alpha}) = \frac{1}{T}\beta^2$ and $As Var(\hat{\beta}^2) = \frac{2}{T}\beta^4$, and the estimators of α and β are asymptotically independent.

3.2.4 The VGA Maximum Likelihood Estimator

The VGA estimator accounts for the difference between the fixed effects estimates and the true factor values when the cohort sizes are large but finite. From (3.20) we deduce that

$$\hat{a}_{k,t} \simeq a_{k,t} + \frac{1}{\sqrt{n_k}}\Sigma_{k,t}^{1/2}v_{k,t}, \quad (3.25)$$

where the errors (v_{kt}) are (multivariate) standard normal, independent of each other, and independent of the $a_{k,t}$'s. Therefore, by integrating out the unobservable canonical factors, we get

$$\hat{a}_t \approx N[\mu(\theta), \Omega(\theta) + \hat{\Sigma}_{n,t}], \quad (3.26)$$

where $\hat{\Sigma}_{n,t} = \text{diag}[\hat{\Sigma}_{k,t}/n_k]$, and $\hat{\Sigma}_{k,t}$ is a consistent estimator of $\Sigma_{k,t}$.
The variance granularity adjusted log-likelihood function is

$$\mathcal{L}^{VGA}(\theta) \propto -\frac{1}{2}\sum_{t=1}^{T} \log \det[\Omega(\theta) + \hat{\Sigma}_{n,t}] \quad (3.27)$$

$$-\frac{1}{2}\sum_{t=1}^{T}[\hat{a}_t - \mu(\theta)]'[\Omega(\theta) + \hat{\Sigma}_{n,t}]^{-1}[\hat{a}_t - \mu(\theta)]. \quad (3.28)$$

Compared to the CSA log-likelihood function (3.22), the variance has been adjusted to account for the variability of the fixed effects estimators of the canonical factors. The VGA maximum likelihood estimator of θ is

$$\hat{\theta}^{\text{VGA}} = \arg\max_{\theta} \mathcal{L}^{\text{VGA}}(\theta). \tag{3.29}$$

For large n and T ($n, T \to \infty$, $T/n \to 0$), the asymptotic distribution of the VGA estimator is the same as that of the CSA estimator given in (3.24). In particular, the VGA estimator is consistent at speed $1/\sqrt{T}$ and is asymptotically normal. The VGA estimator differs from the CSA estimator in its higher order asymptotic properties – more specifically, in terms of the bias at order $1/n$ (see Chapter 4, Section 4.3).

3.3 Closed-Form Expressions of the Estimators

The CSA and VGA log-likelihood functions have closed-form expressions; in particular, they do not involve the multiple integrals appearing in the finite sample likelihood function [see equation (3.16)]. In important special cases of a static qualitative model with factors, it is also possible to obtain closed-form expressions of the CSA maximum likelihood estimators themselves and of their asymptotic variance [see Gouriéroux and Monfort (2010)]. Next we describe such simplifications.

3.3.1 Just-Identified Canonical Factors

Let us denote by $p_{j,k,t} = p(j; a_{k,t})$ the true elementary probabilities and by $p_{k,t} = (p_{1,k,t}, \ldots, p_{J,k,t})'$ the associated vector of probabilities for cohort k and time t. Under the assumption of just-identification $S = J - 1$, we can write

$$p_{k,t} = \Pi(a_{k,t}), \tag{3.30}$$

where Π is a one-to-one function of $I\!R^{J-1}$ onto the simplex of $I\!R^J$; that is, the set of discrete probability distributions:

$$\left\{ (p_1, \ldots, p_J)', \text{ with } p_j \geq 0, j = 1, \ldots, J, \sum_{j=1}^{J} p_j = 1 \right\}.$$

In several examples (see the later discussion and Sections 3.4 and 3.5), function Π can be inverted to express the canonical factors in terms of elementary probabilities as

$$a_{k,t} = c(p_{k,t}), \quad \text{say.} \tag{3.31}$$

It is easily checked that the solution of optimization (3.18) is such that

$$\hat{p}_{k,t} = \Pi(\hat{a}_{k,t}), \tag{3.32}$$

where $\hat{p}_{k,t} = (n_{1,k,t}/n_k, \ldots, n_{J,k,t}/n_k)'$ are the observed cross-sectional frequencies of the alternatives at date t. We deduce the closed-form expression of the fixed effects ML estimators of the canonical factors:

$$\hat{a}_{k,t} = c(\hat{p}_{k,t}). \tag{3.33}$$

It follows that [see, e.g., Gouriéroux and Monfort (1989), Example 7.19, and the δ-method]

$$\sqrt{n}_k(\hat{a}_{k,t} - a_{k,t}) \xrightarrow{d} N\left(0, \frac{\partial c(p_{k,t})}{\partial p'_{k,t}}[\text{diag}(p_{k,t}) - p_{k,t}p'_{k,t}]\frac{\partial c(p_{k,t})'}{\partial p_{k,t}}\right) \tag{3.34}$$

and that the variance-covariance matrix $\Sigma_{k,t}$ in (3.21) is consistently estimated by

$$\hat{\Sigma}_{k,t} = \frac{\partial c(\hat{p}_{k,t})}{\partial p'_{k,t}}(\text{diag }\hat{p}_{k,t} - \hat{p}_{k,t}\hat{p}'_{k,t})\frac{\partial c(\hat{p}_{k,t})'}{\partial p_{k,t}}. \tag{3.35}$$

To summarize the derivations of the fixed effects ML estimator of the canonical factor and of their estimated asymptotic variance become simple, if the canonical factor can be interpreted as a reparameterization of the qualitative model by $J - 1$ real parameters. Such real parameterization has often been considered in the literature on qualitative models for the purpose of introducing quantitative exogenous variables. We review next such standard reparameterizations for the main qualitative models. For expository purposes we keep the index j, but omit indexes k and t. We provide the function Π and the function c for each example.

Example 3.1. Dichotomous Probit Model ($J = 2$)

$$p_1 = \Phi(a_1), \quad p_2 = 1 - \Phi(a_1).$$

This corresponds to the Merton (1974)–Vasicek (1991) default model described in Section 3.1. The probability p_1 is displayed as a function of the canonical factor a_1 in Figure 3.2. This mapping from $I\!R$ to $(0, 1)$ is one to one. We deduce $a_1 = \Phi^{-1}(p_1)$, where Φ^{-1} is the quantile function of the standard normal distribution, called the probit function.

Example 3.2. Dichotomous Logit Model ($J = 2$)

$$p_1 = [1 + \exp(-a_1)]^{-1}, \quad p_2 = \exp(-a_1)[1 + \exp(-a_1)]^{-1}.$$

The probability p_1 is displayed as a function of the canonical factor a_1 in Figure 3.3.

We deduce that $a_1 = \log[p_1/(1 - p_1)]$ and function c is the inverse of the logistic function; that is the logit function [see Berkson (1944)].

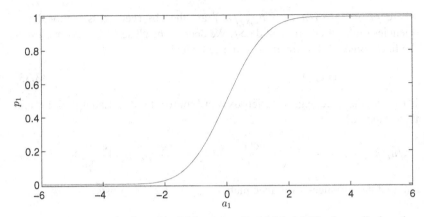

Figure 3.2. Parameterization of the Dichotomous Probit Model. The figure displays the probability p_1 as a function of the canonical factor a_1 in the dichotomous probit model.

Example 3.3. Multinomial Logit Model (any $J \geq 2$) [See McFadden (1973, 1976)]

The model is reparameterized as

$$p_j = \exp(a_j)[\sum_{l=1}^{J} \exp(a_l)]^{-1}, \quad j = 1, \ldots, J,$$

with the convention $a_1 = 0$. We get

$$a_j = \log(p_j/p_1), \quad j = 2, \ldots, J.$$

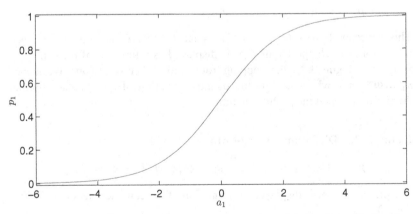

Figure 3.3. Parameterization of the Dichotomous Logit Model. The figure displays the probability p_1 as a function of the canonical factor a_1 in the dichotomous logit model.

The canonical factors are log transforms of appropriate **odd ratios**. For the case of $J = 3$ alternatives, we display in Figure 3.4 the canonical factors a_2 and a_3 as functions of the elementary probabilities (p_1, p_2, p_3).

The vector function (a_2, a_3) is a rather complicated one-to-one mapping from the simplex in $I\!R^3$ onto $I\!R^2$. The component function a_2 admits large positive (resp. negative) values close to the boundary of the simplex with $p_2 = 0$ and $p_1 > 0$ (resp. $p_1 = 0$ and $p_2 > 0$). We have $a_2 = 0$ on the intersection of the simplex with the plane $p_1 = p_2$, which corresponds to the lightest part of the colored surface. The point $p_1 = 0$, $p_2 = 0$, $p_3 = 1$ is singular, because function a_2 can admit any real value in a neighborhood of this point. The component function a_3 features a similar behavior, interchanging p_3 with p_2. For instance, the lightest part of the colored surface is obtained for $p_1 = p_3$, that is, $2p_1 + p_2 = 1$.

Example 3.4. Ordered Polytomous Probit Model (any $J \geq 2$)
The model is reparameterized as

$$p_j = \Phi(a_j) - \Phi(a_{j-1}), \quad j = 1, \ldots, J,$$

with the convention $a_0 = -\infty, a_J = +\infty$. We deduce

$$a_j = \Phi^{-1}(p_1 + \cdots + p_j). \tag{3.36}$$

This new parameterization does not completely fulfill our assumptions. Indeed, parameters $a_j, j = 1, \ldots, J$, are real, but are constrained to form an increasing sequence. However, the Gaussian assumption on the canonical factor [see (3.14)] is still relevant if it concerns a parallel shift on the canonical factors only; that is, if we write

$$a_{jt} = \alpha_j + \beta F_t, \tag{3.37}$$

with $\alpha_1 \leq \alpha_2 \leq \ldots \leq \alpha_{J-1}$, where F_t is a Gaussian random variable. Indeed, because scalar parameter β is independent of the alternative, the ordering of the intercepts implies a similar ordering for the canonical factors.

The Gaussian distribution of the random vector a_t implied by (3.37) is degenerate, because of the deterministic relationships between the canonical factors associated with the different alternatives. We have already encountered a similar feature in the SRF model with several cohorts in Section 3.1. Because of this degeneracy, the results of Section 3.2 on the rate of convergence of the estimators do not apply. In particular, some of the parameters among α_j and β have a micro-interpretation and feature a convergence rate $1/\sqrt{nT}$. The estimators of parameters α_j and β and their asymptotic properties can be derived by using the results presented in Chapter 4, where we consider models with both macro- and micro-parameters (see in particular Section 4.3 on rating migration models based on ordered qualitative specifications).

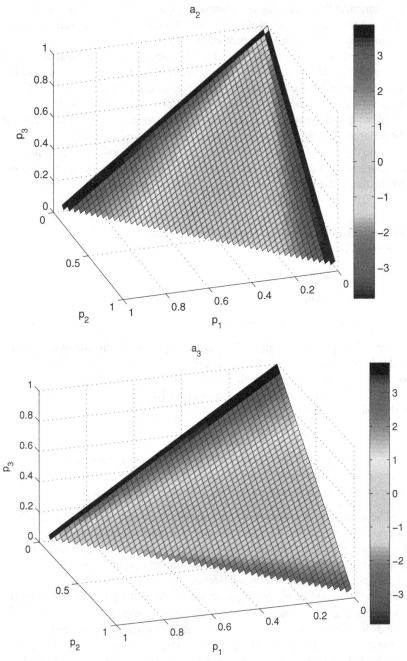

Figure 3.4. Canonical Factors in the Multinomial Logit Model. The upper panel displays the level-color map of the canonical factor a_2 as a function of the elementary probabilities (p_1, p_2, p_3) in the multinomial logit model with $J = 3$ alternatives. Colors on the simplex correspond to function values. The lower panel displays the level-color map for the canonical factor a_3.

3.3.2 Gaussian Factor Analysis of the Canonical Factors

To structure the cross dependence between the canonical factors, let us introduce a linear Gaussian factor model for the distribution of a_t. The model is defined by

$$a_t = \alpha + \beta F_t + \eta w_t, \quad t = 1, \ldots, T, \tag{3.38}$$

where α [resp. β] is a vector of dimension KS [resp. a matrix of dimension (KS, L)], η is a positive scalar, (F_t) are independent Gaussian vectors $F_t \sim IIN(0, Id)$ with size $L < KS$, and w_t are independent standard Gaussian vectors with size KS; that is, $w_t \sim IIN(0, Id)$. Moreover, the factors (F_t) and the errors (w_t) are independent. We deduce that the distribution of the canonical factors vector is

$$a_t \sim N(\alpha, \beta\beta' + \eta^2 Id). \tag{3.39}$$

Thus, model (3.38) implies a special structure of the variance-covariance matrix of the canonical factors. Indeed, the cross-covariances are captured by means of a matrix $\beta\beta'$ of reduced rank L, where L is the number of underlying static factors.

Remark 3.3. It is important to compare the static factor model (3.38) with the latent factor model (3.3) that is usually introduced in the SRF model for default. Model (3.3) includes idiosyncratic error terms $u_{i,k,t}$, whose effects vanish by cross-sectional aggregation. This explains why the associated model for canonical factors reduces to $a_t = \alpha + \beta F_t$; that is, it does not include the error terms w_t. When $K \geq 2$, the non-invertibility of the matrix $\Omega = V(a_t) = \beta\beta'$ and the degeneracy of the CSA likelihood function result [see Section 3.1.3]. More importantly from a financial point of view, by implicitly setting $\eta = 0$, the basic SRF model neglects the cohort-specific source of risk and consequently underestimates the required capital. Thus, with $K \geq 2$, it is preferable to include in the SRF model an additional error term w_t in the canonical factors as in (3.38), which corresponds to cohort-specific effects. Finally, when we have a single cohort $(K = 1)$, it is not possible to introduce an additional error term w_t in the canonical factor, because the associated parameter η is not identified.

The vector of parameters in model (3.38) is $\theta = [\alpha', (vec\beta)', \eta]'$, where the *vec* operator stacks the columns of a matrix into a vector. However, the factors F and the factor sensitivities β are defined up to a linear orthogonal transformation. Therefore, without loss of generality, we can impose the identification restrictions:

Identification restrictions. $\beta_k'\beta_l = 0$, *for any* $k \neq l$, *where* $\beta_l, l = 1, \ldots, L$, *denotes the columns of matrix* β.

50 Granularity Theory with Applications to Finance and Insurance

Let us now derive the CSA estimator of parameter θ. Let us denote

$$\bar{a}_T = \frac{1}{T} \sum_{t=1}^{T} \hat{a}_t \qquad (3.40)$$

as the historical mean of the estimated canonical factors, and

$$\hat{V}_T = \frac{1}{T} \sum_{t=1}^{T} (\hat{a}_t - \bar{a}_T)(\hat{a}_t - \bar{a}_T)' \qquad (3.41)$$

as their historical variance-covariance matrix. The spectral decomposition of the historical variance-covariance matrix $\hat{V}_T$ provides a decreasing sequence of nonnegative eigenvalues $\hat{\lambda}_{1,T} \geq \hat{\lambda}_{2,T} \geq \cdots$, with associated orthonormal eigenvectors $\hat{e}_{1,T}, \hat{e}_{2,T}, \cdots$. Proposition 3.1 provides the explicit expressions of the CSA maximum likelihood estimator of parameter θ.

Proposition 3.1. *The CSA maximum likelihood estimators of the components of parameter θ are*

$$\hat{a}_T = \bar{a}_T, \quad \hat{\eta}_T^2 = [Tr(\hat{V}_T) - \sum_{l=1}^{L} \hat{\lambda}_{l,T}]/(KS - L),$$

$$\hat{\beta}_{l,T} = (\hat{\lambda}_{l,T} - \hat{\eta}_T^2)^{1/2} \hat{e}_{l,T}, \quad l = 1, \ldots, L.$$

Proof. See Appendix 3.7.

These maximum likelihood estimators are based on the **spectral decomposition** of matrix $\hat{V}_T$, also known as **singular value decomposition** [SVD; see, e.g., Anderson (2003) and Appendix A, Review A.4]. The asymptotic variance-covariance matrix also has an explicit expression [see, e.g., Gouriéroux and Monfort (2010), Section 3.3, and Gouriéroux and Jasiak (2012)].[5]

3.3.3 The Estimation Steps

Under the conditions of Sections 3.3.1 and 3.3.2, the estimation steps can be summarized as follows:

Step 1: Reparameterize the qualitative model in the appropriate way to obtain $a_t = c(p_t)$, with real values.
Step 2: Compute the observed frequencies $\hat{p}_t$ and deduce the estimated canonical factors as $\hat{a}_t = c(\hat{p}_t)$.
Step 3: Compute the historical mean $\bar{a}_T$ and variance $\hat{V}_T$ of the estimated canonical factors.

[5] The initial derivation of these variances in Lawley and Maxwell (1971) provides only approximated variance-covariance matrices [see also Jennrich and Thayer (1977)].

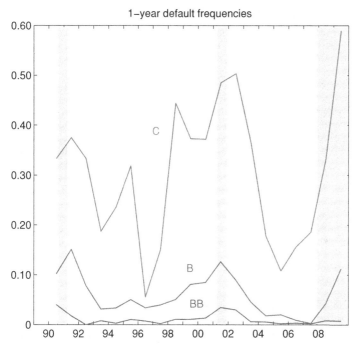

Figure 3.5. S&P U.S. Corporate Default Frequencies for Rating Classes BB, B, and C. The figure displays the series of yearly S&P U.S. corporate default frequencies for rating classes BB, B, and C in the 1990–2009 period. Shaded periods correspond to NBER recessions in the United States.

Step 4: Obtain the CSA estimates of α, β, η^2 from the spectral decomposition of matrix $\hat{V}_T$ (see Proposition 3.1).

Step 5: Finally, obtain the VGA estimates by optimizing numerically the VGA log-likelihood function with the CSA estimate as the starting value of the optimization algorithm.

3.3.4 Illustration: Factor Model for Corporate Default

As an illustration of these steps, we estimate a factor model for corporate default. The binary variable $Y_{i,k,t}$ is a firm's default indicator ($J = 2$; see Section 3.1), and the cohorts $k = 1, 2, 3$ correspond to the non-investment-grade rating classes BB, B, and C in Standard & Poor's (S&P) rating system ($K = 3$). The series of 1-year default frequencies $\bar{Y}_{k,t}$ are displayed in Figure 3.5 for the 1990–2009 period ($T = 20$). These default frequencies are deduced from the S&P rating transition matrices, which are computed from a large pool of U.S. large and medium-sized firms (see Section 4.5 for a more detailed description of the data). The cohort size n_k is of the order of thousands of firms for rating classes BB and B and of the order of hundreds of firms for rating class C.

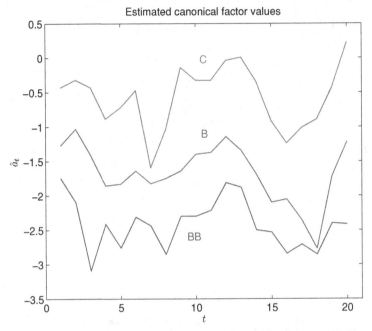

Figure 3.6. Estimated Canonical Factor Values for Rating Classes BB, B, and C. The figure displays the yearly series of estimated canonical factor values $\hat{a}_{k,t}$ for rating classes BB, B, and C in the 1990–2009 period.

As expected, at any given date the default frequencies are ranked in terms of the riskiness of the speculative rating class. Moreover, the series of default frequencies of the three rating classes feature a similar countercyclical pattern, with peaks of default intensity associated with recessions in the U.S. economy (1990–1991, 2001, and 2008–2009).

Because the risk variable is dichotomous, we have a single canonical factor for each rating class ($S = 1$), and the vector of canonical factors a_t is trivariate. We adopt a probit specification (see Example 3.1). The series of estimated canonical factor values $\hat{a}_{k,t} = \Phi^{-1}(\bar{Y}_{k,t})$ for the three rating classes are displayed in Figure 3.6. The estimated canonical factor values are the quantiles of the standard Gaussian distribution for the percentiles that correspond to the default frequencies in Figure 3.5. Steps 1 and 2 of the estimation methodology are completed.

Let us now apply steps 3–4. The historical mean and variance of the estimated canonical factor vectors are

$$\bar{a}_T = \begin{pmatrix} -2.423 \\ -1.671 \\ -0.566 \end{pmatrix}, \qquad \hat{V}_T = \begin{pmatrix} 0.126 & 0.094 & 0.085 \\ 0.094 & 0.174 & 0.129 \\ 0.085 & 0.129 & 0.200 \end{pmatrix}. \qquad (3.42)$$

The spectral decomposition of matrix $\hat{V}_T$ is characterized by the three eigenvalues

$$\hat{\lambda}_{1,T} = 0.379, \qquad \hat{\lambda}_{2,T} = 0.072, \qquad \hat{\lambda}_{3,T} = 0.049,$$

with associated orthonormal eigenvectors:

$$\hat{e}_{1,T} = \begin{pmatrix} 0.447 \\ 0.613 \\ 0.652 \end{pmatrix}, \qquad \hat{e}_{2,T} = \begin{pmatrix} 0.702 \\ 0.212 \\ -0.680 \end{pmatrix}, \qquad \hat{e}_{3,T} = \begin{pmatrix} 0.555 \\ -0.761 \\ 0.335 \end{pmatrix}.$$

The first eigenvalue $\hat{\lambda}_{1,T}$ of matrix $\hat{V}_T$ is significantly larger than the other two. Moreover, the components of the eigenvector associated with $\hat{\lambda}_{1,T}$ have the same sign across rating classes, whereas the eigenvectors associated with the other two eigenvalues have components of both signs. Intuitively, these findings are compatible with a single common factor having a similar impact on the default risk of the three rating classes. Hence, we use a Gaussian single-factor model for the canonical factors as in Equation (3.38) with $L = 1$.

Let us compute the CSA estimates of the model parameters. From Proposition 3.1, the CSA estimate of the vector of intercepts is $\hat{\alpha}_T = \bar{a}_T$ given in (3.42), whereas the CSA estimates of the vector of sensitivities β and idiosyncratic variance η^2 are

$$\hat{\beta}_T = \begin{pmatrix} 0.252 \\ 0.346 \\ 0.368 \end{pmatrix}, \qquad \hat{\eta}_T^2 = 0.060.$$

As expected, the estimated intercepts are increasing with regard to the riskiness of the rating class. The sensitivities to the common factor have the same sign across rating classes and are larger in magnitude for the riskier rating classes B and C than for rating class BB. The sign of the eigenvector associated with the largest eigenvalue of $\hat{V}_T$ has been selected to obtain positive factor sensitivities and interpret the common factor as a default risk factor. From equation (3.39), the estimates of the unconditional variances of the canonical factors are 0.124, 0.180, and 0.195 for rating classes BB, B, and C, respectively. Hence, for rating class BB the systematic factor and the idiosyncratic (i.e., rating-class-specific) factor each contribute about one-half of the unconditional variance of the canonical factor. For rating classes B and C the proportions are about two-thirds from the systematic factor and one-third from the idiosyncratic factor.

3.4 Stochastic Intensity Model with Factor

A discrete random variable with a fixed number K of admissible values can be identified with a polytomous qualitative variable by considering the set of values as the set of alternatives. This interpretation is especially interesting for duration variables that represent the time to some given event, such as default or prepayment in credit analysis and death or lapse for life insurance contracts.

3.4.1 Distribution of a Duration Variable

There exist alternative characterizations of the distribution of a discrete-time duration variable Y, with values $k = 1, \ldots, K$. We can consider the elementary probabilities:

$$\pi_k = P[Y = k], \quad k = 1, \ldots, K.$$

We can also consider the successive **intensities** of event occurrence. These intensities measure the short-term probability of occurrence of the event by means of the following conditional probabilities:

$$p_k = P[Y = k | Y \geq k], \quad k = 1, \ldots, K. \tag{3.43}$$

The elementary probabilities and the intensities are in a one-to-one relationship. Indeed, we have

$$p_k = \pi_k / \sum_{l=k}^{K} \pi_l, \tag{3.44}$$

and

$$\pi_k = \left[\prod_{l=1}^{k-1} (1 - p_l) \right] p_k. \tag{3.45}$$

An approach based on intensity has at least three advantages. First, the intensities p_k, $k = 1, \ldots, K - 1$ can be fixed independently between 0 and 1 (with $p_K = 1$), whereas the elementary probabilities are subject to the unit mass restriction. Second, the sample counterparts of the intensities in an i.i.d. framework are asymptotically independent,[6] Gaussian with mean p_k and variance $p_k(1 - p_k)/n_k$, where n_k is the number of individuals in the **population-at-risk** (PaR) (i.e., with duration larger than or equal to k). Third, intensities allow for an appropriate treatment of two competing notion of times: calendar time with the time origin being the birth of Jesus Christ and individual time with the time origin the beginning of the contract.

3.4.2 Stochastic Intensity with Factor

Let us now consider a large population of contracts originated at different consecutive dates. This population is assumed to be homogeneous; in particular

---

[6] Indeed, it is easily checked that the log-likelihood function is a sum $\sum_{k=1}^{K} \mathcal{L}_k(y, p_k)$, for example. The asymptotic independence follows from the expression of the information matrix, because the Hessian of the log-likelihood function becomes a diagonal matrix.

that all the contracts have the same contractual term K, say. We assume that we monitor the contracts over a given period of time $t = 1, \ldots, T$ and observe whether they close or do not close before their contractual term. Thus, at any given date t, we can observe K different categories of contracts that are still alive, depending on whether they originate at date $t - 1, t - 2, \ldots$, or $t - K$. Among them, only the first $K - 1$ categories can lead to a contract dying strictly before the contractual term. The number of contracts of age k still alive at the beginning of period t is time dependent and denoted by $n_{k,t}$, with $k = 1, \ldots, K - 1$. The probability that such a contract (i, k), $i = 1, \ldots, n_{k,t}, k = 1, \ldots, K - 1$, is closing at period t is

$$P_t[Y_{i,k,t} = 1] = p_{k,t}, \tag{3.46}$$

where $p_{k,t}$ is the intensity for age k and date t.

The introduction of an unobservable stochastic time factor in an intensity model allows for differentiated effects of the factors depending on the age of the contract. For instance, for loans and a single risk factor, these effects are expected to be smaller at the beginning of the contract or close to the contractual term than they are in the middle of the contract. A stochastic intensity model with factor and logit specification of the intensities is

$$P[Y_{i,k,t} = 1|F_t, \varepsilon_{k,t}] = [1 + \exp(\alpha_k + \beta_k F_t + \eta \varepsilon_{k,t})]^{-1}, \tag{3.47}$$

where F_t is the common factor and $\varepsilon_{k,t}$ are age-specific errors.

3.4.3 The Consequences of Stochastic Intensity

Without stochastic intensity effects $F_{k,t}$ and $\varepsilon_{k,t}$, and with constant α_k, the intensities

$$P[Y_{i,k,t} = 1] = (1 + \exp \alpha)^{-1}$$

imply a lifetime following a geometric distribution. The introduction of stochastic variables in the intensities has two effects. At the individual level, the marginal distribution of the lifetime is no longer geometric, but can feature negative duration dependence; that is, an intensity function decreasing with the age. At the joint level, the presence of a common factor creates complicated patterns of dependence between the lifetimes of two individuals of the same cohort.

3.4.4 Longevity Risk

Lee and Carter (1972) first used stochastic intensity with a dynamic factor to analyze mortality in a given population. The Lee-Carter methodology described next is still the basic model used for life insurance and the design and pricing of pension funds. [See, e.g., Blake, Cairns, and David (2006); Gouriéroux and Monfort (2008) for recent work on longevity risk prediction].

Let us denote by $p_{k,t}$ the mortality intensity of an individual of age k at period t. This intensity is specified as

$$\log\left(\frac{p_{k,t}}{1 - p_{k,t}}\right) = \alpha_k + \beta_k F_t, \quad k = 1, \ldots, K, \quad t = 1, \ldots, T, \quad (3.48)$$

where α_k and β_k are parameters and F_t is a stochastic factor. Model (3.48) corresponds to model (3.47) with $\eta = 0$ after a change of sign on α_k and β_k. The logit transform ensures that $p_{k,t}$ is between 0 and 1.[7] Because the unobservable factor values are identifiable up to an affine transformation, we can set $E[F_t] = 0$ and $V[F_t] = 1$.

Then, Lee and Carter propose the use of published mortality tables, which provide a sample counterpart $\hat{p}_{k,t}$ of $p_{k,t}$, and they write the approximate factor model as

$$\log\left(\frac{\hat{p}_{k,t}}{1 - \hat{p}_{k,t}}\right) = \alpha_k + \beta_k F_t + u_{k,t}, \quad (3.49)$$

where $u_{k,t}$ is a Gaussian error term. Then they estimate α_k by $\hat{\alpha}_k = \frac{1}{T}\sum_{t=1}^{T} \log\left(\frac{\hat{p}_{k,t}}{1-\hat{p}_{k,t}}\right)$ and deduce approximations of β_k and F_t by applying a singular value decomposition on the $T \times K$ matrix X with elements $X_{t,k} = \log\left(\frac{\hat{p}_{k,t}}{1-\hat{p}_{k,t}}\right) - \hat{\alpha}_k$. Specifically, the estimates of the factor values are given by vector $\hat{F} = (\hat{F}_1, \ldots, \hat{F}_T)'$, which is the eigenvector of the $T \times T$ matrix XX' associated with the largest eigenvalue and normalized such that $\hat{F}'\hat{F}/T = 1$. The estimates of the factor sensitivities are $\hat{\beta} = (\hat{\beta}_1, \ldots, \hat{\beta}_K)' = X'\hat{F}/T$.

This methodology has been applied to developed countries using the data publicly available in the human mortality database of the University of California Berkeley and the Max Planck Institute.[8] The results for France are summarized in Figures 3.7 and 3.8. The analysis is performed separately for females and males.

From Figure 3.7 we immediately observe that the mortality factor F_t features a (stochastic) downward trend. It corresponds to the general increase in the human life-span; that is, the average annual increase of about three months of residual life-span. This increase varies in time and across genders. Figure 3.8 displays estimated intercepts α_k (left panels) and factor loadings β_k (right panels) for 1-year age classes [$(k - 1, k)$ with $k = 1, \ldots, 111$ years].[9] From the estimated intercepts, we see that the historical average mortality rate in the

---

[7] In their seminal paper, Lee and Carter (1992) use a log-transform that does not ensure this constraint.

[8] Data can be downloaded from the website, www.mortality.org.

[9] The last age class includes people who are 110 years old or older.

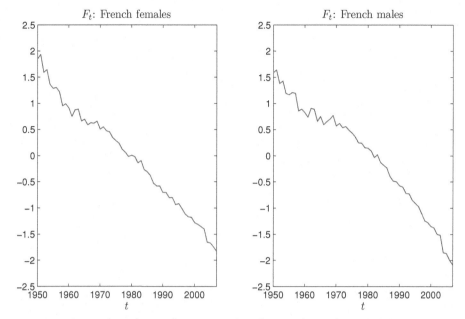

Figure 3.7. Estimated Mortality Factor Values for French Females and Males, 1950–2007. The figure displays the series of estimated mortality factor values for French females (left) and males (right) in the 1950–2007 period. The factor is normalized such that its historical mean is zero and its historical variance is 1.

1950–2007 period features a non-monotonous pattern with respect to age. Mortality is higher for children and old people. Moreover, in age classes between 20 and 80 years, the average mortality is generally larger for males than for females. Factor loadings are positive and overall decreasing with respect to age; that is, the effect of the decreasing mortality trend is less pronounced for older people. The pattern of the factor loadings is similar across females and males, but factor loadings are generally larger for females. Thus, the impact of the decreasing mortality trend seems more important for females.

Let us now discuss the earlier described estimation procedure in view of the general results presented in this chapter. The traditional Lee-Carter model (3.48) corresponds to a qualitative factor model as considered in Section 3.2, where the qualitative observations $Y_{i,k,t} \sim \mathcal{B}(1, p_{k,t})$ are the death events in the different age classes. However, the canonical factors $a_{k,t} = \log\left(\frac{p_{k,t}}{1-p_{k,t}}\right)$ for $k = 1, \ldots, K$ admit a degenerate dependence structure (see Remark 3.3). A nondegenerate dependence structure is obtained by adding age-class-specific mortality risks,

$$a_{k,t} = \alpha_k + \beta_k F_t + \eta \varepsilon_{k,t}, \tag{3.50}$$

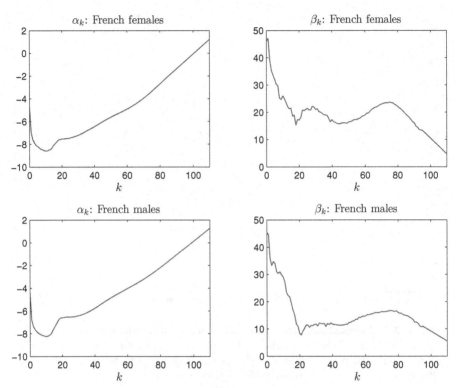

Figure 3.8. Estimated Intercepts and Factor Loadings for French Females and Males, 1950–2007. The figure displays the estimated intercepts α_k and factor loadings β_k for French females and males in 1-year age classes $[k-1, k)$, for $k = 1, \ldots, 111$ years. The factor is normalized such that its historical mean is zero and its historical variance is 1.

where the shocks $\varepsilon_{k,t}$ are $IIN(0, 1)$ across age classes and time dates, and $\eta > 0$ is the standard deviation of the class-specific effects. Model (3.50) can be estimated by means of the CSA approach described in Section 3.3. Specifically, Proposition 3.1 implies that the CSA ML estimators are obtained from the spectral decomposition of the $K \times K$ matrix $X'X/T$. In particular, the estimates of the factor sensitivities correspond to the eigenvector associated with the largest eigenvalue of matrix $X'X/T$ (appropriately rescaled). In Appendix A, Review A.4, we show that the spectral decompositions of matrices XX' and $X'X$ are strongly related; namely, these matrices share the same nonzero eigenvalues and associated eigenvectors. Thus, the CSA ML estimates of the factor sensitivities coincide with those obtained from the standard procedure used in the literature. The CSA approach, however, also provides estimates for the standard deviation of the age class effects. In our empirical illustration using mortality data in France in the 1950–2007 period, the estimates are $\hat{\eta} = 0.089$ for females and $\hat{\eta} = 0.097$ for males. They are small compared to the estimates of the common factor loadings. Hence, age-class-specific mortality effects do not seem very important for the considered datasets.

The basic estimation approach can be improved in several ways:

- Even if the estimation method is close to the CSA approach with a static factor, this factor is clearly dynamic with a trend. This type of extension is considered in Chapter 4.

- It is also possible to take into account the asymptotic variance of $\log\left(\frac{\hat{p}_{k,t}}{1-\hat{p}_{k,t}}\right)$, which depends on the level $p_{k,t}$ and the number of individuals of age k at date t (population-at-risk, PaR). Indeed, for the older age classes, the size of the PaR is small, and the information is less accurate; this effect occurs for the individuals who are intuitively the most sensitive to longevity factors. Accounting for the asymptotic variance of the estimated canonical factors requires VGA estimates of the model parameters [see Section 3.2.4].

- Finally, several factors can be introduced into the analysis. Typically the longevity factors are not necessarily the same for males and females, for workers or executives, and for Europeans and Americans.

3.5 Factor Analysis of Dependence

The general methodology introduced in Sections 3.2–3.3 can also be followed to understand the structure of dependence between two qualitative (or discrete) variables. Indeed, it is important to allow for different factors' effects on the marginal distributions of two qualitative risks or for the dependence between these two risks. For this purpose, it is useful to introduce a suitable reparameterization of the joint distribution of two qualitative variables.

3.5.1 An Appropriate Parameterization for a 2×2 Contingency Table

Let us denote X and Z the two qualitative variables of interest, and $Y = (X, Z)$ the qualitative variable representing both of them. The alternatives for X [resp. Z, Y] are $k, k = 1, \ldots, K$ [resp. $j, j = 1, \ldots, J; (k, j), k = 1, \ldots, K, j = 1, \ldots, J$]. The distribution of Y at date t can be represented in a (K, J) contingency table, where

$$P_t[Y_{i,t} = (k, j)] = p_{k,j,t}.$$

A reparameterization of a contingency table with real parameters, which is able to distinguish between marginal and dependence features, was introduced

Table 3.1. (K, J)
Contingency table

X Z	$1 \ldots j \ldots J$
1	$\vdots$
$\vdots$	$\vdots$
k	$\cdots \; p_{k,j,t} \; \cdots$
$\vdots$	$\vdots$
K	$\vdots$

in the 1980s for the analysis of tendency surveys [see, e.g., Koenig, Nerlove, and Oudiz (1979); Nerlove (1983); Nerlove and Press (1986)]. It is called the **log-linear probability model**. We use this parameterization to introduce the canonical factors. The idea is to separate in the log-probabilities the marginal effects of alternatives k and j from their cross-effects. More precisely, we consider the following decomposition:

$$\log p_{k,j,t} = \mu_t + a_{k,t}^1 + a_{j,t}^2 + a_{k,j,t}^{1,2} \tag{3.51}$$

where

$$\sum_{k=1}^{K} a_{k,t}^1 = 0, \; \sum_{j=1}^{J} a_{j,t}^2 = 0, \; \sum_{k=1}^{K} a_{k,j,t}^{1,2} = 0, \; \forall j, \; \sum_{j=1}^{J} a_{k,j,t}^{1,2} = 0, \; \forall k \tag{3.52}$$

and the leading term μ_t is deduced by the unit mass restriction.

Alternatively, model (3.51) can be seen as a special polytomous logit model:

$$p_{k,j,t} = \exp(a_{k,t}^1 + a_{j,t}^2 + a_{k,j,t}^{1,2}) / \left[\sum_{k,j} \exp(a_{k,t}^1 + a_{j,t}^2 + a_{k,j,t}^{1,2}) \right]. \tag{3.53}$$

3.5.2 Factor Analysis of a Pair of Dichotomous Variables

As an illustration, let us consider a pair of dichotomous variables and denote their alternatives as 0, 1, as is usual in this framework. By taking into account the restrictions in (3.52), all the new parameters can be written as functions of

$a^1_{1,t} = a_{1,t}$ (say), $a^2_{1,t} = a_{2,t}$ (say), and $a^{1,2}_{1,1,t} = a_{3,t}$ (say). We get

$$
\begin{cases}
\log p_{1,1,t} = \mu_t + a_{1,t} + a_{2,t} + a_{3,t}, \\
\log p_{1,0,t} = \mu_t + a_{1,t} - a_{2,t} - a_{3,t}, \\
\log p_{0,1,t} = \mu_t - a_{1,t} + a_{2,t} - a_{3,t}, \\
\log p_{0,0,t} = \mu_t - a_{1,t} - a_{2,t} + a_{3,t},
\end{cases}
\tag{3.54}
$$

and

$$
\begin{cases}
a_{1,t} = \frac{1}{4}(\log p_{1,1,t} + \log p_{1,0,t} - \log p_{0,1,t} - \log p_{0,0,t}), \\
a_{2,t} = \frac{1}{4}(\log p_{1,1,t} + \log p_{0,1,t} - \log p_{1,0,t} - \log p_{0,0,t}), \\
a_{3,t} = \frac{1}{4}(\log p_{11,t} + \log p_{0,0,t} - \log p_{1,0,t} - \log p_{0,1,t}).
\end{cases}
\tag{3.55}
$$

The canonical factors $a_{1,t}$ and $a_{2,t}$ have a positive impact on the probabilities of the events defined by $X = 1$, and $Z = 1$, respectively. To interpret the third canonical factor, note that $a_{3,t}$ can also be written as

$$
a_{3,t} = \frac{1}{4} \log \left(\frac{p_{1,1,t} p_{0,0,t}}{p_{1,0,t} p_{0,1,t}} \right).
\tag{3.56}
$$

It takes value zero if and only if variables X and Z are independent at date t. It takes its maximal value $+\infty$ if either $p_{1,0,t}$ or $p_{0,1,t}$ is equal to zero. The minimal value $-\infty$ is achieved when either $p_{1,1,t}$ or $p_{0,0,t}$ is 0. Thus, $a_{3,t}$ is a measure of the (nonlinear) dependence between X and Z. By introducing different factors for $a_{1,t}$, $a_{2,t}$, and $a_{3,t}$, we can interpret these factors in terms of either marginal or cross-effects.

3.5.3 Illustration: The Effect of the Financial Crisis

We illustrate this methodology with an analysis of the dynamics of the cross-sectional distribution of stock returns during the recent financial crisis. Let us consider the stocks that define the S&P 500 index. Let $r_{i,t}$, for $i = 1, \ldots, n$, $n = 500$, and $r_{m,t}$ denote the return at day t of stock i and the return of the index, respectively. Returns are percentages and concern the time period from May 7, 2007 to May 6, 2011. Figure 3.9 displays the time series of the S&P 500 index returns. It shows a period of large volatility between September 2008 and June 2009 corresponding to the recent financial crisis.

Table 3.2. *Sample* 2 × 2 *contingency table of variables* $X_{i,t}$ *and* $Z_{i,t}$

		$X_{i,t}$		
		0	1	
$Z_{i,t}$	0	0.384	0.366	0.75
	1	0.121	0.129	0.25
		0.505	0.495	

We consider the return $r_{i,t} - r_{m,t}$ of stock i in excess of the market and discretize the support of this variable into four subsets – $I = \{r_{i,t} - r_{m,t} < -\lambda\}$, $II = \{-\lambda \leq r_{i,t} - r_{m,t} < 0\}$, $III = \{0 \leq r_{i,t} - r_{m,t} < \lambda\}$, and $IV = \{r_{i,t} - r_{m,t} \geq \lambda\}$ – where $\lambda > 0$ is a threshold independent of asset and time. The threshold λ is fixed at $\lambda = 1.802$, which corresponds to the 75% quantile of $|r_{i,t} - r_{m,t}|$ across assets and dates in our sample. The subsets I, II, III, and IV correspond to a large negative return, a moderate negative return, a moderate positive return and a large positive return, respectively. At each date t, we compute the cross-sectional frequency of stocks with returns in the subsets I–IV and study the dynamics of these frequencies.

The occurrence of a stock return in a subset I–IV can be characterized by means of two dichotomous variables. Let $X_{i,t} = 1$ if $r_{i,t} - r_{m,t} > 0$ and let

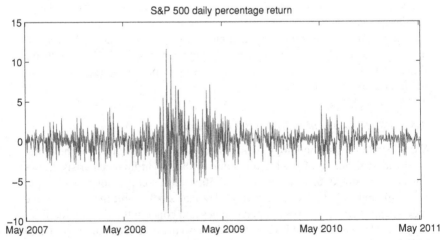

Figure 3.9. Time Series of S&P 500 Daily Percentage Returns, May 7, 2007, to May 6, 2011. The figure displays the time series of daily percentage returns of the S&P 500 index in the period from May 7, 2007, to May 6, 2011.

Table 3.3. 2×2 *contingency table of*
variables $X_{i,t}$ and $Z_{i,t}$ under the
independence assumption

		$X_{i,t}$		
		0	1	
$Z_{i,t}$	0	0.379	0.371	0.75
	1	0.126	0.124	0.25
		0.505	0.495	

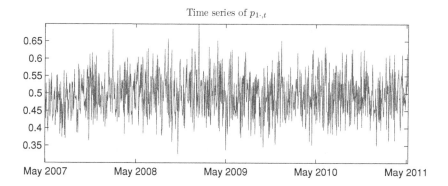

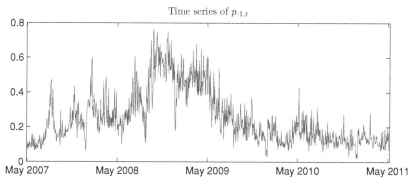

Figure 3.10. Time Series of Probabilities $p_{1\cdot,t}$ and $p_{\cdot1,t}$. The upper panel displays the time series of probability $p_{1\cdot,t} = P_t[X_{i,t} = 1]$ of a positive stock return. The lower panel displays the time series of probability $p_{\cdot1,t} = P_t[Z_{i,t} = 1]$ of a large absolute stock return. Stock returns are in excess of the market return.

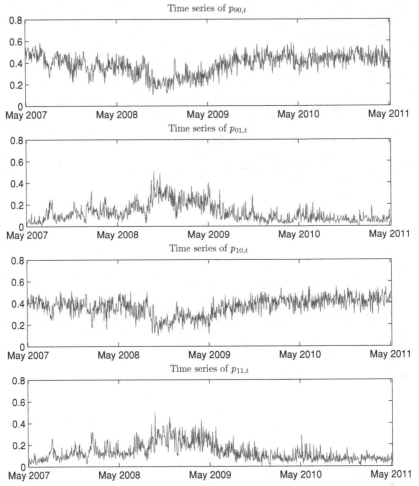

Figure 3.11. Time Series of Probabilities $p_{00,t}$, $p_{01,t}$, $p_{10,t}$, and $p_{11,t}$. This figure displays the time series of probabilities $p_{00,t}$ (first panel), $p_{01,t}$ (second panel), $p_{10,t}$ (third panel), and $p_{11,t}$ (fourth panel), where $p_{kl,t} = P_t[X_{i,t} = k, Z_{i,t} = l]$ for $k, l = 0, 1$.

it equal 0 otherwise. Moreover, let $Z_{i,t} = 1$ if $|r_{i,t} - r_{m,t}| > \lambda$, and let it equal 0 otherwise. Hence, $X_{i,t}$ is the indicator of a positive stock return, and $Z_{i,t}$ is the indicator of a large absolute stock return. Then, subsets I–IV are characterized by $I = \{X_{i,t} = 0, Z_{i,t} = 1\}$, $II = \{X_{i,t} = 0, Z_{i,t} = 0\}$, $III = \{X_{i,t} = 1, Z_{i,t} = 0\}$, and $IV = \{X_{i,t} = 1, Z_{i,t} = 1\}$, respectively.

The sample contingency table of the two dichotomous variables X and Z is displayed in Table 3.2.

The marginal distribution of variable X is such that on average about half of the stocks overperform the market in about half of the trading days. The

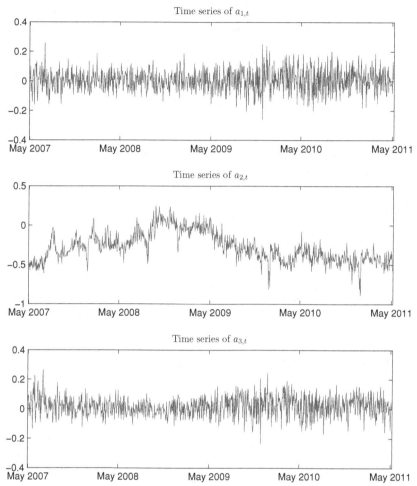

Figure 3.12. Time Series of Factors $a_{1,t}$, $a_{2,t}$, and $a_{3,t}$. This figure displays the time series of factors $a_{1,t}$ (upper panel), $a_{2,t}$ (middle panel), and $a_{3,t}$ (bottom panel).

overperformance of a stock is greater than λ in absolute value in about 25% of the cases, reflecting the choice of threshold λ discussed earlier. To investigate the dependence between the two variables X and Z, we provide in Table 3.3 the contingency table under the assumption that the variables are independent, but with the same marginal distributions as in Table 3.2.

Contingency Tables 3.2 and 3.3 are very similar. This suggests that, in an unconditional, or static, framework, the variables X and Z do not feature a clear pattern of dependence. We now investigate their dependence in a dynamic framework by using factor analysis.

The evolution of the cross-sectional marginal distributions of the dichotomous variables X and Z is given in Figure 3.10. The market return can be interpreted as a weighted average of individual returns. The value of $p_{1\cdot,t} = p_{11,t} + p_{10,t}$ gives information on the skewness of the cross-sectional distribution of individual returns. This marginal probability is equal to 0.5 (resp., larger, smaller than) if the median is equal to the mean (resp., larger, smaller than). From the first panel of Figure 3.10 (see also Table 3.2), we see that the distribution of X is in average moderately left skewed. However, we observe both a large variability in this probability over time and some periodic behavior: periods in which a large number of assets perform better than the market are followed by periods in which much more assets underperform. The marginal probability $p_{\cdot1,t} = p_{11,t} + p_{01,t}$ of Z is a market-adjusted measure of individual risk. During the recent financial crisis, there was simultaneously increased market volatility (see Figure 3.9) and an increase in the market-adjusted risks.

We show in Figure 3.11 the evolutions of the contingency tables and in Figure 3.12 the evolutions of the log-linear parameters. Factor $a_{2,t}$ is another measure of market adjusted risk, with an evolution largely similar to that of $p_{\cdot1,t}$. More interesting is the evolution of the cross-sectional measure of dependence $a_{3,t}$ between X and Z. We might expect a kind of positive risk premium for market-adjusted returns; that is, extreme returns compensated by right-skewed distribution, or equivalently more periods with positive values of factor $a_{3,t}$. This feature is clearly not observed in the third panel of Figure 3.12. This dependence measure is very erratic over time, as if there were a stochastic dependence, and this stochastic dependence fluctuates around 0 corresponding to the cross-sectional independence hypothesis.

3.6 Summary

The maximum likelihood method is complicated in factor models with unobservable factors. It can be approximated by the CSA and VGA approaches. In qualitative models with static factors, these approximated estimation methods are easy to implement if (i) the models are written in terms of well-chosen canonical factors and (ii) the canonical factors are linear functions of a reduced number of Gaussian underlying factors. The methodology can be applied to dichotomous or multinomial probit and logit models, as well as to duration models or log-linear probability models with unobservable factors. The approach is especially relevant for corporate default and longevity analysis.

3.7 Appendix: CSA Maximum Likelihood Estimator in Factor Models

In this appendix we derive the CSA ML estimator (proof of Proposition 3.1). We follow Gouriéroux and Jasiak (2012).

(*) Inverse and Determinant of Matrix Ω

Let us denote by $\tilde{\beta}_l = \beta_l/(\beta_l'\beta_l)^{1/2}$ the column vectors of matrix β rescaled to have a unit norm. The set of vectors $\tilde{\beta}_l$, $l = 1, \ldots, L$, can be completed to obtain the set $\tilde{\beta}_l$, $l = 1, \ldots, KS$, which forms an orthonormal basis of $\mathbb{R}^{SK}$. We get

$$\Omega = V(a_t) = \sum_{l=1}^{L} \beta_l\beta_l' + \eta^2 Id = \sum_{l=1}^{L}(\eta^2 + \beta_l'\beta_l)\tilde{\beta}_l\tilde{\beta}_l' + \eta^2 \sum_{l=L+1}^{KS} \tilde{\beta}_l\tilde{\beta}_l'.$$

The matrices $\tilde{\beta}_l\tilde{\beta}_l'$, for l varying, are orthogonal projectors on mutually orthogonal linear spaces. This provides the spectral decomposition of matrix Ω. We deduce that

$$\det \Omega = (\eta^2)^{KS-L} \prod_{l=1}^{L}(\eta^2 + \beta_l'\beta_l),$$

$$\Omega^{-1} = \sum_{l=1}^{L} \frac{1}{\eta^2 + \beta_l'\beta_l}\tilde{\beta}_l\tilde{\beta}_l' + \sum_{l=L+1}^{KS} \frac{1}{\eta^2}\tilde{\beta}_l\tilde{\beta}_l'$$

$$= -\sum_{l=1}^{L} \beta_l\beta_l' \frac{1}{\eta^2(\eta^2 + \beta_l'\beta_l)} + \frac{1}{\eta^2}Id.$$

(**) The CSA Log-Likelihood Function

We have

$$\frac{1}{T}\mathcal{L}^{CSA}(\theta) \propto -\frac{1}{2}\log \det \Omega(\beta, \eta^2) - \frac{1}{2T}\sum_{t=1}^{T}(\hat{a}_t - \alpha)'\Omega(\beta, \eta^2)^{-1}(\hat{a}_t - \alpha),$$

where we make explicit the dependence of matrix Ω on parameters β and η^2.

(***) CSA Estimator of α

The first-order condition with respect to α is

$$\sum_{t=1}^{T}[\Omega(\beta, \eta^2)]^{-1}(\hat{a}_t - \alpha) = 0$$

$$\Longleftrightarrow \sum_{t=1}^{T}(\hat{a}_t - \alpha) = 0$$

$$\Longleftrightarrow \hat{\alpha}_T = \frac{1}{T}\sum_{t=1}^{T}\hat{a}_t = \bar{a}_T.$$

(****) Concentrated CSA Log-Likelihood Function

Therefore, the log-likelihood function concentrated with respect to α is

$$\frac{1}{T}\tilde{\mathcal{L}}^{\text{CSA}}(\beta, \eta^2) \propto -\frac{1}{2}\log\det\Omega(\beta, \eta^2)$$

$$-\frac{1}{2T}\sum_{t=1}^{T}[(\hat{a}_t - \hat{a}_T)'\Omega(\beta, \eta^2)^{-1}(\hat{a}_t - \hat{a}_T)]$$

$$= -\frac{1}{2}\log\det\Omega(\beta, \eta^2) - \frac{1}{2}Tr[\Omega(\beta, \eta^2)^{-1}\hat{V}_T],$$

where $\hat{V}_T = \frac{1}{T}\sum_{t=1}^{T}(\hat{a}_t - \bar{a}_T)(\hat{a}_t - \bar{a}_T)'$ is the historical variance-covariance matrix of the estimated canonical factors, and Tr denotes the trace operator, which computes the sum of the diagonal elements of a square matrix. From the expressions of $\det\Omega$ and Ω^{-1} derived in (*), we deduce

$$\frac{1}{T}\tilde{\mathcal{L}}^{\text{CSA}}(\beta, \eta^2) \propto -\frac{KS - L}{2}\log\eta^2 - \frac{1}{2}\sum_{l=1}^{L}\log(\eta^2 + \beta_l'\beta_l) - \frac{1}{2\eta^2}Tr(\hat{V}_T)$$

$$+ \frac{1}{2}\sum_{l=1}^{L}\frac{\beta_l'\hat{V}_T\beta_l}{\eta^2(\eta^2 + \beta_l'\beta_l)}.$$

(*****) Estimators of β and η^2

Let us consider the first-order condition with respect to β_l without taking into account the orthogonality restrictions between the sensitivity vectors. We obtain

$$\frac{1}{T}\frac{\partial\tilde{\mathcal{L}}^{\text{CSA}}}{\partial\beta_l} = \left\{-\frac{1}{\eta^2 + \beta_l'\beta_l} - \frac{\beta_l'\hat{V}_T\beta_l}{\eta^2(\eta^2 + \beta_l'\beta_l)^2}\right\}\beta_l + \frac{\hat{V}_T\beta_l}{\eta^2(\eta^2 + \beta_l'\beta_l)} = 0.$$

This first-order condition implies that the vectors $\hat{V}_T\beta_l$ and β_l are proportional, that is, β_l is an eigenvector of matrix $\hat{V}_T$.

Let us denote by $\hat{e}_l$ an eigenvector of $\hat{V}_T$ with unit norm proportional to β_l, and by $\hat{\lambda}_l$ the associated eigenvalue. We have

$$\beta_l = \gamma_l^{1/2}\hat{e}_l,$$

where $\gamma_l = \beta'_l \beta_l$. By substituting in the first-order condition, we obtain an equation that defines γ_l :

$$-\frac{1}{\eta^2 + \gamma_l} - \frac{\hat{\lambda}_l \gamma_l}{\eta^2(\eta^2 + \gamma_l)^2} + \frac{\hat{\lambda}_l}{\eta^2(\eta^2 + \gamma_l)} = 0$$

$$\Longleftrightarrow \gamma_l = \beta'_l \beta_l = \hat{\lambda}_l - \eta^2.$$

Let us finally concentrate with respect to the optimal $\beta'_l s$. We obtain

$$\frac{1}{T} \tilde{\mathcal{L}}^{CSA}(\eta^2)$$

$$\propto -\frac{KS - L}{2} \log \eta^2 - \frac{1}{2} \sum_{l=1}^{L} \log \hat{\lambda}_l - \frac{1}{2\eta^2} Tr(\hat{V}_T) + \frac{1}{2} \sum_{l=1}^{L} \frac{(\hat{\lambda}_l - \eta^2)}{\eta^2}$$

$$= -\frac{KS - L}{2} \log \eta^2 - \frac{1}{2\eta^2} \left[Tr(\hat{V}_T) - \sum_{l=1}^{L} \hat{\lambda}_l \right] - \frac{1}{2} \sum_{l=1}^{L} \log \hat{\lambda}_l - \frac{L}{2}.$$

The first-order condition with respect to η^2 provides

$$\eta^2 = \frac{Tr(\hat{V}_T) - \sum_{l=1}^{L} \hat{\lambda}_l}{KS - L}.$$

Because $Tr(\hat{V}_T) = \sum_{l=1}^{KS} \hat{\lambda}_l$, the corresponding value of the concentrated CSA log-likelihood is equal (up to an additive constant) to

$$-\frac{KS - L}{2} \log \left(\sum_{l=L+1}^{KS} \hat{\lambda}_l \right) - \frac{1}{2} \sum_{l=1}^{L} \log \hat{\lambda}_l.$$

This value is maximized when the eigenvalues $\hat{\lambda}_l, l = 1, \dots, L$, are selected as the L largest eigenvalues of matrix $\hat{V}_T$. This proves Proposition 3.1.

References

Anderson, T. (2003). *An Introduction to Multivariate Statistical Analysis*, 3rd edition. Wiley.

Basel Committee on Banking Supervision (2001). "The New Basel Capital Accord," Consultative Document of the Bank for International Settlements, April 2001, Part 2: Pillar 1.

Basel Committee on Banking Supervision (2003). "The New Basel Capital Accord," Consultative Document of the Bank for International Settlements, April 2003, Part 3: Pillar 2.

Berkson, J. (1944). "Application of the Logistic Function to Bioassay," *Journal of the American Statistical Association*, 39, 357–365.

Blake, D., A., Cairns, and K. David (2006). "A Two Factor Model for Stochastic Mortality with Parameter Uncertainty: Theory and Calibration," *Journal of Risk and Insurance*, 73, 687–718.

Gouriéroux, C., and J. Jasiak (2012). "Granularity Adjustment for Default Risk Factor Model with Cohorts," *Journal of Banking and Finance*, 36, 1464–1477.

Gouriéroux, C., and A. Monfort (1989). *Statistics and Econometric Models*, Cambridge University Press.

Gouriéroux, C., and A. Monfort (1996). *Simulation Based Estimation Methods*, Oxford University Press.

Gouriéroux, C., and A. Monfort (2008). "Queshatic Stochastic Intensity and Prospective Mortality Tables," *Insurance: Mathematics and Economics*, 43, 174–184.

Gouriéroux, C., and A. Monfort (2010). "Granularity in Qualitative Factor Model," *Journal of Credit Risk*, 5, Winter 2009/10.

Jennrich, R., and D. Thayer (1977). "A Note on Lawley's Formulas for Standard Errors in Maximum Likelihood Factor Analysis," Psychometrika, 38, 571–580.

Koenig, H., Nerlove, M., and G., Oudiz (1979). "Modèles log-linéaires pour l'analyse des données qualitatives," *Annales de l'INSEE*, 36, 31–83.

Lawley, D., and A., Maxwell (1971). *Factor Analysis as a Statistical Method*, 2nd edition Elsevier.

Lee, R., and L. Carter (1972). "Modeling and Forecasting US Mortality," *Journal of the American Statistical Association*, 87, 659–675.

McFadden, D. (1973). "Conditional Analysis of Qualitative Choice Behavior," in *Frontiers of Econometrics*, ed. by P. Zarembka, 105–142, Academic.

McFadden, D. (1976). "Quantal Choice Analysis: A Survey," *Annals of Economic and Social Measurement*, 5, 363–390.

Merton, R. (1974). "On the Pricing of Corporate Debt: The Risk Structure of Interest Rates," *Journal of Finance*, 29, 449–470.

Nerlove, M. (1983). "Expectations, Plans and Realizations in Theory and Practice," *Econometrica*, 51, 1251–1279.

Nerlove, M., and S. Press (1986). "Multivariate Log-Linear Probability Models," in *Advances in Statistical Analysis and Statistical Computing: Theory and Application*, ed. by R. Mariano, 117–174, JAI Press.

Vasicek, O. (1991). "Limiting Loan Loss Probability Distribution," DP KMV Corporation.

4   Nonlinear Dynamic Panel Data Model

In this chapter, we present the application of granularity theory to estimation of general nonlinear dynamic panel data models with common factors. These models can feature nonlinear dynamics in both the measurement and state equations. Intuitively, the specification distinguishes between the dynamics at the individual level through the lagged individual observations (micro-dynamics), and the dynamics at the aggregate level through the factors (macro-dynamics). Consequently, the parameterization of these models involves both macro-parameters and micro-parameters.

In Section 4.1, we explain why the GA methodology remains simple in qualitative models with dynamic Gaussian latent factors. Indeed, in these specifications with macro-parameters only, both the CSA and GA approximated models are linear state space models, for which the standard Kalman filter applies. The results for general models with both macro- and micro-parameters and nonlinear factor dynamics are described in Section 4.2. We explain how to derive estimators of the micro- and macro-parameters that are asymptotically efficient when both the cross-sectional dimension n and the time dimension T tend to infinity. We also provide approximations of the factor values (see Chapter 5). As expected, the rates of convergence differ: they are $1/\sqrt{nT}$ for the micro-parameters, $1/\sqrt{T}$ for the macro-parameters, and $1/\sqrt{n}$ for the factor values. A sketch of the proof of the asymptotic results is given in Section 4.3, where we also introduce the CSA and GA maximum likelihood estimators of the parameters. The application to stochastic migration models is presented in Section 4.4. These models are used for a joint analysis of the corporate rating migrations in an homogeneous set of companies. An empirical analysis using S&P rating data for U.S. companies in the 1990–2009 period is presented in Section 4.5.

4.1 Qualitative Model with Gaussian Dynamic Factor

4.1.1 The Model

The static qualitative factor model of Section 3.2 with J alternatives and K cohort can be extended to include factor dynamics. Let us assume individual qualitative observations such that

$$P[Y_{i,k,t} = j|a_t] = p(j; a_{k,t}), \quad j = 1, \ldots, J, \quad k = 1, \ldots, K,$$
$$t = 1, \ldots, T, \tag{4.1}$$

where $a_t = (a'_{1,t}, \ldots, a'_{K,t})' \in I\!R^{KS}$ denotes the canonical factor. Moreover, suppose that the canonical factors are noisy linear transformations of a smaller number $L < KS$ of underlying macro-factors $F_t \in I\!R^L$ with a Gaussian vector autoregressive (VAR) dynamic

$$a_t = \alpha + \beta F_t + \eta w_t, \tag{4.2}$$

where

$$F_t = \Phi F_{t-1} + \varepsilon_t, \tag{4.3}$$

and the errors (w_t), (ε_t) are independent, such that $w_t \sim IIN(0, Id)$ and $\varepsilon_t \sim IIN(0, \Omega)$, say. Model (4.1)–(4.3) is a state space model with static nonlinear measurement equations (4.1) and a Gaussian dynamic linear state equation (4.2)–(4.3).

4.1.2 Approximated Linear State Space Model

For large cross-sectional dimensions n_k of the cohorts, the nonlinear state space model can be approximated by a Gaussian linear state space model, for which standard software programs based on the linear Kalman filter are available.[1] These programs can be used for parameter estimation, prediction of the future individual qualitative variables, or filtering of the unobservable factor values.

Let us consider the fixed effects maximum likelihood estimator of the canonical factor values [see Section 3.2.2]:

$$\hat{a}_{k,t} = \arg\max_{a_{k,t}} \sum_{j=1}^{J} n_{j,k,t} \log p(j; a_{k,t}). \tag{4.4}$$

Under identification conditions, we know from (3.20) that, asymptotically,

$$\hat{a}_t \overset{d}{\sim} N\left(a_t, \hat{\Sigma}_{n,t}\right), \tag{4.5}$$

---

[1] See, e.g., the *sspace* object in EVIEWS or the Kalman function in the *Control and System Toolbox* in MATLAB.

where the asymptotic variance is given by the block-diagonal matrix $\hat{\Sigma}_{n,t} =$ diag$[\hat{\Sigma}_{k,t}/n_k]$ and the matrices $\hat{\Sigma}_{k,t}$ are the estimates of matrices $\Sigma_{k,t}$ in equation (3.21). Moreover, the vectors $\hat{a}_t$, t varying, are asymptotically independent. Thus, the nonlinear static measurement equations written on individual qualitative observations $Y_{i,k,t}$, $i = 1, \ldots, n_k$, $k = 1, \ldots, K$, $t = 1, \ldots, T$ can be asymptotically replaced by the linear measurement equations (4.5) written on the aggregate statistics $\hat{a}_t$, $t = 1, \ldots, T$. In other words, the initial model can be replaced by the following VGA linear state space model:

State equation:

$$F_t = \Phi F_{t-1} + \varepsilon_t, \quad \varepsilon_t \sim IIN(0, \Omega); \tag{4.6}$$

VGA measurement equation:

$$\hat{a}_t = \alpha + \beta F_t + u_t, \quad u_t \sim IIN(0, \eta^2 Id + \hat{\Sigma}_{n,t}). \tag{4.7}$$

The GA appears by means of the additional variance-covariance matrix $\hat{\Sigma}_{n,t}$ in the measurement equation. If $n_k = \infty$, for any $k = 1, \ldots, K$, this term would disappear. This yields the CSA linear state space model:

State equation:

$$F_t = \Phi F_{t-1} + \varepsilon_t, \quad \varepsilon_t \sim IIN(0, \Omega); \tag{4.8}$$

CSA measurement equation:

$$\hat{a}_t = \alpha + \beta F_t + u_t, \quad u_t \sim IIN(0, \eta^2 Id). \tag{4.9}$$

Thus, both the CSA and VGA approximated models are linear state space models and can be analyzed by the standard linear Kalman filter (see Appendix A, Review Appendix A.5). The Kalman filter is used to estimate parameters α, β, Φ, Ω, and η and to filter the latent factor values.

4.2 Asymptotically Efficient Estimators

4.2.1 The Model

Let us now consider the general nonlinear dynamic model with an unobservable factor (see Chapter 1, Section 1.3). For expository purposes, the model is presented for a single cohort. It is defined by its transition densities, which are parameterized as follows:

State equation: The conditional density of factor F_t given $F_{t-1} = f_{t-1}$ is $g(f_t|f_{t-1}; \theta)$.

Measurement equations: The conditional density of $y_{i,t}$ given $y_{i,t-1}$ and f_t is $h(y_{i,t}|y_{i,t-1}, f_t; \beta)$.

Conditional on the factor path, the individual histories $(y_{i,t})$, $i = 1, \cdots, n$, are independent Markov processes, with the same transition density $h(y_{i,t}|y_{i,t-1}, f_t; \beta)$ between $t-1$ and t; that transition density depends on the factor value f_t. The factor varies stochastically in time according to a Markov process with transition density $g(f_t|f_{t-1}; \theta)$. The model involves a vector of micro-parameters β that characterize the dynamics at the individual level (micro-dynamics), as well as a vector of macro-parameters θ that characterize the dynamics of the factor (macro-dynamics). The unknown true values of these parameters are denoted β_0 and θ_0, respectively. When the unobservable stochastic factors (F_t) are integrated out, the model for the observable variables features both cross-sectional dependence and non-Markovian serial dependence.

If the variables $y_{i,t}$, $i = 1, \ldots, n$, and f_t were observable at each date, the joint density (conditional on the initial observations) would be

$$l^*(\underline{y_T}, \underline{f_T}; \beta, \theta) = [\prod_{t=1}^{T} g(f_t|f_{t-1}; \theta)] \prod_{t=1}^{T} \prod_{i=1}^{n} h(y_{it}|y_{i,t-1}, f_t; \beta). \quad (4.10)$$

Thus, the latent log-likelihood function could be decomposed as

$$\mathcal{L}^*(\underline{y_T}, \underline{f_T}; \beta, \theta) = \log l^*(\underline{y_T}, \underline{f_T}; \beta, \theta)$$

$$= \mathcal{L}^M(\underline{f_T}; \theta) + \sum_{t=1}^{T} \mathcal{L}^{CS}(\tilde{y}_t|\tilde{y}_{t-1}, f_t; \beta), \quad (4.11)$$

where

$$\mathcal{L}^M(\underline{f_T}; \theta) = \sum_{t=1}^{T} \log g(f_t|f_{t-1}; \theta), \quad (4.12)$$

is the log-likelihood corresponding to the macroeconomic factor, called the **latent macro log-likelihood function**, and

$$\mathcal{L}^{CS}(\tilde{y}_t|\tilde{y}_{t-1}, f_t; \beta) = \sum_{i=1}^{n} \log h(y_{i,t}|y_{i,t-1}, f_t; \beta), \quad (4.13)$$

is the log-likelihood corresponding to individual transitions between dates $t-1$ and t. It is called the **latent cross-sectional micro log-likelihood function**.

The different log-likelihood functions described in (4.11)–(4.13) are latent, because they treat the latent factors as observable. As already mentioned, the true log-likelihood function is deduced by integrating out the unobservable factors. It is given by

$$\log l(\underline{y_T}; \beta, \theta),$$

where

$$l(\underline{y_T}; \beta, \theta) = \int \cdots \int [\prod_{t=1}^{T} g(f_t|f_{t-1}; \theta)] \prod_{t=1}^{T} \prod_{i=1}^{n} h(y_{i,t}|y_{i,t-1}, f_t; \beta) \prod_{t=1}^{T} df_t.$$

(4.14)

This log-likelihood function has a complicated expression, which involves a multiple integral with a huge dimension equal to T times the number of factors. In particular, the dimension of this integral tends to infinity with time dimension T.

When n and T are large, it is possible to derive asymptotically efficient estimators of both types of parameters without having to compute the high-dimensional integral in (4.14). This is shown next.

4.2.2 The Estimation Method

If micro-parameter β were known, the factor value at date t could be approximated by the **fixed effects estimator:**

$$\hat{f}_{n,t}(\beta) = \arg \max_{f_t} \mathcal{L}^{CS}(\tilde{y}_t|\tilde{y}_{t-1}, f_t; \beta)$$

$$= \arg \max_{f_t} \sum_{i=1}^{n} \log h(y_{i,t}|y_{i,t-1}, f_t; \beta).$$

(4.15)

The term "fixed effects" is used because estimator $\hat{f}_{n,t}(\beta)$ is computed by treating f_t as a parameter in the latent cross-sectional micro-likelihood; that is, by considering the factor values as fixed time effects.

However, micro-parameter β is unknown, and thus the factor approximations $\hat{f}_{n,t}(\beta)$ are unknown as well. But these values can be reintroduced in the latent micro-likelihood functions, aggregated over time, to obtain a function of the observations $\underline{y_T}$ and parameter β only. This leads to an estimator of β defined by

$$\hat{\beta}_{n,T} = \arg \max_{\beta} \sum_{t=1}^{T} \sum_{i=1}^{n} \log h[y_{i,t}|y_{i,t-1}, \hat{f}_{n,t}(\beta); \beta].$$

(4.16)

Equivalently, it can also be derived by considering the solution in β in the joint optimization problem:

$$\max_{\beta, f_1, \dots, f_T} \sum_{t=1}^{T} \sum_{i=1}^{n} \log h(y_{i,t}|y_{i,t-1}, f_t; \beta).$$

(4.17)

The definition of the estimator through (4.17) shows that the unknown factor values have been treated as nuisance parameters. Such an approach might create an **incidental parameter** problem, because the number of nuisance parameters tends to infinity with T [Neyman and Scott (1948)]. This problem does not exist in our framework, where the cross-sectional dimension is much larger than the time dimension (see Proposition 4.1 and the discussion thereafter).

The estimator of the micro-parameter can be introduced in the expression of the fixed effects estimator of the factor value to obtain an approximation of factor value at date t:

$$\hat{f}_{n,T,t} = \hat{f}_{n,t}(\hat{\beta}_{n,T}). \tag{4.18}$$

These approximated factor values can serve as proxies for the unobserved factor values. This leads to the following estimator of the macro-parameter θ:

$$\hat{\theta}_{n,T} = \arg\max_{\theta} \sum_{t=1}^{T} \log g(\hat{f}_{n,T,t} | \hat{f}_{n,T,t-1}; \theta). \tag{4.19}$$

The estimator $\hat{\theta}_{nT}$ maximizes the latent macro log-likelihood $\mathcal{L}^M$ after replacing the factor values by their proxies.

Remark 4.1. The models presented in Chapters 2 and 3 and in Section 4.1 were models with macro-parameters only. In such cases, the fixed effects estimator of the first step is a function of the individual observations only; that is,

$$\hat{f}_{n,T,t} = \hat{f}_{n,t} = \arg\max_{f_t} \sum_{i=1}^{n} \log h(y_{i,t} | y_{i,t-1}, f_t). \tag{4.20}$$

4.2.3 Asymptotic Properties of the Estimators

The asymptotic properties of the estimators of micro- and macro-parameters introduced earlier were derived in Gagliardini and Gouriéroux (2014) (see also the discussion in Section 4.3). Their asymptotic distribution involves information matrices corresponding to the latent macro-likelihood and cross-sectional micro-likelihood. More precisely, the cross-sectional information matrix at date t is

$$I^{CS}(t) = E_0 \left[-\frac{\partial^2 \log h(y_{i,t} | y_{i,t-1}, f_t; \beta_0)}{\partial(\beta', f')' \partial(\beta', f')} | \underline{f_t} \right]. \tag{4.21}$$

It involves the conditional expectation of the second-order derivative matrix of the micro log-density with regard to the micro-parameter and the factor value, given the current and past history of factor values $\underline{f_t} = (f_t, f_{t-1}, \cdots)$. This information matrix can be written in block form as follows:

$$I^{CS}(t) = \begin{bmatrix} I_{\beta\beta}(t) & I_{\beta f}(t) \\ I_{f\beta}(t) & I_{ff}(t) \end{bmatrix}. \tag{4.22}$$

The macro information matrix is

$$I^M = E_0 \left[-\frac{\partial^2 \log g(f_t | f_{t-1}; \theta_0)}{\partial \theta \partial \theta'} \right]. \tag{4.23}$$

We have the following proposition valid under the set of regularity conditions detailed in Gagliardini and Gouriéroux (2014):

Proposition 4.1. *If the dimensions n, T tend to infinity such that $T^b/n = O(1)$, for $b > 1$, then*

(i) *The estimators are consistent and asymptotically normal:*

$$\begin{bmatrix} \sqrt{nT}(\hat{\beta}_{n,T} - \beta_0) \\ \sqrt{T}(\hat{\theta}_{n,T} - \theta_0) \end{bmatrix} \xrightarrow{d} N \left(\begin{bmatrix} 0 \\ 0 \end{bmatrix}, \begin{bmatrix} (I^*_{\beta\beta})^{-1} & 0 \\ 0 & (I^M)^{-1} \end{bmatrix} \right),$$

where

$$I^*_{\beta\beta} = E_0[I_{\beta\beta}(t) - I_{\beta f}(t) I_{ff}(t)^{-1} I_{f\beta}(t)].$$

(ii) *The estimators are asymptotically efficient.*

(iii) *For any date t, conditional on the factor path we have*

$$\sqrt{n}(\hat{f}_{nT,t} - f_t) \xrightarrow{d} N[0, I_{ff}(t)^{-1}].$$

All estimators converge to their corresponding true values when both n and T tend to infinity at suitable relative rates; namely, when n is infinitely larger than T in the limit. However, the convergence rates of the estimators differ: they are equal to $1/\sqrt{nT}$ for the micro-parameters, $1/\sqrt{T}$ for the macro-parameters, and $1/\sqrt{n}$ for the factor values. Estimators $\hat{\beta}_{n,T}$ and $\hat{\theta}_{n,T}$ are asymptotically independent. Thus, asymptotically the inference on β and θ can be done separately. In other words, parameters β (resp. θ) are actually micro-parameters (resp. macro-parameters), because they do not include macro-information (resp. micro-information).

The estimators $\hat{\beta}_{n,T}$ and $\hat{\theta}_{n,T}$ are asymptotically efficient in the sense that they are asymptotically equivalent to the maximum likelihood estimators that maximize the true likelihood function (4.14). Intuitively, when both n and T are large, estimators $\hat{\beta}_{n,T}$ and $\hat{\theta}_{n,T}$ have the lowest possible variance within a very large class of regular consistent estimators. Let us now discuss the expressions of the asymptotic variance-covariance matrices of the estimators. The information matrix I^M corresponds to the Fisher information on θ when the factor values are observable. Thus, for large n, the replacement of these values $f_t, t = 1, \ldots, T$, by their approximations $\hat{f}_{n,T,t}, t = 1, \ldots, T$, has no effect on the estimator of macro-parameter θ. This is because the approximation errors of order $O_p(1/\sqrt{n})$ on the factor values are irrelevant for the estimation of parameter θ at rate $1/\sqrt{T}$, when $T/n \to 0$.

The information matrix $I_{\beta\beta}^*$ is the information matrix for β in the micro-model with parameters β, $f_1, \ldots, f_T$. It does not coincide with $E_0[I_{\beta\beta}(t)]$, because the estimation errors on the factor values have to be taken into account for estimation of the micro-parameters at rate $1/\sqrt{nT}$. However, we observe that the matrix $I_{\beta\beta}^*$ does not depend on the selected dynamic factor model. We deduce that $\hat{\beta}_{n,T}$ is both asymptotically efficient and semi-parametrically efficient [see Gagliardini and Gouriéroux (2014) and Appendix A, Review Appendix A.2].

Finally, the panel data literature emphasizes the role of incidental parameters; that is, the fact that in some models the number of unknown parameters increases with sample size [see Lancaster (2000) for a discussion of incidental parameters in panel data models with individual effects]. In our panel data model with a common factor, the incidental parameters are the factor values, whose number increases with the time dimension T. If the cross-sectional dimension n were fixed, the presence of incidental parameters would imply the inconsistency of $\hat{\beta}_{n,T}$, even for large T. By assuming that n also tends to infinity faster than T, we obtain not only the convergence but also the asymptotic efficiency.

4.3 Likelihood Expansions, CSA, and GA Maximum Likelihood Estimators

The asymptotic properties of the estimators of micro- and macro-parameters presented in Section 4.2 rely on asymptotic expansions of the complicated likelihood function of the model. In this section, we describe the principle of this expansion [see Gagliardini and Gouriéroux (2014) for the complete proofs]; the same principle is also used for prediction purposes (see Chapter 5). Moreover, these asymptotic expansions of the likelihood function are the basis for deriving the CSA and GA maximum likelihood estimators.

4.3.1 First-Order Expansion of the Log-Likelihood Function

The joint density of the observations is [see (4.14)]

$$l(\underline{y}_T; \beta, \theta) = \int \cdots \int \prod_{t=1}^{T} \prod_{i=1}^{n} h(y_{i,t}|y_{i,t-1}, f_t; \beta) \prod_{t=1}^{T} g(f_t|f_{t-1}; \theta) \prod_{t=1}^{T} df_t$$

$$= \int \cdots \int \exp\left\{ \sum_{t=1}^{T} \sum_{i=1}^{n} \log h(y_{i,t}|y_{i,t-1}, f_t; \beta) \right\} \prod_{t=1}^{T} g(f_t|f_{t-1}; \theta) \prod_{t=1}^{T} df_t.$$

For large n the integral with respect to the factor values can be approximated by expanding the integrand around its maximum with regard to the factor along the lines of the **Laplace approximation** [see Jensen (1995), Arellano, Bonhomme (2009), and Appendix 4.8.1]. We obtain the following expansion

Proposition 4.2. *If n, T tend to infinity, with $T^b/n = O(1)$, for $b > 1$, we have*

$$\mathcal{L}_{n,T}(\beta, \theta) = \frac{1}{nT} \log l(\underline{y_T}; \beta, \theta)$$

$$= \mathcal{L}_{n,T}^*(\beta) + \frac{1}{n}\mathcal{L}_{1,n,T}(\beta, \theta) + o_p(1/n), \tag{4.24}$$

where

$$\mathcal{L}_{n,T}^*(\beta) = \frac{1}{nT} \sum_{t=1}^{T} \sum_{i=1}^{n} \log h[y_{i,t}|y_{i,t-1}, \hat{f}_{n,t}(\beta); \beta],$$

$$\mathcal{L}_{1,n,T}(\beta, \theta) = -\frac{1}{2}\frac{1}{T} \sum_{t=1}^{T} \log \det I_{n,t}(\beta) + \frac{1}{T} \sum_{t=1}^{T} \log g[\hat{f}_{n,t}(\beta)|\hat{f}_{n,t-1}(\beta); \theta],$$

and

$$I_{n,t}(\beta) = -\frac{1}{n} \sum_{i=1}^{n} \frac{\partial^2 \log h}{\partial f_t \partial f_t'}(y_{i,t}|y_{i,t-1}, \hat{f}_{n,t}(\beta); \beta).$$

The decomposition of the log-likelihood function in (4.24) explains the main asymptotic results given in Proposition 4.1. Let us first consider the micro-parameters. They are involved in both components of the right-hand side of decomposition (4.24). However, because the second component is negligible with regard to the first one when n is large, the ML estimator of the micro-parameters is equivalent to the estimator based on the optimization of the micro log-likelihood $\mathcal{L}_{n,T}^*$. This is exactly the definition of the fixed effects estimator $\hat{\beta}_{n,T}$ given in Section 4.2.

Let us now consider macro-parameters θ. They are involved in the second term of the expansion (4.24). Because the estimators of the micro-parameters converge faster than the rate $1/\sqrt{T}$, the maximum likelihood estimator of the macro-parameters can be approximated by the solutions of

$$\max_\theta \mathcal{L}_{1,n,T}(\hat{\beta}_{n,T}, \theta)$$

$$\Longleftrightarrow \max_\theta \sum_{t=1}^{T} \log g[\hat{f}_{n,t}(\hat{\beta}_{n,T})|\hat{f}_{n,t-1}(\hat{\beta}_{n,T}); \theta].$$

This yields the estimator $\hat{\theta}_{n,T}$ introduced in Section 4.2. The asymptotic independence between the estimators of the micro- and macro-parameters is due to the additive decomposition of the log-likelihood function in (4.24), where the first component concerns β and the second one θ (because β can be replaced asymptotically by $\hat{\beta}_{n,T}$ in the second component).

In fact, the estimators $(\hat{\beta}_{n,T}, \hat{\theta}_{n,T})$ are asymptotically equivalent to the estimators derived by optimizing the first-order expansion of the log-likelihood function in Proposition 4.2. Let us denote

$$\mathcal{L}_{n,T}^{CSA}(\beta, \theta) = \mathcal{L}_{n,T}^*(\beta) + \frac{1}{n}\mathcal{L}_{1,n,T}(\beta, \theta), \qquad (4.25)$$

as the **cross-sectional asymptotic (CSA) log-likelihood function** and define the **CSA ML estimators** as

$$(\hat{\beta}_{n,T}^{CSA}, \hat{\theta}_{n,T}^{CSA}) = \arg\max_{\beta, \theta} \mathcal{L}_{n,T}^{CSA}(\beta, \theta). \qquad (4.26)$$

The CSA ML estimators are asymptotically equivalent to the estimators $(\hat{\beta}_{n,T}, \hat{\theta}_{n,T})$ and therefore asymptotically efficient.

4.3.2 Granularity Adjustment

The true maximum likelihood estimators of the parameters can be approximated more accurately by considering a second-order expansion of the log-likelihood function with regard to $1/n$ whenever $T^b/n = O(1)$, with $b > 3/2$. We have

$$\mathcal{L}_{n,T}(\beta, \theta) = \mathcal{L}_{n,T}^*(\beta) + \frac{1}{n}\mathcal{L}_{1,n,T}(\beta, \theta) + \frac{1}{n^2}\mathcal{L}_{2,n,T}(\beta, \theta) + o_p(1/n^2), \quad (4.27)$$

where the additional term $\mathcal{L}_{2,n,T}$ has a closed-form expression [see Gagliardini and Gouriéroux (2014)] and does not involve integrals with regard to the unobservable factors. This second-order expansion defines the **GA log-likelihood function**:

$$\mathcal{L}_{n,T}^{GA}(\beta, \theta) = \mathcal{L}_{n,T}^*(\beta) + \frac{1}{n}\mathcal{L}_{1,n,T}(\beta, \theta) + \frac{1}{n^2}\mathcal{L}_{2,n,T}(\beta, \theta). \qquad (4.28)$$

Then, granularity adjusted estimators are defined by maximizing the GA log-likelihood function:

$$(\hat{\beta}_{n,T}^{GA}, \hat{\theta}_{n,T}^{GA}) = \arg\max_{\beta, \theta} \mathcal{L}_{n,T}^{GA}(\beta, \theta). \qquad (4.29)$$

In the general framework, the granularity adjustment is more important for the estimators of the macro-parameters (whose speed of convergence is slower) than for the estimators of micro-parameters. The granularity adjustment allows modification of the bias at order $1/n$ of the CSA estimator $\hat{\theta}_{n,T}^{CSA}$. It is possible to show that the difference between $\hat{\theta}_{n,T}^{GA}$ and the true ML estimator of θ is of order $o_p(1/n)$, whereas this difference is of order $O_p(1/n)$ for the CSA estimator $\hat{\theta}_{n,T}^{CSA}$ and for the estimator $\hat{\theta}_{n,T}$ defined in Section 4.2. Thus, the GA and the true ML estimator of the macro-parameters are equivalent at order $1/n$.

4.3.3 Newton-Raphson Algorithm

It is easily checked that estimators asymptotically equivalent to the GA estimators are obtained by applying a single iteration in an appropriate Newton-Raphson algorithm with the CSA estimator as the starting value [see Appendix 4.8.2]. We have

$$
\begin{pmatrix} \hat{\beta}_{n,T}^{GA} \\ \hat{\theta}_{n,T}^{GA} \end{pmatrix} = \begin{pmatrix} \hat{\beta}_{n,T}^{CSA} \\ \hat{\theta}_{n,T}^{CSA} \end{pmatrix} + \left[-\frac{\partial^2 \mathcal{L}_{n,T}^{CSA}(\hat{\beta}_{n,T}^{CSA}, \hat{\theta}_{n,T}^{CSA})}{\partial(\beta', \theta')' \partial(\beta', \theta')} \right]^{-1}
$$

$$
\cdot \frac{\partial \mathcal{L}_{n,T}^{GA}}{\partial(\beta', \theta')'}(\hat{\beta}_{n,T}^{CSA}, \hat{\theta}_{n,T}^{CSA}), \tag{4.30}
$$

up to order $o_p(1/n^2)$ for the micro-parameters and up to order $o_p(1/n)$ for the macro-parameters.

4.4 Stochastic Migration Model

The Basel 2 accord requires an accurate analysis not only of default risk and default correlation (see Section 3.1) but also of the risk associated with possible rating downgrades and upgrades [BCBS (2001, 2003)]. Indeed, the current rating has a significant impact on the value of the debt, and this effect has to be taken into account when assessing the risk of a credit portfolio. For this purpose, a dynamic analysis of the qualitative rating histories is required, which focuses on rating migration correlation. Unobservable dynamic factors are typically introduced in the models to create downgrade (resp. upgrade) correlation. In response to the demands of regulators, stochastic migration models have been recently introduced in the academic literature, with emphasis on corporate ratings and the business cycle [see, e.g., Gordy and Heitfield (2002), Gagliardini and Gouriéroux (2005a, 2005b), and Feng, Gouriéroux and Jasiak (2008)].

4.4.1 Stochastic Transition Matrices

Let us consider an homogeneous subpopulation and individual qualitative histories $(y_{i,t}, t = 1, \ldots, T)$, for $i = 1, \ldots, n$. Variables $y_{i,t}$ are polytomous qualitative with K possible alternatives, denoted $k = 1, \ldots, K$. In the application to corporate bonds, these alternatives are the possible ratings, such as AAA, AA, A, BBB, ..., D in Standard & Poor's (S&P) rating system. Their number is typically either 8, or 10, depending on whether ratings CCC, CC, and C are grouped together or not. The stochastic migration model described in this section can be applied to other frameworks as well.

As before, the dynamic model is defined by state and measurement equations:

State equation: The transition density of the factor is $g(f_t \mid f_{t-1}; \theta)$.

Measurement equations: These equations are defined by the transition probabilities:

$$P[y_{i,t} = k \mid y_{i,t-1} = l, F_t = f_t; \beta] = \pi_{lk}(f_t; \beta), \text{ say,}$$

for $k, l = 1, \dots, K$.

Because the individual observations are qualitative, the transition pdf of $y_{i,t}$, given $y_{i,t-1}$ and f_t, is characterized by the (K, K) transition matrix:

$$\Pi(f_t; \beta) = [\pi_{lk}(f_t; \beta)]. \tag{4.31}$$

This transition matrix has nonnegative elements, which sum up to one by row. Its diagonal elements provide the probabilities of keeping the same rating between dates $t - 1$ and t, whereas the out-of-diagonal elements are the probabilities of migrating up or down from one rating class to another.

For a given factor history, the individual qualitative rating histories are independent and identically distributed. Each individual rating history is a Markov chain, which is time heterogeneous because the transition matrices evolve in time. When the factor is considered stochastic, we get Markov chains with stochastic transition matrices. This interpretation justifies the alternative names given to this type of model: **stochastic migration model, stochastic transition model**, or **model with stochastic intensity** (see also Section 3.4 for the two-state case with an absorbing state). When the factor is integrated out, the individual histories become dependent and the Markov property is lost. Intuitively, the entire past of all the series is informative and is needed to reconstitute approximately the current factor value.

There exist different migration models according to the specification of the transition matrix. Intuitively, each row of the transition matrix defines a probability distribution for which an ordered polytomous model (see Example 3.4 in Section 3.3) or a multinomial logit model (see Example 3.3 in Section 3.3) can be chosen. Moreover, the models for the different rows can be linked, as seen in the next subsections description of the model usually considered for the analysis of rating histories.

4.4.2 The Dynamic Ordered Qualitative Model for Rating Histories

This model is the direct extension of the SRF model of Section 3.1 to more than two alternatives and to a dynamic framework. In the spirit of Merton's structural model, the rating is based on the level of the log asset-to-liability ratio. More precisely, let us introduce a partition of the real line: $c_0 = -\infty < c_1 < c_2 < \dots < c_{K-1} < c_K = +\infty$. We assume that

$$y_{i,t} = k, \text{ if and only if } c_{k-1} < \log(A_{i,t}/L_{i,t}) \leq c_k \tag{4.32}$$

for $k = 1, \ldots, K$, where $A_{i,t}$ and $L_{i,t}$ denote the asset value and the debt of firm i at date t, respectively. In this way, the rating classes are numbered in order of increasing credit quality, with alternative $k = 1$ typically corresponding to default.[2] Then, we have to define the conditional distribution of the log asset-to-liability ratio given the factor and the past individual histories. We assume that the dependence on the past is through the most recent rating only. The latent model, which extends (3.3), is

$$\log A_{i,t} - \log L_{i,t} = a_l + b_l F_t + \sigma_l u_{i,t} \tag{4.33}$$

for companies with rating $y_{i,t-1} = l$ at date $t - 1$, where $u_{i,t} \sim N(0, 1)$ is independent of F_t. By comparing model (4.33) with equation (3.3), we see that the conditioning with respect to the last rating is equivalent to the creation at each date t of a set of K homogeneous subpopulations, in which the corporations are grouped according to their previous rating.

Under (4.32)–(4.33) the stochastic transition probabilities are given by

$$\pi_{l,k}(f_t; \beta) = \Phi\left(\frac{c_k - a_l - b_l f_t}{\sigma_l}\right) - \Phi\left(\frac{c_{k-1} - a_l - b_l f_t}{\sigma_l}\right), \tag{4.34}$$

where Φ is the standard normal c.d.f. These transition probabilities involve two types of micro-parameters: (1) the parameters $a_l, b_l, \sigma_l, l = 1, \ldots, K$ of the latent model for the individual asset-to-liability ratios and (2) the thresholds $c_k, k = 1, \ldots, K - 1$, used to define the ratings. Whereas a_l, b_l, and σ_l appear in row l of the transition matrix only, the threshold parameters are in all rows, introducing links between them. Moreover, although we focused earlier on a model with a single factor in analogy to Section 3.1, the extension to include a multivariate factor F_t of dimension d, say, is straightforward. In this case, for each row l of the transition matrix we would have a $(d, 1)$ vector b_l of sensitivities to the different factors.

Finally, the measurement equations (4.34) are usually completed by a state equation corresponding to a Gaussian VAR model,

$$F_t = \mu + A F_{t-1} + \varepsilon_t, \quad \varepsilon_t \sim IIN(0, \Omega), \tag{4.35}$$

where A is a (d, d) matrix of autoregressive coefficients.

4.4.3 Identification

Parameter identification has to be considered carefully before applying any estimation method. The vector of model parameters is identified if it is not

---

[2] In Merton's basic model, $c_1 = 0$. In practice the constraint $c_1 = 0$ is generally not introduced, especially because of the regulatory definition of default. For instance, a default can be reported if the lender thinks that a failure of a company is highly probable in the next future, even if this failure has not yet occurred. Thus, threshold c_1 can be strictly positive, and its magnitude depends on the judgment of the lender.

possible to find two distinct parameter vectors that imply the same distribution for the observable variables; that is, for the joint history of the ratings of the n firms [see, e.g., Gouriéroux and Monfort (1995) and Section 3.4]. In the ordered qualitative model for ratings described in Section 4.4.2, the lack of identification can have two causes: the loss in information incurred when passing from the quantitative scoring variable (the asset-to-liability ratio) to the qualitative rating, and from the unobservable factors being defined up to an invertible linear transformation. The identification restrictions have to account for the links between the rows of the transition matrix and to conserve the distinction between micro- and macro-parameters.

For instance, in a stochastic migration model for rating histories with a single factor and absorbing state $k = K$, identification restrictions are $c_1 = a_1 = 0$ and $b_1 = \sigma_1 = 1$. Therefore, the identifiable micro-parameters are $\beta = (a_k, b_k, \sigma_k, c_k, \ k = 2, \ldots, K - 1)$, whereas the macro-parameters are $\theta = (\mu, A, \Omega)$, which are all the parameters of the state equation. In the general case, we denote by β and θ the vectors of identifiable micro- and macro-parameters of the model, once suitable identification restrictions are imposed.

4.4.4 Asymptotically Efficient Estimators

The asymptotically efficient estimators of the micro- and macro-parameters, as well as the factor approximations, are derived from the general results in Section 4.2, shown in equations (4.16), (4.18), and (4.19). For expository purposes, we focus on a single-factor model.

Let us denote by $N_{k,t}$ and $N_{l,k,t}$ the number of companies in rating class k at date t, and the number of companies migrating from class l to class k between dates $t - 1$ and t, respectively. The transition frequencies $\hat{\pi}_{l,k,t} = N_{l,k,t}/N_{l,t-1}$, for $l, k = 1, \ldots, K$, are the empirical counterparts of the stochastic transition probabilities between dates $t - 1$ and t. Then, the cross-sectional micro-density of the model at date t is given by

$$\mathcal{L}^{CS}(\tilde{y}_t | \tilde{y}_{t-1}, f_t; \beta) = \sum_{l=1}^{K} \sum_{k=1}^{K} N_{l,k,t} \log \pi_{l,k,t}(f_t; \beta)$$

$$= \sum_{l=1}^{K} N_{l,t-1} \sum_{k=1}^{K} \hat{\pi}_{l,k,t} \log \left[\Phi \left(\frac{c_k - b_l f_t - a_l}{\sigma_l} \right) \right.$$

$$\left. - \Phi \left(\frac{c_{k-1} - b_l f_t - a_l}{\sigma_l} \right) \right].$$

It follows that the counts $N_{l,t-1}$ and the empirical transition frequencies $\hat{\pi}_{l,k,t}$ for $l, k = 1, \ldots, K$ and $t = 1, \ldots, T$, are summary statistics for the stochastic migration model (conditionally on the initial observations and factor values).

These empirical counts and transition frequencies are freely available from websites of rating agencies or central banks [see, e.g., Gupton, Finger and Bhatia (1997)].

From the cross-sectional micro-density, we get the fixed effects estimators of the factor values given the micro-parameters

$$\hat{f}_{n,t}(\beta) = \arg\max_{f_t} \sum_{l=1}^{K} N_{l,t-1} \sum_{k=1}^{K} \hat{\pi}_{lk,t} \log \left[\Phi\left(\frac{c_k - b_l f_t - a_l}{\sigma_l} \right) \right.$$
$$\left. - \Phi\left(\frac{c_{k-1} - b_l f_t - a_l}{\sigma_l} \right) \right]$$

for $t = 1, \cdots, T$, and the estimator of the micro-parameters:

$$\hat{\beta}_{n,T} = \arg\max_{\beta} \sum_{t=1}^{T} \sum_{l=1}^{K} N_{l,t-1} \sum_{k=1}^{K} \hat{\pi}_{lk,t} \log \left[\Phi\left(\frac{c_k - b_l \hat{f}_{n,t}(\beta) - a_l}{\sigma_l} \right) \right.$$
$$\left. - \Phi\left(\frac{c_{k-1} - b_l \hat{f}_{n,t}(\beta) - a_l}{\sigma_l} \right) \right].$$

The numerical computation of the estimate $\hat{\beta}_{n,T}$ involves two nested optimization problems. For a given β, the factor approximation $\hat{f}_{n,t}(\beta)$ can be computed by a grid search, and then estimate $\hat{\beta}_{n,T}$ is computed by applying the Newton-Raphson algorithm. Estimator $\hat{\beta}_{n,T}$ is used to obtain the cross-sectional approximations of the factor values:

$$\hat{f}_{n,T,t} = \hat{f}_{n,t}(\hat{\beta}_{n,T}). \tag{4.36}$$

Finally, the estimators of the macro-parameters μ, A, and Ω are obtained by replacing the factor proxies in the macro-dynamics and applying maximum likelihood (ML) on the autoregressive model:

$$\hat{f}_{n,T,t} = \mu + A\hat{f}_{n,T,t-1} + \varepsilon_t, \quad \varepsilon_t \sim IIN(0, \Omega), \quad t = 1, \cdots, T. \tag{4.37}$$

For this autoregressive model, the ML estimator coincides with the ordinary least squares (OLS) estimator. When the factor is multivariate and the vector autoregressive (VAR) model (4.37) involves several equations, the OLS estimators of the components of μ and A are computed equation by equation [see, e.g., Gouriéroux and Jasiak (2005)]. The estimator of Ω is obtained from the sample variance-covariance matrix of the estimated regression residuals $\hat{\varepsilon}_t$. The convergence rates of estimators $\hat{\beta}_{n,T}$ and $\hat{\theta}_{n,T} = (\hat{\mu}_{n,T}, \hat{A}_{n,T}, \hat{\Omega}_{n,T})$ are $1/\sqrt{nT}$ and $1/\sqrt{T}$, respectively, and their asymptotic variance-covariance matrices are deduced from Proposition 4.1.

4.4.5 Approximate Linear State Space Model

An alternative estimation methodology writes the stochastic migration model as an approximate linear state space model and applies a procedure similar to the one described in Section 4.1. The basic idea is that the qualitative model (4.34) can be "linearized" by considering the canonical factors for each row of the transition matrix, as in the ordered probit model in Example 3.4 of Section 3.3. More precisely, let us introduce the cumulated transition probabilities

$$\pi_{l,k}^*(f_t; \beta) = P[Y_{i,t} \leq k | Y_{i,t-1} = l, f_t; \beta]$$

$$= \sum_{h=1}^{k} \pi_{l,h}(f_t; \beta)$$

$$= \Phi\left(\frac{c_k - a_l - b_l f_t}{\sigma_l}\right), \tag{4.38}$$

for $l = 1, \ldots, K$ and $k = 1, \ldots, K - 1$. By applying the quantile function of the standard normal distribution to both sides of equation (4.38), we obtain

$$\Phi^{-1}[\pi_{l,k}^*(f_t; \beta)] = \frac{c_k - a_l - b_l f_t}{\sigma_l}. \tag{4.39}$$

These nonlinear transformations of the cumulated transition probabilities play the role of the canonical factors

$$a_t = vec[a_{l,k,t}] \tag{4.40}$$

where

$$a_{l,k,t} = \frac{c_k - a_l - b_l f_t}{\sigma_l} \tag{4.41}$$

is linear with regard to f_t. The canonical factors are cross-sectionally approximated by their sample analogs:

$$\hat{a}_{l,k,t} = \Phi^{-1}\left(\sum_{h=1}^{k} \hat{\pi}_{l,h,t}\right). \tag{4.42}$$

For large cross-sectional size n, the estimated factors are such that $\hat{a}_t \overset{d}{\sim} N(a_t, \Sigma_{n,t})$ asymptotically, conditional on the factors, and the expression of the estimated asymptotic variance-covariance matrix $\hat{\Sigma}_{n,t}$ is derived in Appendix 4.7. In particular, the block of matrix $\hat{\Sigma}_{n,t}$ corresponding to the canonical factors for row l involves the number $N_{l,t-1}$ of companies in class l at date $t - 1$. Then, the parameters can be estimated by applying the Kalman filter on the VGA linear state space model:

Table 4.1. *Distribution of firms in the S&P pool across rating classes in 1990 and in 2009*

	AAA	AA	A	BBB	BB	B	C	Total
1990	147	373	560	347	282	363	48	2120
2009	81	470	1396	1498	1002	1223	190	5860

State equation:

$$F_t = \mu + AF_{t-1} + \varepsilon_t, \quad \varepsilon_t \sim IIN(0, \Omega)$$

VGA measurement equations:

$$\hat{a}_{l,k,t} = \frac{c_k - a_l}{\sigma_l} - \frac{b_l}{\sigma_l} F_t + u_{l,k,t}, \quad vec(u_{l,k,t}) \sim IIN(0, \hat{\Sigma}_{n,t})$$

for $l = 1, \cdots, K - 1$ and $k = 1, \cdots, K$.

Thus, the nonlinear measurement equations for the individual ratings are approximated by linear measurement equations for suitable cross-sectional aggregates. Contrary to the linear state space models in Section 4.1, the variance of the errors in the measurement equations tends to zero as n tends to infinity. This explains the different rates of convergence for the micro-parameters and the macro-parameters, which are $1/\sqrt{nT}$ and $1/\sqrt{T}$, respectively.

4.5 Application to S&P Rating Migration Data

In this section we present an application of stochastic transition models to S&P rating migration data [see Gagliardini and Gouriéroux (2005b) for a similar analysis using data of the French central bank].

4.5.1 Description of the Data

The data consist of $T = 20$ 1-year empirical migration matrices for U.S. firms in the period from 1990 to 2009. The migration matrices are provided by S&P in public reports and are computed on an annual basis from a pool of large and medium-sized U.S. firms. S&P relies on a rating system based on eight classes (in the simplest version): AAA, AA, A, BBB, BB, B, C, and D. Category AAA corresponds to the lowest risk (i.e., the highest credit ranking) and category C to the highest risk. Category D corresponds to default. The rating is assigned by experts based on available information on a firm's business and financial ratios. The pool of monitored firms is updated regularly to replace defaulting firms with new firms. Table 4.1 shows the distributions of the firms in the pool across rating classes in 1990 and in 2009.

Table 4.2. *One-year transition matrix for 2009*

		\multicolumn{9}{c}{2009}								
		AAA	AA	A	BBB	BB	B	C	D	NR
	AAA	87.65	8.64	0	0	0	0	0	0	3.71
	AA	0	76.17	15.96	0.64	0.21	0	0	0	7.02
	A	0	0.36	84.67	7.74	0.43	0.29	0	0.21	6.3
2008	BBB	0	0	2	83.71	5.94	0.8	0.20	0.53	6.81
	BB	0	0	0	3.09	72.95	11.48	0.60	0.70	11.18
	B	0	0	0.16	0	2.29	69.34	8.42	10.14	9.65
	C	0	0	0	0	0	6.32	27.37	48.42	17.89
	D	0	0	0	0	0	0	0	100	0

Transition probabilities are in percentages. Rating classes are ordered from AAA (lowest risk) to D (default). The column NR corresponds to firms that are not rated at the end of 2009.

As shown, the total size n of the pool nearly tripled between 1990 and 2009, increasing from about 2,000 to almost 6,000 firms. The relative importance of rating classes BBB, BB, B, and C increased, whereas that of classes AAA and AA decreased. Possible explanations for this phenomenon are a deterioration of the average credit quality of the firms considered in the pool, an increased severity in the judgment of the rating agency, or the fact that the criteria for following new firms have become increasingly stringent overtime.

The transition matrix in 2009 is displayed in Table 4.2. The rows and columns are arranged in order of increasing risk. There is an additional column for firms that were not rated (NR) at the end of 2009. The NR firms likely failed to report their balance sheets, or their reported data had missing information. The percentages of NR firms ranged between 3% and 18%, tending to increase as the quality of the rating at the beginning of 2009 decreased. Missing data were mainly due to the lack of information disclosure, which might have been voluntary or not.

Similar to other rating agencies, S&P does not provide the row corresponding to the transition frequencies from the NR category to the other categories. Hence, the transition matrix in Table 4.2 has to be transformed into a square matrix by imputing the companies in the NR category to the other rating classes. This transformation is usually done by a proportional assignment, in which, for each row the NR companies are assigned to the other rating classes proportionally to their transition frequencies. It is important to check that the proportional assignment does not induce a selectivity bias. By using migration data of the French central bank, Foulcher, Gouriéroux, and Tiomo (2004) provided evidence that incomplete reporting of balance sheets data is not an indicator of imminent default. This finding supports the practice of proportional assignment and suggests that the increase in the NR percentage

Table 4.3. *Adjusted 1-year transition matrix for 2009*

		AAA	AA	A	BBB	BB	B	C	D
		\multicolumn{8}{c}{2009}							
	AAA	91.02	8.98	0	0	0	0	0	0
	AA	0	81.92	17.16	0.69	0.23	0	0	0
	A	0	0.38	90.36	8.26	0.46	0.31	0	0.22
2008	BBB	0	0	2.15	89.83	6.37	0.86	0.21	0.57
	BB	0	0	0	3.48	82.13	12.93	0.68	0.79
	B	0	0	0.18	0	2.53	76.75	9.32	11.22
	C	0	0	0	0	0	7.70	33.33	58.97
	D	0	0	0	0	0	0	0	100

Transition probabilities are in percentages. Rating classes are ordered from AAA (lowest risk) to C (default).

in the worst rating classes may be due to the fact that disclosing information is not a priority for firms in a difficult situation.

After the transformation was done to eliminate the NR category, the transition matrix in 2009 is displayed in Table 4.3. The largest transition probabilities appear on the main diagonal of the matrix, pointing to a tendency to stability of the ratings. Moreover, the other transition probabilities that are significantly different from zero correspond in general to transitions involving one rating class only. Thus, rating down- or up-grades of more than one rating class over one year are unlikely, except in the riskiest categories. The last column of the matrix displays the default probabilities. As expected, they increase as the rating quality decreases. Finally, the elements in the last row of the transition matrix are all zeros, except a 100% in the last column, reflecting the fact that default is an absorbing state.

Let us now discuss the dynamics of the transition matrices. We focus on up- and downgrade probabilities $ug_{l,t} = \sum_{k=l+1}^{K} \hat{\pi}_{l,k,t}$ and $dg_{l,t} = \sum_{k=1}^{l-1} \hat{\pi}_{l,k,t}$, respectively, indexed by the initial rating class l [see Section 3.3.4 for a description of the time series of default probabilities]. We display the time series of upgrade probabilities $ug_{l,t}$ in Figure 4.1 and the series of downgrade probabilities $dg_{l,t}$ in Figure 4.2. The shaded periods in these figures correspond to recessions in the United States as identified by the National Bureau of Economic Research (NBER).[3]

The transition probabilities vary cyclically over time, with similar patterns across rating classes. Peaks of downgrade probabilities and troughs of upgrade probabilities are associated with the economic recessions in the United States. The variations in these probabilities over the 1990–2009 period have been of

[3] See the website http://www.nber.org/cycles.html.

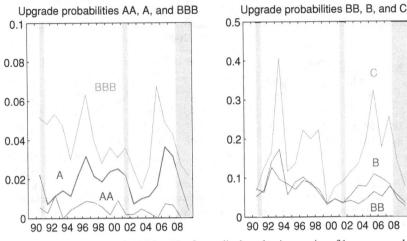

Figure 4.1. Upgrade Probabilities. The figure displays the time-series of 1-year upgrade probabilities for rating classes AA, A, and BBB (left panel) and BB, B, and C (right panel) in the 1990–2009 period. Migration probabilities are in percentages. Shaded periods correspond to NBER recessions in the United States.

the order of 5% to 10% for most rating classes and of the order of 30% for the riskiest rating class C. The evidence in Figures 4.1 and 4.2 supports the idea that transition probabilities are driven by stochastic factors that are common across rating classes, which is at the core of the stochastic transition model.

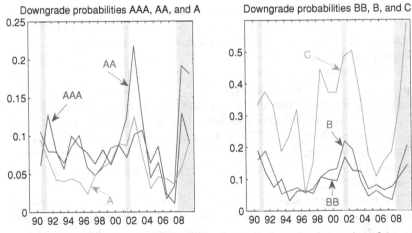

Figure 4.2. Downgrade Probabilities. The figure displays the time-series of 1-year downgrade probabilities for rating classes AAA, AA, and A (left panel) and BB, B, and C (right panel) in the 1990–2009 period. Migration probabilities are in percentages. Shaded periods correspond to NBER recessions in the United States.

4.5.2 Estimation Results

We estimate the ordered qualitative stochastic transition model introduced in Section 4.4.2 with $K = 8$ rating classes by applying the methodology presented in Section 4.4.4. To ensure compatibility with the notation in Section 4.4, we renumber the rating classes of S&P into 1, 2, ..., 8 with $k = 1$ corresponding to default, $k = 2$ corresponding to C, and so on until $k = 8$ corresponding to AAA.

Before applying the estimation procedure, we have to determine the number of factors. For this purpose, in a preliminary step we compute the series of estimated canonical factors $\hat{a}_{l,k,t}$ in (4.42) for k, l, and perform their **principal component analysis** (PCA); that is, the spectral decomposition of the $T \times T$ matrix YY', where the row t of matrix Y is given by $\hat{a}_{l,k,t} - \bar{a}_{l,k}$, k, l varying, with $\bar{a}_{l,k} = \frac{1}{T} \sum_t a_{l,k,t}$ (see Appendix A, Review Appendix A.4). The associated eigenvalues are given in decreasing order in the following table:

81.87	13.92	11.88	9.75	5.58	3.05	2.15	1.66	1.44	0.76
0.50	0.27	0.22	0.10	0.05	0.00	0.00	0.00	0.00	0.00

The first eigenvalue is much larger than the other ones. The second, third, and fourth eigenvalues are about of the same magnitude. The components of the standardized eigenvectors (zero sample mean and unitary variance) corresponding to the four largest eigenvalues are displayed in Figure 4.3 as functions of date t.

The pattern of the eigenvector associated with the largest eigenvalue is compatible with the time evolution of the transition probabilities in Figures 4.1 and 4.2. Indeed, small factor values correspond to a high default and downgrade risk (assuming positive factor sensitivities). The troughs in the factor patterns in the 1990–1991, 2001–2002, and 2008–2009 periods are associated with the troughs in upgrade probabilities and the peaks in downgrade probabilities in Figures 4.1 and 4.2. The pattern of the eigenvector associated with the second largest eigenvalue features a downward trend in the 1990–1996 period and an upward trend in the 1996–2009 period, corresponding to an increase and a decrease in downward risk, respectively. Finally, the patterns of the eigenvectors associated with the third and fourth eigenvalues are rather erratic.

Based on this evidence, we consider a specification with a single factor [see Gagliardini and Gouriéroux (2005b) for a multifactor analysis using French data]. We impose the identification restrictions $a_5 = 0$, $b_5 = \sigma_5 = 1$, and $c_4 = 0$. These identification restrictions concern the parameters of rating class BBB and the threshold between rating classes BBB and BB [see Section 4.4.3]. The estimates of the parameters are displayed in Table 4.4.

The upper panel of Table 4.4 displays the estimates of the threshold parameters c_k. As expected, they are increasing with regard to the rating class index. The middle panel displays the estimates for the parameters in rows $l = 2, 3, \ldots, 8$

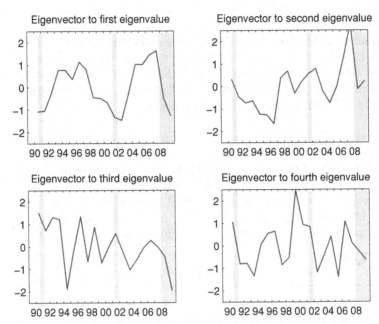

Figure 4.3. Eigenvectors from Principal Component Analysis. The figure displays the patterns of the eigenvectors associated with the four largest eigenvalues in the PCA of the estimated canonical factors. Shaded periods correspond to NBER recessions in the United States.

of the transition matrix, which correspond to rating classes C, B, ..., AAA in the S&P rating system. The intercepts a_l are increasing with respect to the rating index, which confirms that the underlying quantitative score for credit quality is larger for the less risky rating classes. The parameters b_l are the sensitivities of the different rating classes to the common factor. The estimated factor sensitivities are all positive; that is, an increase in the factor improves the underlying quantitative score for credit quality in all rating classes. The idiosyncratic volatility parameters σ_l are generally smaller for the riskier rating categories. Finally, the lower panel in Table 4.4 displays the estimates for the parameters of the factor dynamics. The autoregressive coefficient is positive and corresponds to a quite strong persistence of the factor.

Let us now discuss the approximated factor path and the link with the business cycle literature [see also Nickell, Perraudin and Varotto (2000)]. The approximated factor values $\hat{f}_{n,T,t}$ in (4.36) are displayed in Figure 4.4. The factor estimates are standardized to obtain zero-mean and unit variance in the sample.

The approximated path of the factor in Figure 4.4 is very close to the components of the eigenvector associated with the largest eigenvalue in the

Table 4.4. *Parameter estimates*

$c_1 = -2.635$	$c_2 = -2.517$	$c_3 = -1.818$	$c_4 = 0$
$c_5 = 6.304$	$c_6 = 22.679$	$c_7 = 64.906$	
$a_2 = -2.947$	$b_2 = 0.084$	$\sigma_2 = 0.045$	
$a_3 = -2.888$	$b_3 = 0.230$	$\sigma_3 = 0.141$	
$a_4 = -2.010$	$b_4 = 0.333$	$\sigma_4 = 0.355$	
$a_5 = 0$	$b_5 = 1$	$\sigma_5 = 1$	
$a_6 = 4.524$	$b_6 = 2.849$	$\sigma_6 = 2.397$	
$a_7 = 9.849$	$b_7 = 8.586$	$\sigma_7 = 5.358$	
$a_8 = 78.067$	$b_8 = 8.063$	$\sigma_8 = 15.084$	
$\mu = 1.108$	$A = 0.628$	$\Omega = 0.062$	

Estimated parameters for the factor ordered probit model. Thresholds c, intercepts a, factor sensitivities b, volatilities σ, and parameters of the factor dynamics μ, A, Ω are displayed.

PCA of the estimated canonical factors shown in Figure 4.3. The cyclical pattern of the factor in Figure 4.4 is clearly related to the business cycle: the troughs in the factor pattern are associated with periods of economic recession in the United States. Hence, as expected we find a link between the credit cycle and the business cycle. There are, however, some lead-lag effects between the two cycles. For instance, we observe a long period of decrease in the credit factor from the peak in 1996 until the trough in 2002 that is associated with the economic recession in 2001. In contrast, in the recent economic crisis, a decrease in the credit risk factor occurs at the inception of the recession in 2008 [see also Gagliardini and Gouriéroux (2005b) for a causality analysis between credit and business cycles using French data].

4.5.3 Estimation of Asset and Migration Correlations

The estimated model can be used to estimate asset and migration correlations [De Servigny and Renault (2002, 2004); Gagliardini and Gouriéroux (2005a)]. Let us consider two firms i and j that are currently in rating classes l and k, respectively. The asset correlation between these two firms, conditional on the current factor value F_t, is defined as[4]

$$\rho_{a,lk,t} = corr \left[\log(A_{i,t+1}/L_{i,t+1}), \log(A_{j,t+1}/L_{j,t+1}) | Y_{i,t} = l, Y_{j,t} = k, F_t \right].$$

(4.43)

---

[4] The conditioning set in the definition of asset correlation $\rho_{a,lk,t}$ for firms i and j involves neither the ratings of other firms nor the past values of ratings and factors. Indeed, this additional information is irrelevant due to the conditional independence of the rating histories given the factor path and the Markov property of the factor.

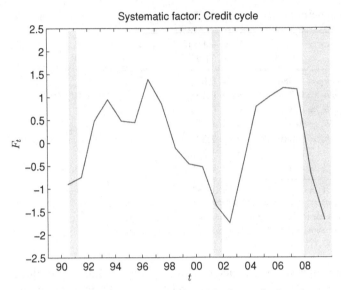

Figure 4.4. Approximated Factor Values. The figure displays the pattern of the approximated factor values $\hat{f}_{n,T,t}$ [see (4.36)] for $t = 1, \ldots, 20$. The factor estimates are standardized to obtain zero mean and unit variance in the sample. Shaded periods correspond to NBER recessions in the United States.

From equations (4.33) and (4.35), we obtain

$$\rho_{a,lk,t} = \frac{b_l b_k V[F_{t+1}|F_t]}{\sqrt{b_l^2 V[F_{t+1}|F_t] + \sigma_l^2}\sqrt{b_k^2 V[F_{t+1}|F_t] + \sigma_k^2}}$$

$$= \frac{b_l b_k}{\sqrt{b_l^2 + \frac{\sigma_l^2}{\Omega}}\sqrt{b_k^2 + \frac{\sigma_k^2}{\Omega}}}.$$

The asset correlation $\rho_{a,lk,t}$ does not depend on the firms' names i and j, but only on their current ratings l and k, because the individual risks are exchangeable within a rating class. Moreover, $\rho_{a,lk,t} \equiv \rho_{a,lk}$ is independent of the date t, because the conditional variance of the Gaussian autoregressive factor is constant. The asset correlation involves both micro-parameters b_l, b_k, σ_l^2, σ_k^2 and macro-parameter Ω, which is scalar in this SRF model.

The asset correlations $\rho_{a,lk}$ for the different rating classes can be arranged in a symmetric matrix, whose row and column indices l, k correspond to the current firms' ratings. The matrix of estimated asset correlations is displayed in Table 4.5.

Estimated asset correlations range from about 3% for firms within rating class AAA to about 26% for firms within rating class C. Hence, the risks in class AAA are mostly driven by the idiosyncratic component, whereas the systematic

Table 4.5. *Matrix of estimated asset correlations between two firms (percentages)*

	AAA	AA	A	BBB	BB	B	C
AAA	2.83	7.66	5.96	5.11	4.81	7.76	8.69
AA	7.66	20.73	16.15	13.84	13.04	21.01	23.54
A	5.96	16.15	12.58	10.78	10.15	16.36	18.33
BBB	5.11	13.84	10.78	9.24	8.70	14.02	15.71
BB	4.81	13.04	10.15	8.70	8.20	13.21	14.80
B	7.76	21.01	16.36	14.02	13.21	21.28	23.84
C	8.69	23.54	18.33	15.71	14.80	23.84	26.71

Row and column indices l and k, respectively, correspond to the current rating classes of the firms.

factor has a significant impact on the risks in class C. This effect can also be seen by comparing the estimated ratios b_l/σ_l for classes $l = 2$ and $l = 8$ in Table 4.4. However, estimated asset correlations are not monotone with regard to the riskiness of the rating class. Indeed, the estimated asset correlation is large and equal to about 20% for class AA, whereas it is equal to about 10% for classes A, BBB, and BB. This finding can be due to the heterogeneity in these latter classes, whose size is large especially in the last part of the sample (see Table 4.1).

Let us now consider the migration correlations. The upgrade correlation between the future ratings of the two firms, conditional on the current ratings and factor value, is defined as

$$\rho_{u,lk,t} = corr\left[\mathbf{1}_{Y_{i,t+1}=l+1}, \mathbf{1}_{Y_{j,t+1}=k+1} | Y_{i,t} = l, Y_{j,t} = k, F_t\right],$$

where l and k are their current ratings. Hence, upgrade correlations are correlations between the indicators for the events of rating upgrades. We show in Appendix 4.C in Section 4.9 that upgrade correlations can be rewritten in terms of conditional moments and cross-moments of the stochastic migration probabilities given the current factor value

$$\rho_{u,lk,t} = \frac{Cov\left[\pi_{l,l+1,t+1}, \pi_{k,k+1,t+1} | F_t\right]}{\sqrt{E[\pi_{l,l+1,t+1}|F_t](1-E[\pi_{l,l+1,t+1}|F_t])}\sqrt{E[\pi_{k,k+1,t+1}|F_t](1-E[\pi_{k,k+1,t+1}|F_t])}},$$

(4.44)

where $\pi_{l,l+1,t+1} = \pi_{l,l+1}(F_{t+1})$ are the stochastic upgrade probabilities. As for asset correlations, the upgrade correlations depend on the current ratings of the two firms, but not on their names. Moreover, they also depend on the current factor value F_t through the conditional distribution of F_{t+1} given F_t, and not only on the conditional variance of the factor. Hence, upgrade correlations are stochastic and time varying. Finally, we can define similarly downgrade

Table 4.6. *Matrix of estimated upgrade correlations between two firms (percentages)*

	AA	A	BBB	BB	B	C
AA	0.04	0.07	0.08	0.10	0.17	0.28
A	0.07	0.11	0.13	0.15	0.26	0.45
BBB	0.08	0.13	0.16	0.19	0.32	0.54
BB	0.10	0.15	0.19	0.22	0.37	0.63
B	0.17	0.26	0.32	0.37	0.64	1.09
C	0.28	0.45	0.54	0.63	1.09	1.85

Row and column indices l and k, respectively, correspond to the current rating classes of the firms. The current factor value is equal to the approximated factor value for the year 2009.

correlations and then have

$$\rho_{d,lk,t} = corr\left[\mathbf{1}_{Y_{i,t+1}=l-1}, \mathbf{1}_{Y_{j,t+1}=k-1} | Y_{i,t} = l, Y_{j,t} = k, F_t\right]$$

$$= \frac{Cov\left[\pi_{l,l-1,t+1}, \pi_{k,k-1,t+1} | F_t\right]}{\sqrt{E[\pi_{l,l-1,t+1}|F_t](1-E[\pi_{l,l-1,t+1}|F_t])}\sqrt{E[\pi_{k,k-1,t+1}|F_t](1-E[\pi_{k,k-1,t+1}|F_t])}}, \quad (4.45)$$

where $\pi_{l,l-1,t+1} = \pi_{l,l-1}(F_{t+1})$ are the stochastic downgrade probabilities. Migration correlations involve the micro-parameters through the transition probabilities and the macro-parameters through the conditional expectations given the current factor value.

We display in Tables 4.6 and 4.7 the matrices of estimated upgrade and downgrade correlations. The current factor value is $F_t = -2.44$, which is the approximated factor value for 2009 found in Section 4.5.2. The conditional

Table 4.7. *Matrix of estimated downgrade correlations between two firms (percentage)*

	AAA	AA	A	BBB	BB	B	C
AAA	0.14	0.49	0.29	0.21	0.25	0.34	0.82
AA	0.49	1.79	1.06	0.75	0.92	1.21	2.93
A	0.29	1.06	0.63	0.45	0.55	0.72	1.74
BBB	0.21	0.75	0.45	0.32	0.39	0.51	1.24
BB	0.25	0.92	0.55	0.39	0.48	0.63	1.53
B	0.34	1.21	0.72	0.51	0.63	0.83	2.02
C	0.82	2.93	1.74	1.24	1.53	2.02	4.95

Row and column indices l and k, respectively, correspond to the current rating classes of the firms. The current factor value is equal to the approximated factor value for the year 2009.

expectations with respect to the factor are computed by Monte Carlo integration based on $1,000,000$ repetitions (see Appendix A, Review Appendix A.1). Estimated upgrade correlations are much smaller than asset correlations, ranging between 0.04% for rating class AAA and about 2% for rating class C. Moreover, estimated upgrade correlations are monotonically increasing with regard to the riskiness of the rating class. Estimated downgrade correlations are typically larger than estimated upgrade correlations. For instance, the estimated downgrade correlation is almost 5% for two firms in rating class C. The impact of the systematic factor is asymmetric with regard to downside and upside risks, being more pronounced for the former.

4.6 Summary

In a general dynamic framework, we have to account for both micro- and macro-dynamics. In this chapter we developed efficient estimation methods for estimating micro- and macro-parameters and showed that they have different rates of convergence. We also explained how to reconstitute the unobservable dynamic common factors. We then applied the approach to the dynamic analysis of corporate ratings by means of a stochastic migration model, as recommended by the Basel 2 accord.

4.7 Appendix A: Asymptotic Variance-Covariance Matrix of the Transition Frequencies

Let us denote $\hat{\pi}_{l,t} = (\hat{\pi}_{l,1,t}, \dots, \hat{\pi}_{l,K,t})'$, $l = 1, \dots, K$, $t = 1, \dots, T$, the rows of the empirical transition matrices. These rows are asymptotically independent conditionally on the factor history such that [see, e.g., Bartholomew (1982)]

$$\sqrt{n}(\hat{\pi}_{l,t} - \pi_{l,t}) \overset{d}{\to} N[0, \; \text{diag}\,(\pi_{l,t}) - \pi_{l,t}\pi_{l,t}']$$

as $n \to \infty$, where n denotes the number of individuals in class l at date $t - 1$. The cumulated transition frequencies $\hat{\pi}_{l,t}^* = (\hat{\pi}_{l,1,t}^*, \dots, \hat{\pi}_{l,K-1,t}^*)'$ defined in (4.38) are also conditionally independent for different rows and dates, with asymptotic Gaussian distribution

$$\sqrt{n}(\hat{\pi}_{l,t}^* - \pi_{l,t}^*) \overset{d}{\to} N[0, \; Q(\text{diag}(\pi_{l,t}) - \pi_{l,t}\pi_{l,t}')Q'],$$

where $Q = [q_{l,k}]$ is the $(K - 1, K)$ matrix with $q_{l,k} = 1$ if $k \leq l$, and $q_{l,k} = 0$, otherwise.

Finally, the rows of the estimated canonical factor

$$\hat{a}_{l,t} = [\Phi^{-1}(\hat{\pi}_{l,1,t}^*), \dots, \Phi^{-1}(\hat{\pi}_{l,K-1,t}^*)]', \quad l = 1, \dots, K, \; t = 1, \dots, T,$$

are also asymptotically independent with asymptotic distribution

$$\sqrt{n}(\hat{a}_{l,t} - a_{l,t}) \xrightarrow{d} N\left(0, \Delta_{l,t} Q[\mathrm{diag}(\pi_{l,t}) - \pi_{l,t}\pi'_{l,t}]Q'\Delta_{l,t}\right),$$

where $\Delta_{l,t} = \mathrm{diag}\{(\phi[\Phi^{-1}(\pi^*_{k,l,t})])^{-1}, k = 1, \ldots, K - 1\}$ by applying the δ-method. The estimated asymptotic variance $\hat{\Sigma}_{n,t}$ of $\hat{a}_t$ is such that the block corresponding to row l is

$$\hat{\Sigma}_{n,l,t} = \frac{1}{N_{l,t-1}} \hat{\Delta}_{l,t} Q[\mathrm{diag}(\hat{\pi}_{l,t}) - \hat{\pi}_{l,t}\hat{\pi}'_{l,t}]Q'\hat{\Delta}_{l,t},$$

where $\hat{\Delta}_{l,t}$ is defined in terms of the empirical transition frequencies.

4.8 Appendix B: Likelihood Expansion and GAML Estimators

4.8.1 Expansion of the Log-Likelihood

We have

$$l(\underline{y_T}; \beta, \theta) =$$

$$\int \ldots \int \exp\left\{\sum_{t=1}^{T}\sum_{i=1}^{n} \log h(y_{i,t}|y_{i,t-1}, f_t; \beta) + \sum_{t=1}^{T} \log g(f_t|f_{t-1}; \theta)\right\} \prod_{t=1}^{T} df_t.$$

Let us now expand the integrand with regard to f_t around $\hat{f}_{n,t}(\beta), t = 1, \ldots, T$, and define

$$\psi_{n,t}(f_t, f_{t-1}) = \sum_{i=1}^{n} \log h(y_{i,t}|y_{i,t-1}, f_t; \beta) - \sum_{i=1}^{n} \log h(y_{i,t}|y_{i,t-1}, \hat{f}_{n,t}(\beta); \beta)$$

$$+ \frac{1}{2}\sqrt{n}(f_t - \hat{f}_{n,t}(\beta))' I_{n,t}(\beta)\sqrt{n}(f_t - \hat{f}_{n,t}(\beta))$$

$$+ \log g(f_t|f_{t-1}; \theta) - \log g(\hat{f}_{n,t}(\beta)|\hat{f}_{n,t-1}(\beta); \theta).$$

Then

$$l(\underline{y_T}; \beta, \theta) = \prod_{t=1}^{T}\prod_{i=1}^{n} h(y_{i,t}|y_{i,t-1}, \hat{f}_{n,t}(\beta); \beta) \prod_{t=1}^{T} g(\hat{f}_{n,t}(\beta)|\hat{f}_{n,t-1}(\beta); \theta)$$

$$\int \ldots \int \exp\left\{-\frac{1}{2}\sum_{t=1}^{T}\sqrt{n}(f_t - \hat{f}_{n,t}(\beta))' I_{n,t}(\beta)\sqrt{n}(f_t - \hat{f}_{n,t}(\beta))\right\}$$

$$\exp\left\{\sum_{t=1}^{T} \psi_{n,t}(f_t, f_{t-1})\right\} \prod_{t=1}^{T} df_t.$$

Let us introduce the change of variable

$$Z_t = \sqrt{n}[I_{n,t}(\beta)]^{1/2}(f_t - \hat{f}_{n,t}(\beta)) \iff f_t = \hat{f}_{n,t}(\beta) + \frac{1}{\sqrt{n}}[I_{n,t}(\beta)]^{-1/2}Z_t.$$

Then

$$l(\underline{y_T}; \beta, \theta)$$

$$= \left(\frac{2\pi}{n}\right)^{TL/2} \prod_{t=1}^{T} [\det I_{n,t}(\beta)]^{-1/2}$$

$$\times \prod_{t=1}^{T} \prod_{i=1}^{n} h(y_{i,t}|y_{i,t-1}, \hat{f}_{n,t}(\beta); \beta) \prod_{t=1}^{T} g(\hat{f}_{n,t}(\beta)|\hat{f}_{n,t-1}(\beta); \theta)$$

$$\frac{1}{(2\pi)^{TL/2}} \int \cdots \int \exp\left\{-\frac{1}{2}\sum_{t=1}^{T} Z_t' Z_t\right\}$$

$$\exp\left\{\sum_{t=1}^{T} \psi_{n,t}\left(\hat{f}_{n,t}(\beta) + \frac{1}{\sqrt{n}}[I_{n,t}(\beta)]^{-1/2}Z_t, \hat{f}_{n,t-1}(\beta)\right.\right.$$

$$\left.\left. + \frac{1}{\sqrt{n}}[I_{n,t-1}(\beta)]^{-1/2}Z_{t-1}\right)\right\} \prod_{t=1}^{T} dZ_t,$$

where L is the dimension of the factor f_t. Thus, we can write

$$l(\underline{y_T}; \beta, \theta) = \left(\frac{2\pi}{n}\right)^{TL/2} \prod_{t=1}^{T} [\det I_{n,t}(\beta)]^{-1/2}$$

$$\times \prod_{t=1}^{T} \prod_{i=1}^{n} h(y_{i,t}|y_{i,t-1}, \hat{f}_{n,t}(\beta); \beta) \prod_{t=1}^{T} g(\hat{f}_{n,t}(\beta)|\hat{f}_{n,t-1}(\beta); \theta) J_{n,T},$$

where

$$J_{n,T} = E\left[\exp\left\{\sum_{t=1}^{T} \psi_{n,t}\left(\hat{f}_{n,t}(\beta) + \frac{1}{\sqrt{n}}[I_{n,t}(\beta)]^{-1/2}Z_t,\right.\right.\right.$$

$$\left.\left.\left. \hat{f}_{n,t-1}(\beta) + \frac{1}{\sqrt{n}}[I_{n,t-1}(\beta)]^{-1/2}Z_{t-1}\right)\right\}\right]$$

is an expectation with regard to independent standard normal random vectors $Z_t, t = 1, \ldots, T$. The result in Proposition 4.2 is deduced by expanding up to order $1/n$ the function within the expectation [see Gagliardini and Gouriéroux (2014) for the detailed derivation].

4.8.2 Newton-Raphson Expansion of the GA Estimator

By definition of the CSA and GA maximum likelihood estimators, we get

$$\frac{\partial \mathcal{L}^{CSA}}{\partial(\beta', \theta')'}(\hat{\beta}^{CSA}, \hat{\theta}^{CSA}) = 0, \quad \frac{\partial \mathcal{L}^{GA}}{\partial(\beta', \theta')'}(\hat{\beta}^{GA}, \hat{\theta}^{GA}) = 0,$$

where we omit the indices n, T in the estimators and log-likelihood functions for expository purposes. By considering the expansion of the second set of first-order conditions around the CSA estimator, we obtain

$$\frac{\partial \mathcal{L}^{GA}}{\partial(\beta', \theta')'}(\hat{\beta}^{CSA}, \hat{\theta}^{CSA}) \simeq -\frac{\partial^2 \mathcal{L}^{GA}(\hat{\beta}^{CSA}, \hat{\theta}^{CSA})}{\partial(\beta', \theta')'\partial(\beta', \theta')} \left[\begin{pmatrix} \hat{\beta}^{GA} \\ \hat{\theta}^{GA} \end{pmatrix} - \begin{pmatrix} \hat{\beta}^{CSA} \\ \hat{\theta}^{CSA} \end{pmatrix} \right].$$

This is equivalent to

$$\begin{pmatrix} \hat{\beta}^{GA} \\ \hat{\theta}^{GA} \end{pmatrix} - \begin{pmatrix} \hat{\beta}^{CSA} \\ \hat{\theta}^{CSA} \end{pmatrix} \simeq \left[-\frac{\partial^2 \mathcal{L}^{GA}(\hat{\beta}^{CSA}, \hat{\theta}^{CSA})}{\partial(\beta', \theta')'\partial(\beta', \theta')} \right]^{-1} \frac{\partial \mathcal{L}^{GA}(\hat{\beta}^{CSA}, \hat{\theta}^{CSA})}{\partial(\beta', \theta')'}$$

$$\simeq \left[-\frac{\partial^2 \mathcal{L}^{CSA}(\hat{\beta}^{CSA}, \hat{\theta}^{CSA})}{\partial(\beta', \theta')'\partial(\beta', \theta')} \right]^{-1} \frac{\partial \mathcal{L}^{GA}(\hat{\beta}^{CSA}, \hat{\theta}^{CSA})}{\partial(\beta', \theta')'}.$$

4.9 Appendix C: Migration Correlations

In this appendix we prove equations (4.44) and (4.45). By the law of iterated expectation, we have

$$E\left[\mathbf{1}_{Y_{i,t+1}=l+1} | Y_{i,t} = l, Y_{j,t} = k, F_t \right]$$
$$= E\left[E\left[\mathbf{1}_{Y_{i,t+1}=l+1} | Y_{i,t} = l, Y_{j,t} = k, F_{t+1}, F_t \right] | Y_{i,t} = l, Y_{j,t} = k, F_t \right]$$
$$= E\left[P\left[Y_{i,t+1} = l+1 | Y_{i,t} = l, Y_{j,t} = k, F_{t+1}, F_t \right] | Y_{i,t} = l, Y_{j,t} = k, F_t \right]$$
$$= E\left[\pi_{l,l+1}(F_{t+1}) | Y_{i,t} = l, Y_{j,t} = k, F_t \right] = E\left[\pi_{l,l+1}(F_{t+1}) | F_t \right].$$

By a similar argument and by using the conditional independence of the rating histories given the factor path, we have

$$E\left[\mathbf{1}_{Y_{i,t+1}=l+1} \mathbf{1}_{Y_{j,t+1}=k+1} | Y_{i,t} = l, Y_{j,t} = k, F_t \right]$$
$$= E\left[P\left[Y_{i,t+1} = l+1, Y_{j,t+1} = k+1 | Y_{i,t} = l, Y_{j,t} = k, F_{t+1}, F_t \right] \right.$$
$$\left. | Y_{i,t} = l, Y_{j,t} = k, F_t \right]$$
$$= E\left[\pi_{l,l+1}(F_{t+1})\pi_{k,k+1}(F_{t+1}) | F_t \right].$$

Thus, we obtain

$$V\left[\mathbf{1}_{Y_{i,t+1}=l+1}|Y_{i,t}=l,\,Y_{j,t}=k,\,F_t\right]=E\left[\pi_{l,l+1}(F_{t+1})|F_t\right]$$
$$\times\left(1-E\left[\pi_{l,l+1}(F_{t+1})|F_t\right]\right)$$

and

$$Cov\left[\mathbf{1}_{Y_{i,t+1}=l+1},\,\mathbf{1}_{Y_{j,t+1}=k+1}|Y_{i,t}=l,\,Y_{j,t}=k,\,F_t\right]$$
$$=Cov\left[\pi_{l,l+1}(F_{t+1}),\,\pi_{k,k+1}(F_{t+1})|F_t\right].$$

Equation (4.44) follows. The proof of (4.45) is similar.

References

Arellano, M., and S. Bonhomme (2009). "Robust Priors in Nonlinear Panel Data Models," *Econometrica*, 77, 489–536.

Basel Committee on Banking Supervision (2001). "The New Basel Capital Accord," Consultative Document of the Bank for International Settlements, April 2001, Part 2: Pillar 1.

Basel Committee on Banking Supervision (2003). "The New Basel Capital Accord," Consultative Document of the Bank for International Settlements, April 2003, Part 3: Pillar 2.

Bartholomew, D. (1982). *Stochastic Models for Social Processes*, 3rd edition, Wiley.

De Servigni, A., and O. Renault (2002). "Default Correlation: Empirical Evidence," Standard & Poor's DP.

De Servigny, A., and O. Renault (2004). *Measuring and Managing Credit Risk*, McGraw-Hill.

Feng, D., C. Gouriéroux, and J. Jasiak (2008). "The Ordered Qualitative Model for Credit Rating Transitions," *Journal of Empirical Finance*, 15, 111–130.

Foulcher, S., C. Gouriéroux, and A. Tiomo (2004). "The Term Structure of Defaults and Ratings," *Insurance and Risk Management*, 72, 207–276.

Gagliardini, P., and C. Gouriéroux (2005a). "Migration Correlation: Definition and Efficient Estimation," *Journal of Banking and Finance*, 29, 865–894.

Gagliardini, P., and C. Gouriéroux (2005b). "Stochastic Migration Models with Application to Corporate Risk," *Journal of Financial Econometrics*, 3, 188–226.

Gagliardini, P., and C. Gouriéroux (2014). "Efficiency in Large Dynamic Panel Models with Common Factors," forthcoming in *Econometric Theory*.

Gordy, M., and E. Heitfield (2002). "Estimating Default Correlation from Short Panels of Credit Rating Performance Data," Working Paper, Federal Reserve Board.

Gouriéroux, C., and J. Jasiak (2005). *Financial Econometrics: Problems, Models and Methods*, Princeton University Press.

Gouriéroux, C., and A. Monfort (1995). *Statistics and Econometric Models*, Cambridge University Press.

Gupton, G., C. Finger, and M. Bhatia (1997). "CreditMetrics," Technical Report, Riskmetrics Group.

Jensen, J. (1995). *Saddlepoint Approximations*, Clarendon Press.

Lancaster, T. (2000). "The Incidental Parameter Problem since 1948," *Journal of Econometrics*, 95, 391–413.

Neyman, J., and E. Scott (1948). "Consistent Estimates Based on Partially Consistent Observations," *Econometrica*, 16, 1–31.

Nickell, P., W. Perraudin, and S. Varotto (2000). "Stability of Rating Transitions," *Journal of Banking and Finance*, 24, 203–227.

5 Prediction and Basket Derivative Pricing

We consider in this chapter an exchangeable set of individual histories, with macro-dynamics only. From Chapter 1, the dynamics are specified by means of a state space model. The measurement equations are defined by the conditional pdf $h(y_{it}|f_t)$ of the individual variables given the common factor. The transition equation is defined by the conditional pdf $g(f_t|f_{t-1})$ of the current factor value given its own past. For expository purposes, we focus in this chapter on a single-factor model, but the results can be generalized to multiple-factor models.

As usual, the joint distribution of individual histories involves multiple integrals with respect to the unobservable factor path. Such multiple integrals are also involved when predicting future values of the individual variables or when trying to reconstitute the unobserved factor values from the observed individual variables, the so-called filtering problem (see Appendix A, Review A.5). Granularity approximations for prediction and filtering problems are the subject of this chapter.

The first section considers granularity adjustments for factor filtering and extends the example considered in Section 2.2 to a general framework. Then, the result is used to deduce the granularity adjustment when predicting a function of future values of the individual variables. The results are illustrated in Section 5.2 by various examples. Under the assumption of the absence of arbitrage opportunities in the market, the problem of derivative pricing becomes a prediction problem after an appropriate discounting (see Appendix B, Review B.2 on arbitrage). This explains why the results of Section 5.1 can be used to obtain approximate prices for derivatives written on an homogeneous basket of individual risks. We give in Section 5.3 examples of such derivatives that have been recently introduced on financial markets. They include **basket default swaps** (BDSs), derivatives written on the iTraxx index, longevity bonds, and **mortality linked securities** (MLS). The corresponding approximated pricing formulas are given and discussed in Section 5.4. Section 5.5 explains how to introduce appropriately designed derivatives for hedging a common risk.

Finally, in Section 5.6 we present a numerical illustration for the approximate pricing of a BDS.

5.1 Approximate Prediction Formulas

We first derive an approximation at order $1/n$ of the predictive distribution of the factor value f_t given all individual histories up to date t. Then, this formula is used to predict future values of the factor and of the individual variables.

5.1.1 Approximate Filtering

Let us assume that the individual histories up to date t are known. They are denoted by $\underline{y}_{i,t}$, for $i = 1, \ldots, n$. The cross-sectional maximum likelihood estimate

$$\hat{f}_{n,t} = \arg\max_{f_t} \sum_{i=1}^{n} \log h(y_{i,t}|f_t) \tag{5.1}$$

provides a first approximation of the unknown factor value. This approximation is based on the cross-sectional information, but neglects the information contained in past observations. Proposition 5.1 explains how the accuracy of the approximation can be increased. It provides a result valid for the predictive distribution itself, which can be characterized by the knowledge of its **Laplace transform**; that is, by the knowledge of the prediction of any exponential transform of f_t. This transformation can be real (moment-generating function) or complex (characteristic function). In the latter case, it provides directly the predictions of sine and cosine transforms of f_t and then of any (continuous) function of f_t by Fourier inversion.

Proposition 5.1 is derived in Appendix 5.8.1.

Proposition 5.1. *We have*

$E[\exp(uf_t)|\underline{y}_{1,t}, \ldots, \underline{y}_{n,t}, \underline{f}_{t-1}]$

$= E[\exp(uf_t)|\underline{y}_{1,t}, \ldots, \underline{y}_{n,t}] + o(1/n)$

$= \exp\{u[\hat{f}_{n,t} + \frac{1}{n}I_{n,t}^{-1}\frac{\partial \log g}{\partial f_t}(\hat{f}_{n,t}|\hat{f}_{n,t-1}) + \frac{1}{2n}I_{n,t}^{-2}K_{n,t}] + \frac{1}{2n}I_{n,t}^{-1}u^2 + o(1/n)\}$,

where $I_{n,t} = -\frac{1}{n}\sum_{i=1}^{n}\frac{\partial^2 \log h}{\partial f_t^2}(y_{i,t}|\hat{f}_{n,t})$ *and* $K_{n,t} = \frac{1}{n}\sum_{i=1}^{n}\frac{\partial^3 \log h}{\partial f_t^3}(y_{it}|\hat{f}_{n,t})$.

At order $1/n$, the predictive distribution of f_t – that is, the filtering distribution – depends on the individual histories by means of a small number of summary statistics: the current and lagged factor approximations $\hat{f}_{n,t}$, $\hat{f}_{n,t-1}$, the estimated cross-sectional information matrix $I_{n,t}$, and statistic $K_{n,t}$, which is a component in the bias at order $1/n$ of the cross-sectional maximum likelihood estimator.

We immediately deduce from Proposition 5.1 the following corollaries:

Corollary 5.1. *The lagged factor values are not informative at order $1/n$ to predict f_t.*

This is a direct consequence of the first equality in Proposition 5.1.

Corollary 5.2. *At order $1/n$, the filtering distribution is Gaussian:*

$$N\left(\hat{f}_{n,t} + \frac{1}{n}[I_{n,t}^{-1}\frac{\partial \log g}{\partial f_t}(\hat{f}_{n,t}|\hat{f}_{n,t-1}) + \frac{1}{2}I_{n,t}^{-2}K_{n,t}], \frac{1}{n}I_{n,t}^{-1}\right).$$

Indeed the Laplace transform of the Gaussian distribution $N(m, \sigma^2)$ is $\exp[um + u^2\sigma^2/2]$, and the result is deduced from Proposition 5.1.

Proposition 5.1 and its corollaries show that the initial non-Gaussian filter can be replaced by an approximate Gaussian filter. This approximate Gaussianity is a numerical result due to a Laplace approximation of the integral underlying the conditional expectation in Proposition 5.1 [see Appendix 5.8.1] and is not a consequence of a Central Limit Theorem.

When n diverges to infinity, the Gaussian distribution in Corollary 5.2 becomes degenerate, with mean $\hat{f}_{n,t}$ and zero variance. For finite n, the GA has two components: the mean and variance of the approximately Gaussian filtering distribution. The macro-dynamics is captured by the adjustment of the mean [see the term $\frac{\partial \log g}{\partial f_t}(\hat{f}_{n,t}|\hat{f}_{n,t-1})$], whereas cross-sectional effects affect both the mean and variance GA.

From the approximate filtering distribution, we deduce an approximation of the prediction of any smooth function $a(f_t)$ of the factor [see Appendix 5.8.2].

Corollary 5.3. *For any twice-differentiable function a, we have*

$$E[a(f_t)|\underline{y_{1,t}}, \ldots, \underline{y_{n,t}}]$$

$$= a(\hat{f}_{n,t}) + \frac{1}{n}\frac{da}{df}(\hat{f}_{n,t})[I_{n,t}^{-1}\frac{\partial \log g}{df_t}(\hat{f}_{n,t}|\hat{f}_{n,t-1}) + \frac{1}{2}I_{n,t}^{-2}K_{n,t}]$$

$$+ \frac{1}{2n}\frac{d^2a}{df^2}(\hat{f}_{n,t})I_{n,t}^{-1} + o(1/n).$$

The filtering formula in Corollary 5.3 is a type of Ito's formula [Ito (1951)] for prediction, which accounts for both the effect of mean and variance GA at order $1/n$.

5.1.2 *Approximate Prediction*

Let us now consider the prediction of a function $\alpha(y_{1,t+h}, \ldots, y_{n,t+h}, f_{t+h})$, say, performed at time t. By the iterated expectation theorem, we know that

$$E[\alpha(y_{1,t+h}, \ldots, y_{n,t+h}, f_{t+h})|\underline{y_{1,t}}, \ldots, \underline{y_{n,t}}, \underline{f_{t-1}}]$$

$$= E[\alpha^*(f_{t+h})|\underline{y_{1,t}}, \ldots, \underline{y_{n,t}}, \underline{f_{t-1}}],$$

where $\alpha^*(f_{t+h}) = E[\alpha(y_{1,t+h}, \ldots, y_{n,t+h}, f_{t+h})|\underline{y_{1,t+h-1}}, \ldots, \underline{y_{n,t+h-1}}, \underline{f_{t+h}}]$ depends on the conditioning variables by means of f_{t+h} only.

Let us denote

$$\alpha^*(h, f_t) = E[\alpha^*(f_{t+h})|\underline{f_t}] = E[\alpha^*(f_{t+h})|\underline{y_{1,t}}, \ldots, \underline{y_{n,t}}, \underline{f_t}]. \quad (5.2)$$

By the iterated expectation theorem, we deduce the following result

Proposition 5.2. *We have*

$$E[\alpha(y_{1,t+h}, \ldots, y_{n,t+h}, f_{t+h})|\underline{y_{1,t}}, \ldots, \underline{y_{n,t}}, \underline{f_{t-1}}]$$

$$= E[\alpha^*(h, f_t)|\underline{y_{1,t}}, \ldots \underline{y_{n,t}}, \underline{f_{t-1}}],$$

where $\alpha^*(h, f)$ is given in (5.2).

Thus, we can apply Corollary 5.3 to deduce the GA for any predictor.

Corollary 5.4. *At order $1/n$ the predictor of $\alpha(y_{1,t+h}, \ldots, y_{n,t+h}, f_{t+h})$ is given by*

$$\alpha^*(h, \hat{f}_{n,t}) + \frac{1}{n}\frac{\partial \alpha^*}{\partial f}(h, \hat{f}_{n,t})[I_{n,t}^{-1}\frac{\partial \log g}{\partial f_t}(\hat{f}_{n,t}|\hat{f}_{n,t-1}) + \frac{1}{2}I_{n,t}^{-2}K_{n,t}]$$

$$+ \frac{1}{2n}\frac{\partial^2 \alpha^*}{\partial f^2}(h, \hat{f}_{n,t})I_{n,t}^{-1}.$$

The predictions for different horizons h are simply derived by combining the functions $h \to \alpha^*(h, \hat{f}_{n,t})$, $\frac{\partial \alpha^*}{\partial f}(h, \hat{f}_{n,t})$, $\frac{\partial^2 \alpha^*(h, \hat{f}_{n,t})}{\partial f^2}$ with weights independent of the prediction horizon and of the quantity to be predicted.

5.1.3 *Approximate Linear State Space Models*

When the factor dynamics are Gaussian autoregressive, the approximate filtering distribution in Corollary 5.2 coincides up to order $o(1/n)$, with the filtering distribution derived from the Kalman filter applied to an approximate linear state space model (see Appendix A, Review A.5 on the Kalman filter). Specifically, let us assume that factor (f_t) follows a Gaussian autoregressive process

$$f_t = \mu + \gamma f_{t-1} + \eta u_t, \quad u_t \sim IIN(0, 1), \quad (5.3)$$

where the autoregressive coefficient γ is such that $|\gamma| < 1$. Then, let us consider the linear state space model defined by the measurement equation

$$\xi_{n,t} = f_t + \frac{1}{\sqrt{n}} I_{n,t}^{-1/2} \varepsilon_t, \quad \varepsilon_t \sim IIN(0, 1), \tag{5.4}$$

where $\xi_{n,t} = \hat{f}_{n,t} + \frac{1}{2n} I_{n,t}^{-2} K_{n,t}$, and the transition equation given in (5.3). In the measurement equation, the variable $\xi_{n,t}$ is the cross-sectional factor approximation $\hat{f}_{n,t}$ adjusted by a bias correction term at order $1/n$, whereas the variance of the error is $\frac{1}{n} I_{n,t}^{-1}$ and vanishes when n diverges to infinity. In Appendix 5.8.3 we show that the filtering distribution of factor f_t obtained by applying the Kalman filter to the linear state space model (5.3)–(5.4) equals the Gaussian distribution in Corollary 5.2 up to terms of order $o(1/n)$. Moreover, Gagliardini, Gouriéroux, and Monfort (2012) show that the approximate linear state space model (5.3)–(5.4) can be used to compute estimators of the macro-parameters μ, γ, η that are asymptotically equivalent to GA maximum likelihood estimators (see also Chapters 3 and 4 for similar results when variables $y_{i,t}$ are qualitative). Hence, by appropriately linearizing the original nonlinear state space model, we can compute jointly macro-parameter estimates and filtering distributions by applying the standard Kalman filter.

5.2 Examples

In the standard cases, the GA adjustments for the mean and variance have simple expressions. However, function $\alpha^*(h, f)$ can be difficult to derive for large horizon h and complicated function α. We see in Section 5.5 a case in which it is easily approximated at order $1/n$. In this section, we present several examples of computations of mean and variance GA coefficients.

5.2.1 Gaussian Linear Factor Model

The individual variables are real valued, such that

$$y_{i,t} = a + b f_t + \sigma u_{it}, \tag{5.5}$$

where the error terms u_{it} are $IIN(0, 1)$ conditional on factor f_t. Because the factor f_t is unobservable, the factor can be transformed such that we have $a = 0$ and $b = 1$. This corresponds to the linear single risk factor (LSRF) model of Chapter 2 extended to include a factor dynamic. Then, the **microdensity** is

$$\prod_{i=1}^{n} h(y_{i,t}|f_t) = \frac{1}{(2\pi\sigma^2)^{n/2}} \exp\{-\frac{n}{2}\log\sigma^2 - \frac{1}{2\sigma^2}\sum_{i=1}^{n}(y_{it} - f_t)^2\}.$$

The cross-sectional maximum likelihood estimator is $\hat{f}_{n,t} = \frac{1}{n}\sum_{i=1}^{n} y_{i,t}$, and we have $I_{n,t} = 1/\sigma^2$, $K_{n,t} = 0$.

5.2.2 Stochastic Volatility Model with Factor

The individual observations are such that

$$y_{i,t} = f_t^{1/2} u_{i,t}, \tag{5.6}$$

where factor (f_t) is a positive Markov process and the error terms $u_{i,t}$ are $IIN(0, 1)$ conditional on factor f_t. The microdensity is

$$\prod_{i=1}^{n} h(y_{i,t}|f_t) = \frac{1}{(2\pi)^{n/2}} \exp\{-\frac{n}{2} \log f_t - \frac{1}{2f_t} \sum_{i=1}^{n} y_{it}^2\}.$$

The cross-sectional maximum likelihood estimator of f_t is $\hat{f}_{n,t} = \frac{1}{n} \sum_{i=1}^{n} y_{i,t}^2$. It is equal to a cross-sectional realized variance. Moreover, we have $I_{n,t} = 1/(2\hat{f}_{n,t}^2)$ and $K_{n,t} = 2/(\hat{f}_{n,t}^3)$.

5.2.3 Dichotomous Qualitative Model with Factor

The individual variables are dichotomous qualitative; they are independent conditionally on the value of a common factor f_t with Bernoulli distribution such that $y_{i,t} \sim B(1, f_t)$. The factor f_t takes values in the interval $(0, 1)$. The cross-sectional estimator of f_t is $\hat{f}_{n,t} = \bar{y}_{n,t} = \frac{1}{n} \sum_{i=1}^{n} y_{i,t}$, and we have

$$I_{n,t} = 1/[\bar{y}_{n,t}(1 - \bar{y}_{n,t})], \quad K_{n,t} = 2(1 - 2\bar{y}_{n,t})/[\bar{y}_{n,t}(1 - \bar{y}_{n,t})]^2. \tag{5.7}$$

5.2.4 Gamma Model with Factor

In this case the individual observations are independent conditionally on factor f_t with common distribution $\gamma(f_t, \lambda)$; thus, factor f_t is a stochastic degree of freedom with positive real values. The microdensity is

$$\prod_{i=1}^{n} h(y_{i,t}|f_t) = \frac{1}{\Gamma(f_t)^n} \exp(-\lambda \sum_{i=1}^{n} y_{i,t})(\prod_{i=1}^{n} y_{i,t})^{f_t-1} \lambda^{nf_t} \mathbf{1}_{\min_i y_{i,t}>0},$$

where Γ denotes the gamma function. The cross-sectional maximum likelihood estimator of f_t, derived by maximizing $\prod_{i=1}^{n} h(y_{i,t}|f_t)$ with respect to f_t does not admit a closed form expression. It is given by

$$\hat{f}_{n,t} = \psi^{-1} \left(\frac{1}{n} \sum_{i=1}^{n} \log y_{i,t} + \log \lambda \right),$$

where $\psi(s) = \frac{d \log \Gamma(s)}{ds}$ is the digamma function, and we have

$$I_{n,t} = \frac{d\psi}{ds}(\hat{f}_{n,t}) \text{ and } K_{n,t} = -\frac{d^2\psi}{ds^2}(\hat{f}_{n,t}).$$

5.2.5 Beta Model with Factor

The individual observations take value in the interval $(0,1)$. They are independent conditionally on factor f_t, with density

$$h(y_{i,t}|f_t) = \frac{\Gamma(f_t)}{\Gamma(\alpha f_t)\Gamma[(1-\alpha)f_t]} y_{i,t}^{\alpha f_t - 1}(1 - y_{i,t})^{(1-\alpha)f_t - 1} \mathbf{1}_{0 < y_{i,t} < 1}, \quad (5.8)$$

where α is a scalar parameter in $(0, 1)$ and f_t a positive factor. For this beta distribution, the conditional mean $E(y_{i,t}|f_t) = \alpha$ is constant. Moreover, the conditional variance of a variable on $[0, 1]$ is upper bounded

$$V(y_{i,t}|f_t) \leq E(y_{i,t}|f_t)[1 - E(y_{i,t}|f_t)] = \alpha(1 - \alpha),$$

and the upper bound is reached when the total mass is distributed on the two-point set $\{0, 1\}$. It is easily checked that

$$f_t + 1 = \alpha(1 - \alpha)/V(y_{i,t}|f_t)$$

measures the concentration of the distribution. Thus, we obtain a beta model with a stochastic concentration parameter.

As in example in Section 5.2.4, the cross-sectional maximum likelihood does not admit a simple closed form expression. It is given by

$$\hat{f}_{n,t} = \psi_\alpha^{-1}\left(\frac{1}{n}\sum_{i=1}^{n}[\alpha \log y_{i,t} + (1-\alpha)\log(1 - y_{i,t})]\right),$$

where $\psi_\alpha(s) = \alpha\psi(\alpha s) + (1 - \alpha)\psi[(1 - \alpha)s] - \psi(s)$, and $\psi(s) = \frac{d\log\Gamma(s)}{ds}$. Moreover, we have

$$I_{n,t} = \frac{d\psi_\alpha}{ds}(\hat{f}_{n,t}) \text{ and } K_{n,t} = -\frac{d^2\psi_\alpha}{ds^2}(\hat{f}_{n,t}).$$

5.3 Basket Derivatives

A basket derivative is a derivative written on a large number of individual risks $y_{i,t}$, for $i = 1, \ldots, n$. These risks can correspond to individual asset returns or simply to individual risky events that are not necessarily traded on financial markets, such as human lifetimes [see the example of longevity in Section 3.4.3]. Let us denote by t the current date; a European basket derivative with time-to-maturity h will pay the contractual amount $a(y_{1,t+h}, \ldots, y_{n,t+h})$, say, at date $t + h$. Its current price is denoted by $\pi_t(a, h)$.

Various basket derivatives have recently been introduced for securitized products, with the aim of facilitating an appropriate hedging of some common risks.

5.3.1 Basket Default Swap

Let us consider at date t a set of loans $i = 1, \ldots, n$ called the basket. A basket default swap (BDS) with maturity $t + h$ will pay \$1, say, at time $t + h$, if the proportion of loans with default at date $t + h$ in the basket is larger than a given contractual threshold α, with $\alpha \in (0, 1)$. Thus, the design of the BDS is determined by the composition of the basket, the maturity, and the threshold of the default frequency.

Let us represent the individual loan histories by means of the default indicator $y_{i,t}$, such that $y_{i,t} = 1$ if the loan i is defaulted at time t and $y_{i,t} = 0$ otherwise. The payoff of the BDS is

$$a(y_{i,t+h}, \ldots, y_{n,t+h}; \alpha) = \mathbf{1}_{\bar{y}_{n,t+h} > \alpha},$$

where $\bar{y}_{n,t+h} = \frac{1}{n} \sum_{i=1}^{n} y_{i,t+h}$ is the default frequency.

Let us assume that the basket is homogeneous and that, at a given date, the default indicators of the loans that are still alive are independent, with identical Bernoulli distributions $\mathcal{B}(1, f_t)$, say, conditionally on a common factor f_t. This factor is the stochastic default probability. In the limiting case of a basket of infinite size, we have $\bar{y}_{n,t+1} \sim f_{t+1}$. Thus, the short-term BDS is a derivative to hedge extreme values of f_{t+1}. When n is large but finite, the interpretation of the BDS as an hedging product is similar, but the insurance against common factor movements cannot be perfect, because the factor values are never observed.

5.3.2 CDO Tranche

A **collateralized debt obligation (CDO) tranche** is also based on a contractual basket of loans, with payoff at $t + h$ of the type

$$a(y_{1,t+h}, \ldots, y_{n,t+h}; \alpha_1, \alpha_2) = (\bar{y}_{n,t+h} - \alpha_1)^+ - (\bar{y}_{n,t+h} - \alpha_2)^+,$$

where α_1 and α_2 are called the **attachment** and **detachment points**, respectively, with $\alpha_2 > \alpha_1$, and $X^+ = \max(X, 0)$. The payoff of the CDO tranche as a function of the default frequency at maturity is displayed in Figure 5.1.

The payoff function is nonlinear and corresponds to the payoff of a portfolio that is long in a call option written on $\bar{y}_{n,t+h}$ with strike α_1 and short in a call option with strike α_2 [see, e.g., Laurent and Gregory (2005) and Lamb, Perraudin and Van Landschoot (2008) on the pricing of CDOs].

5.3.3 Derivatives on iTraxx

Credit default swaps (CDSs) are life insurance contracts written on individual companies and are traded on secondary financial markets. In the simplest case of a **digital CDS**, the payoff is equal to \$1, if the corporation defaults between t and $t + h$ and \$0, otherwise.

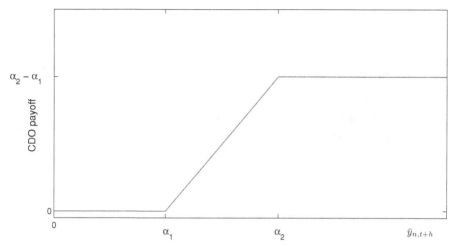

Figure 5.1. Payoff of a CDO Tranche. The figure displays the payoff of a CDO tranche as a function of the default frequency $\bar{y}_{n,t+h}$ at maturity. Thresholds α_1 and α_2 are the attachment and detachment points, respectively.

Such CDSs are regularly traded on the market under a variety of names. The price of such a CDS for maturity h is always smaller than the price of the risk-free zero-coupon bond with the same maturity. The ratio of the prices at t of the CDS and of the associated risk-free bond is a quantity $y_{i,t,h}$ between 0 and 1, which can be interpreted as the market price at t of default of the firm between t and $t + h$.

We expect that the common factor involved in individual default occurrences will also have an effect on the associated CDS prices. For this reason, some indexes of CDS prices analogous to an average

$$\bar{y}_{n,t,h} = \frac{1}{n} \sum_{i=1}^{n} y_{i,t,h},$$

are regularly published. Examples are the **iTraxx indexes** covering the European and Asian markets and the **CDX indexes** for North American markets. These indexes can be used as support for writing derivatives. For instance, a synthetic CDO tranche written on iTraxx, with time-to-maturity 1, will pay at $t + 1$

$$a(y_{1,t+1,h}, \dots, y_{n,t+1,h}) = (\bar{y}_{n,t+1,h} - \alpha_1)^+ - (\bar{y}_{n,t+1,h} - \alpha_2)^+.$$

Even if the design of the payoff is similar for a CDO tranche written on a basket of loans and for the derivatives written on CDS indices, the two types of options are different, because they are written on different types of individual risks; default occurrences and levels of CDS prices, respectively.

5.3.4 Securitization in Insurance

Similar principles have been followed in insurance to hedge longevity risk; that is, the uncertain length of an individual's life-span. In practice the derivatives are written on observed mortality rates of individuals. **Longevity bonds** are computed on a given subpopulation in a country, such as the generations of males born in the United States between 1960 and 1965. **Mortality linked securities (MLS)** correspond to a portfolio of life insurance contracts securitized by an insurance company.

5.4 Derivative Pricing

5.4.1 No-Arbitrage and Stochastic Discount Factor

The no-arbitrage condition is that condition in which it is impossible to make a positive gain at some future date with an initial zero (or negative) investment (see Appendix B, Review B.2). The no-arbitrage condition is equivalent to the existence of a pricing operator, characterized by a **stochastic discount factor (SDF)** [Harrison and Kreps (1979)]. More precisely, let us consider an information set at date t, which includes the current and past values of variables observed by the investors. In our framework this information set is

$$J_t = (\underline{y_{1,t}}, \ldots, \underline{y_{n,t}}, \underline{f_{t-1}}). \tag{5.9}$$

Thus, the investors know the individual risks, but have an imperfect knowledge of the common factor: they know its past, but not its current value. Then, a stochastic discount factor for period $(t, t+1)$ is a positive function $m_{t,t+1}$, which depends on information J_{t+1}.

Under the no-arbitrage assumption, there exists an SDF such that the prices at date t of European derivative assets with payoff a_{t+h} at $t+h$ can be written as

$$\pi_t(a, h) = E_t[m_{t,t+1} \ldots m_{t+h-1,t+h} a_{t+h}], \tag{5.10}$$

where E_t denotes the expectation conditional on the information J_t at time t.

From now on, we assume that the SDF depends on the information by means of f_t only; that is, $m_{t,t+1} = m(f_t)$.

5.4.2 Pricing Basket Derivatives

Let us now consider an homogeneous set (basket) of risks $y_{i,t}$, with $i = 1, \ldots, n$, $t = 1, \ldots T$, satisfying the assumptions described in the introduction to this chapter. At $t+h$ a basket derivative pays an amount $a(y_{1,t+h}, \ldots, y_{n,t+h})$. Its price at date t is

$$\pi_t(a, h) = E_t[m_{t,t+1} \ldots m_{t+h-1,t+h} a(y_{1,t+h}, \ldots, y_{n,t+h})]. \tag{5.11}$$

By the iterated expectation theorem and by using the assumptions on the state and measurement equations, the price can also be written as

$$\pi_t(a, h) = E_t[m(f_t)\psi(f_t, a, h)], \tag{5.12}$$

where

$$\psi(f_t, a, h) = E[m(f_{t+1})\dots m(f_{t+h-1})a(y_{1,t+h}, \dots, y_{n,t+h})|\underline{f_t}, \underline{y_{1t}}, \dots, \underline{y_{n,t}}]. \tag{5.13}$$

Thus, the price of the initial basket derivative with time-to-maturity h is equal to the price of a virtual short-term derivative written on f_t with payoff $\psi(f_t, a, h)$ at $t + 1$. Function $m(f_t)\psi(f_t, a, h)$ corresponds to function $\alpha^*(f_t, h)$ in Proposition 5.2.

We have seen in Corollary 5.2 that the conditional distribution of f_t given J_t can be approximated at order $1/n$ by the Gaussian distribution with the pdf given by

$$\hat{\varphi}_{n,t}(f_t) = \frac{1}{\sigma_{n,t}}\phi\left(\frac{f_t - \mu_{n,t}}{\sigma_{n,t}}\right), \tag{5.14}$$

where ϕ is the pdf of the standard Gaussian distribution and

$$\mu_{n,t} = \hat{f}_{n,t} + \frac{1}{n}[I_{n,t}^{-1}\frac{\partial \log g}{\partial f_t}(\hat{f}_{n,t}|\hat{f}_{n,t-1}) + \frac{1}{2}I_{n,t}^{-2}K_{n,t}], \quad \sigma_{n,t}^2 = \frac{1}{n}I_{n,t}^{-1}.$$

We deduce the following proposition

Proposition 5.3. *The price of the basket derivative paying* $a(y_{1,t+h}, \dots, y_{n,t+h})$ *at $t + h$ is such that*

$$\pi_t(a, h) = \int m(f_t)\psi(f_t, a, h)\hat{\varphi}_{n,t}(f_t)df_t + o(1/n),$$

where function ψ is defined in (5.13) and pdf $\hat{\varphi}_{n,t}$ is given in (5.14).

Up to order $1/n$, the basket derivative price can be approximated by a function of $\hat{f}_{n,t}$, $\hat{f}_{n,t-1}$, $I_{n,t}$ and $K_{n,t}$ only. This approximated price does not require any past observation of the common factor, which is important for the two following reasons:

(1) First, even if the investors observe the lagged factor values, the economist do not. Nevertheless, the economists can approximate the derivative price rather accurately by taking into account the cross-sectional information.

(2) Second, the values of the underlying factor could be deduced from the prices of highly traded derivatives written on the $y_{i,t+h}$. Because these factor values are not needed to compute the approximate derivative price, the approximate pricing formula in Proposition 5.3 can be used

at the creation of a new derivative market to propose a coherent system of quotes for derivatives. In this situation, the SDF $m(.)$ is not a market correction for risk, but reflects the risk aversion and choices of the monopolistic firm, which is quoting first. The SDF has to be updated during the emergence of this derivative market to account for the adjustment of derivative prices to demand and supply.

5.5 Derivatives Written on a Factor Proxy

5.5.1 The Derivatives and Their Prices

As mentioned earlier, basket derivatives are usually introduced into financial markets as instruments to hedge the common risks. Because the common factor is not observed, the derivatives are usually written on a suitable proxy of this factor that reflects its risk dynamics. In this section, we derive another approximate pricing formula in which the derivatives are written on the cross-sectional maximum likelihood estimator of factor f_t [see Gagliardini and Gourieroux (2011) for the proof]. We focus on derivatives with an exponential payoff, because they are the basis for the pricing of derivatives with a more general payoff (see Section 5.6).

Proposition 5.4. *The true price at time t of the derivative with payoff* $\exp(u\,\hat{f}_{n,t+h})$ *at time $t+h$ is*

$$\pi_{n,t}(u,h) = \int m(f_t)\psi_n(f_t,u,h)\hat{\varphi}_{n,t}(f_t)df_t + o(1/n),$$

where

$$\psi_n(f_t,u,h)$$
$$= E[m(f_{t+1})\ldots m(f_{t+h-1})\exp(uf_{t+h} - \frac{u}{2n}I_{t+h}^{-2}\beta_{t+h} + \frac{u^2}{2n}I_{t+h}^{-1})|f_t],$$

and pdf $\hat{\varphi}_{n,t}$ is given in (5.14), with

$$I_{t+h} = E\left[\frac{-\partial^2 \log h(y_{i,t+h}|f_{t+h})}{\partial f^2}|f_{t+h}\right],$$

$$\beta_{t+h} = Cov\left[\frac{\partial \log h(y_{i,t+h}|f_{t+h})}{\partial f}, \frac{\partial^2 \log h(y_{i,t+h}|f_{t+h})}{\partial f^2} + \left(\frac{\partial \log h(y_{i,t+h}|f_{t+h})}{\partial f}\right)^2 |f_{t+h}\right].$$

Compared to the general result in Proposition 5.3, in the framework of Proposition 5.4 we exploit the large size n of the basket to approximate function $\psi(f_t, u, h)$ by means of an expectation with regard to the factor path $\psi_n(f_t, u, h)$, up to order $o(1/n)$. This simplifies considerably the numerical calculation of the approximate derivative price.

A BDS is an example of a basket derivative whose payoff is written on the ML estimate of the systematic risk factor. In a short-term BDS, the individual

Table 5.1. *Adjustment coefficients*

Gaussian linear factor model	$I_t = 1/\sigma^2$	$\beta_t = 0$
Stochastic volatility model with factor	$I_t = 1/(2f_t^2)$	$\beta_t = 0$
Dichotomous qualitative model with factor	$I_t = 1/[f_t(1-f_t)]$	$\beta_t = 0$
Gamma model with factor	$I_t = \dfrac{d\psi}{ds}(f_t)$	$\beta_t = \dfrac{d^2\psi}{ds^2}(f_t)$
Beta model with factor	$I_t = \dfrac{d\psi_a}{ds}(f_t)$	$\beta_t = \dfrac{d^2\psi_a}{ds^2}(f_t)$

risks are measured by the 0–1 default occurrences, with Bernoulli distribution $\mathcal{B}(1, f_t)$. The cross-sectional ML estimator of f_t is equal to the observed default frequency $\hat{f}_{n,t} = \bar{y}_{n,t}$ [see Section 5.2.3]. This is exactly the proxy of the factor used as support for the BDS.

Let us now consider a CDO tranche on iTraxx. The underlying individual risks correspond to the implied default probabilities, which are equal to the ratios of the CDS prices by the associated risk-free zero-coupon bonds. The individual risk corresponds to a real variable taking a value between 0 and 1. A beta model with factor [see Section 5.2.5] is a natural choice for describing these risks. Unfortunately, the CDO tranche is written on the average $\bar{y}_{n,t}$, which is not equal to the cross-sectional ML estimator.

The adjustment coefficients I_t and β_t in Proposition 5.4 are given in Table 5.1 for the models introduced in Section 5.2.

5.5.2 SRF Model for Default Correlation

Let us consider basket derivatives written on a default frequency $\hat{f}_{n,t} = \bar{y}_{n,t}$, where the individual risks $y_{i,t}$ are 0–1 variables with distribution $\mathcal{B}(1, f_t)$. From Table 5.1 we obtain $I_{t+1} = 1/[f_{t+1}(1 - f_{t+1})]$ and $\beta_{t+1} = 0$. We deduce that the true price of the exponential derivative with short time-to-maturity $h = 1$ is

$$\pi_{n,t}(u, 1)$$

$$= \int m(f_t)E\left(\exp[uf_{t+1} + \frac{u^2}{2n}f_{t+1}(1 - f_{t+1})]|f_t\right)\hat{\varphi}_{n,t}(f_t)df_t + o(1/n),$$

$$(5.15)$$

where $\hat{\varphi}_{n,t}$ is the Gaussian pdf (5.14) with

$$\mu_{n,t} = \hat{f}_{n,t} + \frac{1}{n}[\hat{f}_{n,t}(1 - \hat{f}_{n,t})\frac{\partial \log g}{\partial f_t}(\hat{f}_{n,t}|\hat{f}_{n,t-1}) + (1 - 2\hat{f}_{n,t})],$$

$$\sigma_{n,t}^2 = \frac{\hat{f}_{n,t}[1 - \hat{f}_{n,t}]}{n}.$$

One GA term appears by means of the term $\frac{u^2}{2n} f_{t+1}(1 - f_{t+1})$ in formula (5.15). It involves the uncertainty of the probability of default at date $t + 1$, because $V[\hat{f}_{n,t+1}|f_{t+1}] = \frac{f_{t+1}(1 - f_{t+1})}{n}$. An increase in this uncertainty – for instance, if n diminishes – implies an increase in the derivative price; that is, in the price of the corresponding insurance product.

5.6 Approximate Pricing of Basket Default Swaps

In this section we present a numerical illustration for the approximate pricing of a basket default swap [see Gagliardini and Gourieroux (2011)].

5.6.1 The Risk Factor Model

The risk variables $y_{i,t}$ are binary default indicators for an homogeneous portfolio of corporate loans. Their joint distribution is given by a dynamic version of the Merton (1974)–Vasicek (1991) value of the firm model [see Chapter 3, Section 3.1.2]. We have $y_{i,t} = 1$ if $A_{i,t} < L_{i,t}$ and $y_{i,t} = 0$ otherwise, where $A_{i,t}$ and $L_{i,t}$ denote the firm asset and liability, respectively. The log asset/liability ratios follow a linear single risk factor model

$$\log(A_{i,t}/L_{i,t}) = -\Phi^{-1}(PD) + \sqrt{\rho}F_t + \sqrt{1 - \rho}u_{i,t}, \qquad (5.16)$$

where shocks $u_{i,t}$ are $IIN(0, 1)$ across firms and time dates, $PD \in (0, 1)$ and $\rho \in (0, 1)$. The systematic factor F_t follows a Gaussian autoregressive process

$$F_t = \gamma F_{t-1} + \sqrt{1 - \gamma^2}\varepsilon_t, \qquad (5.17)$$

where $\varepsilon_t \sim IIN(0, 1)$ and the autoregressive coefficient γ is such that $|\gamma| < 1$. The stationary distribution of F_t is standard Gaussian. Then, the parameterization in (5.16) is such that PD is the unconditional default probability of a firm, whereas ρ is the contemporaneous correlation between the log asset/liability ratios of two firms.

The time unit is 1 year. We set an unconditional 1-year default probability equal to $PD = 0.04$. We consider three values for the asset correlation: $\rho = 0.01, 0.10, 0.30$. They cover the range of asset correlation values that are compatible with default correlation estimates reported in the literature [De Servigny and Renault (2002, 2004); Gagliardini and Gouriéroux (2005)], as well as values suggested by the Basel 2 accord [BCBS (2001, 2003)]. The portfolio size is $n = 1,000$.

Model (5.16)–(5.17) is such that the default indicators $y_{i,t}$, for i varying, are i.i.d. conditional on factor F_t, with Bernoulli distribution $\mathcal{B}(1, f_t)$, where the transformed factor f_t is the conditional default probability:

$$f_t = P[\log(A_{i,t}/L_{i,t}) < 0|F_t] = \Phi\left(\frac{\Phi^{-1}(PD) - \sqrt{\rho}F_t}{\sqrt{1 - \rho}}\right) \qquad (5.18)$$

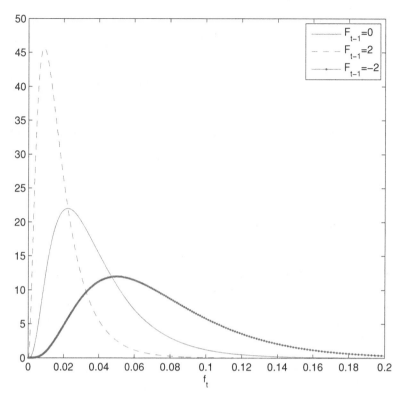

Figure 5.2. Transition pdf of Transformed Factor f_t. The figure plots the conditional distribution of factor f_t given lagged value f_{t-1}, for different values of f_{t-1}. The conditioning values f_{t-1} are given in terms of their corresponding Gaussian factor values F_{t-1}: $F_{t-1} = 0$, $F_{t-1} = 2$, and $F_{t-1} = -2$, respectively. Asset correlation is $\rho = 0.10$.

[see example 5.2.3 in Section 5.2]. The transition density of the Markov process (f_t) is deduced from (5.17) and (5.18),

$$g(f_t|f_{t-1}) = \frac{1}{\sqrt{1 - \gamma^2}} \phi \left(\frac{F_t - \gamma F_{t-1}}{\sqrt{1 - \gamma^2}} \right) \frac{\sqrt{1 - \rho}}{\sqrt{\rho}} \frac{1}{\phi[\Phi^{-1}(f_t)]}, \quad (5.19)$$

where $F_t = \frac{\Phi^{-1}(PD) - \sqrt{1 - \rho}\Phi^{-1}(f_t)}{\sqrt{\rho}}$. This transition pdf is displayed in Figure 5.2 for different values of the lagged factor when asset correlation is $\rho = 0.10$. The lagged value f_{t-1} has an impact on both the location and the variance of the distribution of f_t. Moreover, the transition pdf is right skewed.

5.6.2 Approximate Filtering Distribution

To assess the accuracy of the Gaussian approximation in Proposition 5.1 and its corollaries, let us now compare the distribution of factor f_t given the investor information J_t and the Gaussian approximate filtering distribution in Corollary 5.2. The pdf of f_t conditional on $J_t = (\underline{f_{t-1}}, y_{1,t}, \ldots, \underline{y_{n,t}})$ is given by

$$g(f_t|J_t) = \frac{g(\underline{f_t}, y_{1,t}, \ldots, y_{n,t})}{\int g(\underline{f_t}, y_{1,t}, \ldots, \underline{y_{n,t}})df_t} = \frac{\prod_{i=1}^{n} h(y_{i,t}|f_t)g(f_t|f_{t-1})}{\int \prod_{i=1}^{n} h(y_{i,t}|f_t)g(f_t|f_{t-1})df_t}$$

$$= \frac{f_t^{n\bar{y}_{n,t}}(1 - f_t)^{n(1-\bar{y}_{n,t})}g(f_t|f_{t-1})}{\int f_t^{n\bar{y}_{n,t}}(1 - f_t)^{n(1-\bar{y}_{n,t})}g(f_t|f_{t-1})df_t} \qquad (5.20)$$

and depends on the conditioning information J_t by means of the current default frequency $\bar{y}_{n,t}$ and lagged factor f_{t-1} only. The Gaussian approximation of the filtering distribution is obtained from Corollary 5.2 with the factor approximation equal to the default frequency $\hat{f}_{n,t} = \bar{y}_{n,t}$, statistics $I_{n,t}$, $K_{n,t}$ given in (5.7) [see Section 5.2.3], and the partial derivative of the factor log-transition density $\frac{\partial \log g}{\partial f_t}(\hat{f}_{n,t}|\hat{f}_{n,t-1})$ computed from (5.19). The approximate filtering distribution depends on the default history by means of current and lagged default frequencies $\hat{f}_{n,t}$ and $\hat{f}_{n,t-1}$ only.

In Figure 5.3 we display the predictive distribution of f_t given investor information J_t for $\hat{f}_{n,t} = 0.04$ and different values of the lagged factor f_{t-1}. In Figure 5.4 we display the approximate filtering distribution of f_t for $\hat{f}_{n,t} = 0.04$ and different values of the lagged default frequency $\hat{f}_{n,t-1}$. Asset correlation is $\rho = 0.10$.

By comparing Figures 5.2 and 5.3, it is seen that the default history is very informative for the distribution of the unobservable factor. Indeed, by including default frequency $\hat{f}_{n,t}$ in the conditioning set, the distribution of f_t given f_{t-1} is less dispersed and is much closer to a Gaussian distribution. Moreover, this distribution is rather insensitive to the lagged factor value f_{t-1}, as explained by Corollary 5.1. Similarly, the Gaussian approximation of the filtering distribution in Figure 5.4 is quite independent of the lagged default frequency $\hat{f}_{n,t-1}$. Finally, by comparing Figures 5.3 and 5.4 we deduce that the Gaussian approximation of the filtering distribution is rather accurate.

5.6.3 Approximate Pricing of a BDS

Let us now consider the approximate pricing of a short-term BDS. For expository purposes, we consider the SDF $m_{t,t+1} = 1$; that is, we set the risk-free rate and the risk premium for systematic risk equal to zero. The derivative payoff is $a(y_{1,t+1}, \ldots, y_{n,t+1}) = \mathbf{1}_{\hat{f}_{n,t+1}>\alpha}$, with $\alpha \in (0, 1)$ [see Section 5.3.1]. By using the Fourier transform inversion formula [see, e.g., Proposition 2

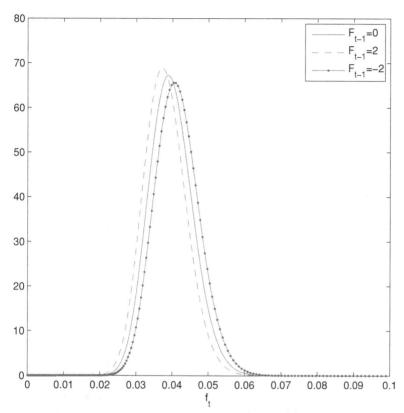

Figure 5.3. Predictive Distribution of f_t Given the Investor Information. The figure plots the conditional distribution of factor f_t given investor information J_t, such that $\hat{f}_{n,t} = 0.04$ and for different values of f_{t-1}. The conditioning values of f_{t-1} are given in terms of their corresponding Gaussian factor values F_{t-1}; $F_{t-1} = 0$, $F_{t-1} = 2$, and $F_{t-1} = -2$, respectively. Asset correlation is $\rho = 0.10$.

in Duffie, Pan, and Singleton (2000)], it is possible to write the price $\pi_t(\alpha, 1)$ of such a derivative as an integral transform of the prices of derivatives with an exponential payoff. More precisely, we have

$$\pi_t(\alpha, 1) = \frac{1}{2} + \frac{1}{\pi} \int_0^\infty \frac{Im\left[\tilde{\pi}_t(iv, 1)\exp\left(-iv\alpha_t\right)\right]}{v} dv, \tag{5.21}$$

where i is the imaginary unit, Im denotes the imaginary part of a complex number, and

$$\tilde{\pi}_t(u, 1) = E\left[\exp(u\,\hat{f}_{n,t+1})|J_t\right]. \tag{5.22}$$

We use equation (5.12) and Proposition 5.3 to derive the true and approximate prices of derivatives with an exponential payoff and then apply transformation

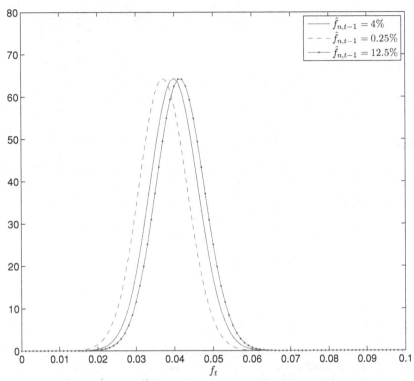

Figure 5.4. Approximate Filtering Distribution of f_t. The figure plots the approximate distribution of f_t given past default history, such that $\hat{f}_{n,t} = 0.04$ and for different values of $\hat{f}_{n,t-1}$. Asset correlation is $\rho = 0.10$.

(5.21) to obtain the true and approximated prices of the BDS. The advantage of this approach using Fourier transform inversion is that function ψ in (5.13) can be computed in closed form for exponential derivatives, up to an expectation with regard to the factor value. More precisely, by the iterated expectation theorem we have

$$\psi(f_t, u, 1) = E\left[\exp(u\hat{f}_{n,t+1})|\underline{f_t}, \underline{y_{1,t}}, \ldots, \underline{y_{n,t}}\right]$$

$$= E\left[E\left[\exp(u\hat{f}_{n,t+1})|\underline{f_{t+1}}, \underline{y_{1,t}}, \ldots, \underline{y_{n,t}}\right]|\underline{f_t}, \underline{y_{1,t}}, \ldots, \underline{y_{n,t}}\right].$$

Then, by using that the risks $y_{i,t+1}$ are i.i.d. $\mathcal{B}(1, f_{t+1})$ given $\underline{f_{t+1}}, \underline{y_{1,t}}, \ldots, \underline{y_{n,t}}$, we obtain

$$\psi(f_t, u, 1) = E\left[(1 + (e^{u/n} - 1)f_{t+1})^n |\underline{f_t}, \underline{y_{1,t}}, \ldots, \underline{y_{n,t}}\right]$$

$$= E\left[(1 + (e^{u/n} - 1)f_{t+1})^n |\underline{f_t}\right].$$

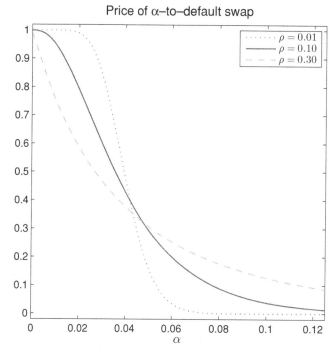

Figure 5.5. True Price of a BDS. The figure plots the price of the BDS at 1-year time-to-maturity as a function of threshold α, for three values of asset correlation: $\rho = 0.01$ (dotted line), $\rho = 0.10$ (solid line), and $\rho = 0.30$ (dashed line). The available information is such that $\hat{f}_{n,t} = f_{t-1} = 0.04$.

Thus, the true and approximated prices of the exponential derivatives are $\tilde{\pi}_t(u, 1) = \int \psi(f_t, u, 1)g(f_t|J_t)df_t$ and $\tilde{\pi}_{n,t}(u, 1) = \int \psi(f_t, u, 1)\hat{\varphi}_{n,t}(f_t)df_t$, respectively, where the pdf $g(\cdot|J_t)$ given the investor information and the approximate filtering distribution $\hat{\varphi}_{n,t}(\cdot)$ are derived in Section 5.6.2. The true price depends on the available information by means of $\hat{f}_{n,t}$ and f_{t-1}, whereas the approximate price depends on the default history by means of $\hat{f}_{n,t}$ and $\hat{f}_{n,t-1}$. The expectations with regard to f_{t+1} in function ψ and to f_t in the true and approximated prices, respectively, can be computed by Monte Carlo integration. The integral in (5.21) can be computed by numerical integration.

In Figures 5.5 and 5.6 we display the true and approximate BDS price for time-to-maturity $h = 1$ year, respectively, as a function of threshold α and for different values of default correlation. In Figure 5.5 the available information is such that $\hat{f}_{n,t} = f_{t-1} = 0.04$, and in Figure 5.6 the default history is such that $\hat{f}_{n,t} = \hat{f}_{n,t-1} = 0.04$.

The true BDS price is clearly a decreasing function of the threshold α. Its pattern corresponds to the (risk-neutral) conditional survivor function of the

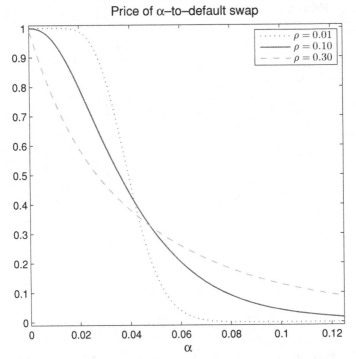

Figure 5.6. Approximate Price of a BDS. The figure plots the approximate price of the BDS at 1-year time-to-maturity as a function of threshold α for three values of asset correlation: $\rho = 0.01$ (dotted line), $\rho = 0.10$ (solid line), and $\rho = 0.30$ (dashed line). The past default history is such that $\hat{f}_{n,t} = \hat{f}_{n,t-1} = 0.04$.

future default frequency $\hat{f}_{n,t+1}$ given the available information. For small values of the asset correlation, the BDS price is close to 1 for α smaller than the current default frequency $\hat{f}_{n,t} = 0.04$; it is close to 0 for α larger than $\hat{f}_{n,t} = 0.04$. In the latter case the BDS price corresponds to the market price of a rare joint default event. The default correlation parameter ρ has a significant impact on the BDS price. Figure 5.5 shows that an increase in the asset correlation ρ implies an increase in the BDS price for α above $\hat{f}_{n,t}$ and a decrease for α below $\hat{f}_{n,t}$. This is due to the positive effect of asset correlation ρ on the conditional variance of $\hat{f}_{n,t+1}$ given the available information. By comparing Figures 5.5 and 5.6 we deduce that the approximation of the BDS price provided by Proposition 5.3 is rather accurate.

5.7 Summary

In factor models the prediction and filtering formulas involve large-dimensional integrals. However, for large exchangeable panels, these formulas can be approximated under closed form at order $1/n$, where n is the cross-sectional dimension. These approximations correspond to the standard prediction and filtering formulas applied to an appropriately linearized state space model. These approximated prediction formulas can be applied at order $1/n$ to compute the prices of derivatives written on a basket of individual risks.

5.8 Appendix: Approximation of the Filtering Distribution

5.8.1 Proof of Proposition 5.1

Let us first derive an approximation for the conditional Laplace transform of f_t given $\underline{y_{1,t}}, \ldots, \underline{y_{n,t}}$ and f_{t-1}:

$$
\mathcal{L}_{n,t}(u) = E\left[\exp\left(uf_t\right)|\underline{y_{1,t}}, \ldots, \underline{y_{n,t}}, f_{t-1}\right]
$$

$$
= \frac{\displaystyle\int e^{uf_t} g(f_t|f_{t-1}) \prod_{i=1}^{n} h\left(y_{i,t}|f_t\right) df_t}{\displaystyle\int g(f_t|f_{t-1}) \prod_{i=1}^{n} h\left(y_{i,t}|f_t\right) df_t}, \tag{5.23}
$$

which depends only on $\underline{y_{1,t}}, \ldots, \underline{y_{n,t}}$ and f_{t-1}.

Let us expand the microdensity around the estimate $\hat{f}_{n,t}$ defined in (5.1). We obtain

$$
\sum_{i=1}^{n} \log h\left(y_{i,t}|f_t\right) = \sum_{i=1}^{n} \log h\left(y_{i,t}|\hat{f}_{n,t}\right)
$$

$$
+ \frac{1}{2}\frac{1}{n} \sum_{i=1}^{n} \frac{\partial^2 \log h}{\partial f_t^2}\left(y_{i,t}|\hat{f}_{n,t}\right)\left[\sqrt{n}\left(f_t - \hat{f}_{n,t}\right)\right]^2
$$

$$
+ \frac{1}{6\sqrt{n}}\frac{1}{n} \sum_{i=1}^{n} \frac{\partial^3 \log h}{\partial f_t^3}\left(y_{i,t}|\hat{f}_{n,t}\right)\left[\sqrt{n}\left(f_t - \hat{f}_{n,t}\right)\right]^3
$$

$$
+ \frac{1}{24n}\frac{1}{n} \sum_{i=1}^{n} \frac{\partial^4 \log h}{\partial f_t^4}\left(y_{i,t}|\hat{f}_{n,t}\right)\left[\sqrt{n}\left(f_t - \hat{f}_{n,t}\right)\right]^4
$$

$$
+ o\left(1/n\right).
$$

Let us introduce the change of variable:

$$
X = I_{n,t}^{1/2}\sqrt{n}\left(f_t - \hat{f}_{n,t}\right) \iff f_t = \hat{f}_{n,t} + \frac{1}{\sqrt{n}}I_{n,t}^{-1/2}X.
$$

Then, we have

$$\sum_{i=1}^{n} \log h\left(y_{i,t}|f_t\right)$$

$$= \sum_{i=1}^{n} \log h\left(y_{i,t}|\hat{f}_{n,t}\right) - \frac{1}{2}X^2 + \frac{1}{6\sqrt{n}}J_{n,t}X^3 + \frac{1}{24n}Q_{n,t}X^4 + o(1/n),$$

where

$$J_{n,t} = I_{n,t}^{-3/2} K_{n,t} \quad \text{and} \quad Q_{n,t} = I_{n,t}^{-2} \frac{1}{n}\sum_{i=1}^{n} \frac{\partial^4 \log h}{\partial f_t^4}\left(y_{i,t}|\hat{f}_{n,t}\right).$$

Thus

$$\prod_{i=1}^{n} h\left(y_{i,t}|f_t\right)$$

$$= \prod_{i=1}^{n} h\left(y_{i,t}|\hat{f}_{n,t}\right) \exp\left(-\frac{1}{2}X^2\right) \exp\left(\frac{1}{6\sqrt{n}}J_{n,t}X^3 + \frac{1}{24n}Q_{n,t}X^4 + o(1/n)\right)$$

$$= \prod_{i=1}^{n} h\left(y_{i,t}|\hat{f}_{n,t}\right) \exp\left(-\frac{1}{2}X^2\right)$$

$$\left[1 + \frac{1}{6\sqrt{n}}J_{n,t}X^3 + \frac{1}{24n}Q_{n,t}X^4 + \frac{1}{72n}J_{n,t}^2 X^6 + o(1/n)\right]. \tag{5.24}$$

Similarly, we have an expansion for $\log g(f_t|f_{t-1})$ as

$$\log g(f_t|f_{t-1}) = \log g\left(\hat{f}_{n,t} + \frac{1}{\sqrt{n}}I_{n,t}^{-1/2}X|f_{t-1}\right)$$

$$= \log g\left(\hat{f}_{n,t}|f_{t-1}\right) + \frac{1}{\sqrt{n}}I_{n,t}^{-1/2}A_{n,t}X + \frac{1}{2n}I_{n,t}^{-1}B_{n,t}X^2 + o(1/n),$$

where

$$A_{n,t} = \frac{\partial \log g}{\partial f_t}\left(\hat{f}_{n,t}|f_{t-1}\right) \quad \text{and} \quad B_{n,t} = \frac{\partial^2 \log g}{\partial f_t^2}\left(\hat{f}_{n,t}|f_{t-1}\right).$$

Thus

$$g(f_t | f_{t-1})$$

$$= g\left(\hat{f}_{n,t} | f_{t-1}\right) \exp\left(\frac{1}{\sqrt{n}} I_{n,t}^{-1/2} A_{n,t} X + \frac{1}{2n} I_{n,t}^{-1} B_{n,t} X^2 + o(1/n)\right)$$

$$= g\left(\hat{f}_{n,t} | f_{t-1}\right) \left[1 + \frac{1}{\sqrt{n}} I_{n,t}^{-1/2} A_{n,t} X + \frac{1}{2n} I_{n,t}^{-1} B_{n,t} X^2 + \frac{1}{2n} I_{n,t}^{-1} A_{n,t}^2 X^2\right.$$

$$\left. + o(1/n)\right]. \tag{5.25}$$

Finally, we have an expansion for $\exp(u f_t)$:

$$\exp(u f_t) = \exp\left(u \hat{f}_{n,t}\right) \exp\left(\frac{u}{\sqrt{n}} I_{n,t}^{-1/2} X\right)$$

$$= \exp\left(u \hat{f}_{n,t}\right) \left[1 + \frac{u}{\sqrt{n}} I_{n,t}^{-1/2} X + \frac{u^2}{2n} I_{n,t}^{-1} X^2 + o(1/n)\right]. \tag{5.26}$$

Let us now substitute expansions (5.24)–(5.26) into the numerator in equation (5.23) (the denominator is obtained by setting $u = 0$). We have

$$\int e^{u f_t} g(f_t | f_{t-1}) \prod_{i=1}^{n} h\left(y_{i,t} | f_t\right) df_t = e^{u \hat{f}_{n,t}} \prod_{i=1}^{n} h\left(y_{i,t} | \hat{f}_{n,t}\right) g\left(\hat{f}_{n,t} | f_{t-1}\right)$$

$$E_X \left[\left(1 + \frac{u}{\sqrt{n}} I_{n,t}^{-1/2} X + \frac{u^2}{2n} I_{n,t}^{-1} X^2 + o(1/n)\right)\right.$$

$$\left(1 + \frac{1}{\sqrt{n}} I_{n,t}^{-1/2} A_{n,t} X + \frac{1}{2n} I_{n,t}^{-1} \left(B_{n,t} + A_{n,t}^2\right) X^2 + o(1/n)\right)$$

$$\left.\left(1 + \frac{1}{6\sqrt{n}} J_{n,t} X^3 + \frac{1}{24n} Q_{n,t} X^4 + \frac{1}{72n} J_{n,t}^2 X^6 + o(1/n)\right)\right],$$

where the expectation E_X is with regard to the standard normal variable X. Because odd power moments of X are equal to zero, the terms of order $1/\sqrt{n}$ [and similarly the terms of order $1/(n\sqrt{n})$, if the expansion is considered up to order $1/n^2$] cancel, and the expectation is equal to

$$1 + \frac{u}{n}\left[I_{n,t}^{-1} A_{n,t} + \frac{1}{2} I_{n,t}^{-1/2} J_{n,t}\right] + \frac{1}{2n} u^2 I_{n,t}^{-1} + \Lambda_{n,t} + O(1/n^2),$$

where

$$\Lambda_{n,t} = \frac{1}{2n} I_{n,t}^{-1} \left(B_{n,t} + A_{n,t}^2\right) + \frac{1}{2n} I_{n,t}^{-1/2} J_{n,t} A_{n,t} + \frac{1}{8n} Q_{n,t} + \frac{1}{72n} J_{n,t}^2 E\left[X^6\right]$$

is independent of u. Thus, we deduce

$\mathcal{L}_{n,t}(u)$

$$= e^{u\hat{f}_{n,t}} \frac{1 + \frac{u}{n}\left(I_{n,t}^{-1}A_{n,t} + \frac{1}{2}I_{n,t}^{-1/2}J_{n,t}\right) + \frac{1}{2n}u^2 I_{n,t}^{-1} + \Lambda_{n,t} + O(1/n^2)}{1 + \Lambda_{n,t} + O(1/n^2)}$$

$$= e^{u\hat{f}_{n,t}}\left[1 + \frac{u}{n}\left(I_{n,t}^{-1}A_{n,t} + \frac{1}{2}I_{n,t}^{-1/2}J_{n,t}\right) + \frac{u^2}{2n}I_{n,t}^{-1} + \Lambda_{n,t} + O\left(\frac{1}{n^2}\right)\right]$$

$$\cdot\left(1 - \Lambda_{n,t} + O\left(\frac{1}{n^2}\right)\right)$$

$$= e^{u\hat{f}_{n,t}}\left[1 + \frac{u}{n}\left(I_{n,t}^{-1}A_{n,t} + \frac{1}{2}I_{n,t}^{-1/2}J_{n,t}\right) + \frac{u^2}{2n}I_{n,t}^{-1} + O\left(\frac{1}{n^2}\right)\right].$$

By definition of $J_{n,t}$ and $A_{n,t}$, we conclude

$$\mathcal{L}_{n,t}(u) = e^{u\hat{f}_{n,t}}\left\{1 + \frac{u}{n}\left(I_{n,t}^{-1}\frac{\partial \log g}{\partial f_t}\left(\hat{f}_{n,t}|f_{t-1}\right) + \frac{1}{2}I_{n,t}^{-2}K_{n,t}\right) + \frac{1}{2n}u^2 I_{n,t}^{-1}\right\}$$

$$+ O(1/n^2),$$

and

$$\mathcal{L}_{n,t}(u) = \exp\left\{u\hat{f}_{n,t} + \frac{u}{n}\left(I_{n,t}^{-1}\frac{\partial \log g}{\partial f_t}\left(\hat{f}_{n,t}|f_{t-1}\right) + \frac{1}{2}I_{n,t}^{-2}K_{n,t}\right)\right.$$

$$\left. + \frac{1}{2n}u^2 I_{n,t}^{-1} + O(1/n^2)\right\}.$$

Another approximation valid at order $1/n$ can be obtained by replacing f_{t-1} by $\hat{f}_{n,t-1}$. We have

$$\mathcal{L}_{n,t}(u) = \exp\left\{u\hat{f}_{n,t} + \frac{u}{n}\left(I_{n,t}^{-1}\frac{\partial \log g}{\partial f_t}\left(\hat{f}_{n,t}|\hat{f}_{n,t-1}\right) + \frac{1}{2}I_{n,t}^{-2}K_{n,t}\right)\right.$$

$$\left. + \frac{1}{2n}u^2 I_{n,t}^{-1} + o(1/n)\right\}.$$

Then, Proposition 5.1 follows.

5.8.2 Proof of Corollary 5.3

Let us expand function a at second order around $\hat{f}_{n,t}$:

$$a(f_t) = a\left(\hat{f}_{n,t}\right) + \frac{da}{df}\left(\hat{f}_{n,t}\right)\left(f_t - \hat{f}_{n,t}\right) + \frac{1}{2}\frac{d^2a}{df^2}\left(\hat{f}_{n,t}\right)\left(f_t - \hat{f}_{n,t}\right)^2$$

$$+ o\left(\left(f_t - \hat{f}_{n,t}\right)^2\right).$$

Then, by computing the conditional expectation with regard to the Gaussian density for f_t given in Corollary 5.2, Corollary 5.3 follows.

5.8.3 Approximate Linear State Space Model and Kalman Filter

Let us prove that the filtering distribution obtained by applying the Kalman filter on the linear state space model (5.3)–(5.4) equals the Gaussian distribution in Corollary 5.2 up to order $o(1/n)$. For expository purposes we set $\mu = 0$ (the proof for $\mu \neq 0$ is similar).

From the Kalman filter (see Appendix A, Review A.5), the distribution of f_t given the history $\xi_{n,t}, \xi_{n,t-1}, \ldots$ is Gaussian, with mean $\hat{f}_{t|t}$ and variance $\hat{\Sigma}_{t|t}$ satisfying recursive equations. To write these equations, let $\hat{f}_{t|t-1}$ and $\hat{\Sigma}_{t|t-1}$ denote the conditional mean and variance of factor f_t, respectively, given the lagged information $\xi_{n,t-1}, \xi_{n,t-2}, \ldots$. Then, from Review A.5 we have

$$\hat{f}_{t|t} = \hat{f}_{t|t-1} + K_{t|t}(\xi_{n,t} - \hat{f}_{t|t-1})$$
$$= \gamma(1 - K_{t|t})\hat{f}_{t-1|t-1} + K_{t|t}\xi_{n,t}, \tag{5.27}$$

and

$$\Sigma_{t|t} = (1 - K_{t|t})\Sigma_{t|t-1}, \tag{5.28}$$

where the Kalman gain $K_{t|t}$ is such that

$$K_{t|t} = \frac{\Sigma_{t|t-1}}{\Sigma_{t|t-1} + \dfrac{1}{n}I_{n,t}^{-1}}, \tag{5.29}$$

and

$$\Sigma_{t|t-1} = \gamma^2 \Sigma_{t-1|t-1} + \eta^2. \tag{5.30}$$

From equations (5.28)–(5.30) we deduce

$$\Sigma_{t|t} = \frac{1}{n}I_{n,t}^{-1} + o(1/n), \tag{5.31}$$

$$\Sigma_{t|t-1} = \eta^2 + O(1/n), \quad K_{t|t} = 1 - \frac{1}{n\eta^2}I_{n,t}^{-1} + o(1/n).$$

Then, from equation (5.27) we obtain

$$\hat{f}_{t|t} = \frac{\gamma}{n\eta^2}I_{n,t}^{-1}\hat{f}_{t-1|t-1} + \xi_{n,t} - \frac{1}{n\eta^2}I_{n,t}^{-1}\xi_{n,t} + o(1/n)$$
$$= \hat{f}_{n,t} + \frac{1}{2n}I_{n,t}^{-2}K_{n,t} - \frac{1}{n\eta^2}I_{n,t}^{-1}(\hat{f}_{n,t} - \gamma\hat{f}_{t-1|t-1}) + o(1/n).$$

We deduce

$$\hat{f}_{t|t} = \hat{f}_{n,t} + \frac{1}{2n}I_{n,t}^{-2}K_{n,t} - \frac{1}{n\eta^2}I_{n,t}^{-1}(\hat{f}_{n,t} - \gamma\hat{f}_{n,t-1}) + o(1/n). \tag{5.32}$$

Then, by using that $\frac{\partial \log g}{\partial f_t}(f_t|f_{t-1}) = -\frac{f_t - \gamma f_{t-1}}{\eta^2}$, from equations (5.31) and (5.32) the conclusion follows.

References

Basel Committee on Banking Supervision (2001). "The New Basel Capital Accord," Consultative Document of the Bank for International Settlements, April 2001, Part 2: Pillar 1.

Basel Committee on Banking Supervision (2003). "The New Basel Capital Accord," Consultative Document of the Bank for International Settlements, April 2003, Part 3: Pillar 2.

De Servigny, A., and O. Renault (2002). "Default Correlation: Empirical Evidence," S&P, October.

De Servigny, A., and O. Renault (2004). *Measuring and Managing Credit Risk*, McGraw-Hill.

Duffie, D., J. Pan, and K. Singleton (2000). "Transform Analysis and Asset Pricing for Affine Jump Diffusions," *Econometrica*, 68, 1343–1376.

Gagliardini, P., and C. Gouriéroux (2005). "Stochastic Migration Models with Application to Corporate Risk," *Journal of Financial Econometrics*, 3, 188–226.

Gagliardini, P., and C. Gourieroux (2011). "Approximate Derivative Pricing in Large Classes of Homogeneous Assets with Systematic Risk," *Journal of Financial Econometrics*, 9, 237–280.

Gagliardini, P., C. Gouriéroux, and A. Monfort (2012). "Microinformation, Nonlinear Filtering and Granularity," *Journal of Financial Econometrics*, 10, 1–51.

Harrison, J., and D. Kreps (1979). "Martingales and Arbitrage in Multiperiod Securities Markets," *Journal of Economic Theory*, 20, 381–408.

Ito, K. (1951). "On Stochastic Differential Equations," *Memoirs of the American Mathematical Society*, 4, 1–51.

Lamb, R., W. Perraudin, and A. Van Landschoot (2008). "Dynamic Pricing of Synthetic Collaterized Debt Obligation," Imperial College W.P.

Laurent, J. P., and J. Gregory (2005). "Basket Default Swaps, CDO's and Factor Copulas," *Journal of Risk*, 7, 103–122.

Merton, R. (1974). "On the Pricing of Corporate Debt: The Risk Structure of Interest Rates," *Journal of Finance*, 29, 449–470.

Vasicek, O. (1991). "Limiting Loan Loss Probability Distribution," KMV Technical Report.

6 Granularity for Risk Measures

The current interest in risk measures is explained by recent regulatory changes in the finance and insurance industries. New measures of risk have been introduced that are now commonly used for risk management and risk control. They are the basis for determining the regulatory capital required to hedge the risk of a portfolio or of a business line in a balance sheet.

The main risk measures – the **Value-at-Risk (VaR)**, the **expected shortfall (ES)** or TailVaR, and the **distortion risk measures (DRM)** – are introduced in Section 6.1. Section 6.2 deals with the local analysis of risk measures; that is, their sensitivity to shocks on the distribution of the portfolio value. This local analysis is used in Section 6.3 to determine the granularity adjustment for theoretical risk measures for large homogeneous portfolios in a static factor model. The extension to dynamic factor models is discussed in Section 6.4, where we consider how to account for the unobservability of the current and lagged factor values. We finally consider in Section 6.5 the computation of risk measures for large portfolios of derivative assets written on a factor proxy (see also Chapter 5).

6.1 Risk Measures

Let us consider a given portfolio of assets. This portfolio can include stocks, corporate bonds, consumer loans, mortgages, or life insurance contracts. At date t, the value W_t of this portfolio is known, but its future value W_{t+h} at horizon h is unknown. This uncertainty is summarized in the **profit and loss (P&L)** distribution, which gives the conditional distribution of W_{t+h} given the information available at time t. To hedge this uncertainty some reserves R are introduced. With these reserves, which receive a zero return, the total value of the portfolio at date $t + h$ becomes $W_{t+h} + R$.

6.1.1 Value-at-Risk

Let us fix a probability of loss α, where $\alpha = 1\%$, 5%, or 10%, per instance. The **reserve level** can be chosen such that

$$P_t(W_{t+h} + R < 0) = \alpha, \tag{6.1}$$

where P_t denotes the conditional P&L distribution. By solving equation (6.1), we see that the corresponding reserve level is the opposite of the α-quantile of the P&L distribution. This level of reserve,

$$R = R(t, h, \alpha), \tag{6.2}$$

depends on date t (in particular on the information available at this date), on horizon h (there is a term structure of risk and a term structure of reserve), and on the loss probability α. The reserve $R(t, h, \alpha)$ is a decreasing function of α.

When the assets in the portfolio are stocks traded on the market, the portfolio value W_t generally features a nonstationary evolution, which can make it difficult to determinate R. To circumvent this technical difficulty, it has been proposed to introduce the Value-at-Risk defined by

$$VaR(t, h, \alpha) = R(t, h, \alpha) + W_t. \tag{6.3}$$

Thus, the VaR is characterized by

$$P_t[W_{t+h} - W_t < -VaR(t, h, \alpha)] = \alpha \tag{6.4}$$

and is the opposite of the conditional α-quantile of the distribution of change in portfolio value (see Figure 6.1). The VaR defined on these changes of portfolio value features a more stationary evolution than the reserve.

The reserve and VaR can equivalently be defined from the **loss and profit (L&P)** distribution as

$$P_t(-W_{t+h} < R) = 1 - \alpha \equiv \alpha^*, \tag{6.5}$$

$$P_t(W_t - W_{t+h} < VaR) = 1 - \alpha \equiv \alpha^*. \tag{6.6}$$

From (6.5), the level of reserve is the $(1 - \alpha)$-quantile of the L&P distribution. In this approach, $\alpha^* = 1 - \alpha$ takes large values such as 99%, 95%, or 90%. Definitions (6.1)–(6.4) and (6.5)–(6.6) are equivalent, but their choice depends on the interest. The P&L definition is generally considered by banks, which focus on profits, whereas the L&P definitions are typically adopted by regulatory and supervision authorities, which are more concerned with controlling losses.

With primary products such as consumer loans or mortgages, which are not directly traded on financial markets, the benchmark value W_t corresponds to the accounting value, which is generally the contractual value of the loan or mortgage. This value does not account for default risk and systematically overestimates the "true" value of the portfolio. The difference $W_t - W_{t+h}$ measures

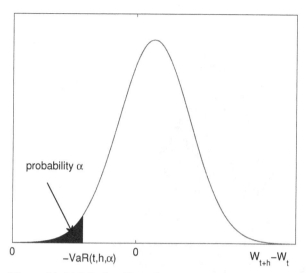

Figure 6.1. VaR Defined from the P&L Distribution. The Value-at-Risk $VaR(t, h, \alpha)$ is the opposite of the quantile at level α of the conditional distribution of $W_{t+h} - W_t$ given date t information (P&L distribution). The shaded area corresponds to a probability of α.

the loss due to default and is always positive. The associated VaR is called **CreditVaR** (see Figure 6.2).

Example 6.1. Gaussian P&L Distribution

Let us consider a Gaussian P&L distribution

$$W_{t+h}|I_t \sim N(m_t, \sigma_t^2),$$

where I_t is the available information, and m_t and σ_t^2 are the conditional mean and variance of the future portfolio value, respectively. We have

$$P_t[W_{t+h} + R < 0] = \alpha$$

$$\Longleftrightarrow P_t[m_t + \sigma_t Z + R < 0] = \alpha$$

$$\Longleftrightarrow P_t\left(Z < -\frac{R + m_t}{\sigma_t}\right) = \alpha$$

$$\Longleftrightarrow \Phi\left(-\frac{R + m_t}{\sigma_t}\right) = \alpha$$

$$\Longleftrightarrow -R = m_t + \sigma_t \Phi^{-1}(\alpha) = Q_t(\alpha), \text{ say,} \qquad (6.7)$$

where Z denotes a standard normal variable, and

$$Q_t(\alpha) = m_t + \sigma_t \Phi^{-1}(\alpha), \qquad (6.8)$$

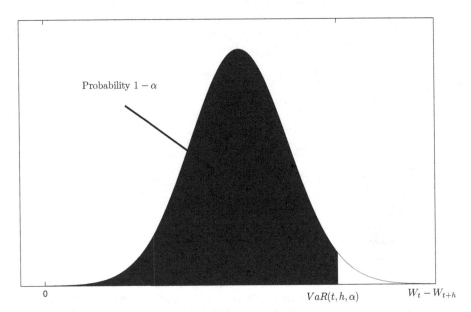

Figure 6.2. CreditVaR defined from the L&P Distribution. The CreditVaR $VaR(t, h, \alpha)$ is the quantile at level $1 - \alpha$ of the conditional distribution of $W_t - W_{t+h}$ given date t information (L&P distribution). The shaded area corresponds to a probability of $1 - \alpha$.

is the quantile function; that is, the inverse of the c.d.f. of the profit and loss distribution. Because α is small in practice, $\Phi^{-1}(\alpha)$ is negative, and from (6.7), we see that the reserve diminishes when the expected portfolio value increases and that it increases when its variance increases. In practice, P&L distributions often feature fat tails and the Gaussian model just described is inappropriate, leading to an underestimation of the risk and of the reserve.

The levels of the reserves, which are the quantiles, are natural measures of risk. They are easy to understand by professionals and are largely used in the industry. From the regulatory point of view, the required capital has to be defined without ambiguity, and therefore I_t, h, and α have to be fixed. These quantities typically depend on the type of risk – for example, market risk, credit risk, etc. – and on the level of sophistication of the risk model. For instance, for credit risk in the "standard approach" of Basel 2 (Pillar 1) one generally chooses $h = 1$ year and $\alpha = 5\%$, while the information set I_t corresponds to the absence of information. Then, the P&L distribution reduces to an unconditional distribution, called **historical** in Basel 2 terminology. However, for internal models of risk management (which correspond to Pillar 2 of Basel 2) and in the "advanced approach," several conditional quantiles have to be followed jointly to take into account the effect of information, the term structure of risk, and the severity of risk control [see Basel Committee on Banking Supervision (1995, 2001)].

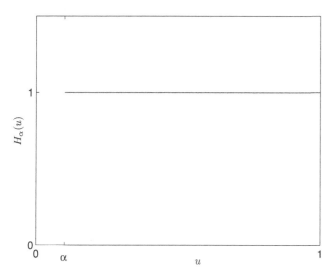

Figure 6.3. VaR Distortion Measure. The distortion measure for the VaR at level α is the point mass measure with c.d.f. $H_\alpha(u) = \mathbf{1}_{u \geq \alpha}$.

6.1.2 Distortion Risk Measures

The set of all quantile risk measures, which are the VaRs for all risk levels α and terms h, is highly informative, because it provides the entire P&L distribution for all horizons. However, when a single VaR is selected – for instance to define the required capital – this risk measure has a drawback: it accounts for the probability of loss, but not for the magnitude of the loss when a loss arises. An extended set of risk measures is obtained by considering weighted combinations of opposite quantiles.

Definition 6.1. *Let us consider a profit and loss distribution with quantile function Q and a positive probability measure H. A distortion risk measure (DRM) is defined by*

$$\pi(Q, H) = - \int_0^1 Q(u) d H(u).$$

The measure H is called the distortion measure.

This family of risk measures has been extensively studied in papers by Wang (1996, 2000). For a DRM to have desirable properties as a risk measure, function H has to be concave (see Appendix B, Review Appendix B.3).

Example 6.2. VaR
The VaR at level α corresponds to the limiting case of a point mass distortion measure $H_\alpha(u) = \mathbf{1}_{u \geq \alpha}$ (see Figure 6.3). The lack of concavity of the indicator

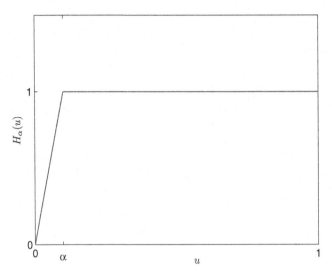

Figure 6.4. Distortion Measure for the TailVaR. The distortion measure for the TailVaR at level α is the uniform distribution on $[0, \alpha]$ with c.d.f. $H_\alpha(u) = min\{u/\alpha, 1\}$.

function explains some drawbacks of the VaR (α) when used as a single measure of risk.

Example 6.3. TailVaR
When $H_\alpha(u) = \min(u/\alpha, 1)$, with $\alpha \in (0, 1)$ (see Figure 6.4), we obtain the equally weighted average of VaR on the interval $[0, \alpha]$

$$\pi(Q, H_\alpha) = -\int_0^\alpha \frac{Q(u)}{\alpha} du$$

$$= -\frac{1}{\alpha} \int_{-\infty}^{Q(\alpha)} v \, dF(v) \quad \text{[by change of variable } v = Q(u)]$$

$$= E[-W | W < Q(\alpha)],$$

which measures the expected loss behind the VaR. This measure is also called the **expected shortfall** [Acerbi and Tasche (2002)].

6.2 Local Analysis of VaR

Let us now analyze the sensitivity of a risk measure with respect to a small change in the P&L distribution.

6.2.1 Bahadur's Expansion

Let us consider a sequence of one-dimensional continuous distributions with c.d.f. F_n and positive density f_n, tending to a probability distribution with c.d.f. F and positive density f as the index n tends to infinity. We assume that the limiting density is differentiable. These assumptions imply the existence of the quantile functions Q_n and Q defined by

$$F_n[Q_n(u)] = u, \quad F[Q(u)] = u, \quad \forall u \in (0, 1). \tag{6.9}$$

Proposition 6.1. (Bahadur's expansion) *We have*

$$Q_n(u) - Q(u) \simeq -\frac{F_n[Q(u)] - F[Q(u)]}{f[Q(u)]}.$$

Proof. From definitions (6.9) of the quantile functions, we deduce that

$$0 = F_n[Q_n(u)] - F[Q(u)]$$
$$= F_n[Q_n(u)] - F_n[Q(u)] + F_n[Q(u)] - F[Q(u)],$$

and thus

$$F_n[Q_n(u)] - F_n[Q(u)] = -(F_n[Q(u)] - F[Q(u)]).$$

By considering a first-order expansion of the left hand side, we get

$$f_n[Q(u)][Q_n(u) - Q(u)] \simeq -(F_n[Q(u)] - F[Q(u)]).$$

Equivalently we have

$$Q_n(u) - Q(u) \simeq -\frac{F_n[Q(u)] - F[Q(u)]}{f_n[Q(u)]}$$

$$\simeq -\frac{F_n[Q(u)] - F[Q(u)]}{f[Q(u)]},$$

which is the result of Proposition 6.1.

QED

The first-order expansion of the quantile function was derived in Bahadur (1966) and is largely used in nonparametric estimation of the quantile function [see, e.g., Koenker (2005)] or of the VaR [see, e.g., Gouriéroux (2010)]. As seen in Section 6.3, in the applications to portfolio risk measures, the difference $F_n - F$ is of order $1/n$, where n is the portfolio size. By Proposition 6.1, the same order is expected for the difference between the quantile functions.

6.2.2 Interpretation in Terms of Variables

It is useful to give an interpretation of Bahadur's expansion in terms of random variables. For this purpose, let us assume that F_n is the distribution of a sum

$Y_n = Y + W_n$, where variable W_n tends to zero when n tends to infinity. Then the limiting distribution F is simply the distribution of Y. Proposition 6.2 is proved in Appendix 6.7.

Proposition 6.2. *Let us assume that F_n is the distribution of $Y_n = Y + W_n$, with W_n tending to zero as $n \to \infty$. Let us also assume that Y has a continuous distribution with positive differentiable density f, that W_n is second-order integrable conditional on $Y = y$, and that $E(W_n^2 | Y = y)$ is differentiable with respect to y. Then, Bahadur's expansion can also be written as*

$$Q_n(u) - Q(u) \simeq E[W_n | Y = Q(u)]$$

$$- \frac{1}{2} \frac{\partial \log f[Q(u)]}{\partial y} E[W_n^2 | Y = Q(u)] - \frac{1}{2} \frac{\partial E[W_n^2 | Y = Q(u)]}{\partial y}. \qquad (6.10)$$

Equivalently, the sum of the last two terms in the right hand side of approximation (6.10) is equal to

$$- \frac{1}{2 f[Q(u)]} \frac{\partial}{\partial y} \left\{ f(y) E[W_n^2 | Y = y] \right\}_{y = Q(u)}.$$

We refer to Gagliardini and Gouriéroux (2013) and Fermanian (2014) for discussion of the regularity conditions. The interpretation in terms of random variables was first derived in the literature when $W_n = \varepsilon_n W$, where ε_n is a scalar tending to zero [see Gouriéroux, Laurent, and Scaillet (2000); Tasche (2000); Wilde (2001); Pykhtin and Dev (2002); Martin and Wilde (2003); Gordy (2003, 2004)]. In this case, we obtain

$$Q_n(u) - Q(u) \simeq \varepsilon_n E[W | Y = Q(u)]$$

$$- \frac{\varepsilon_n^2}{2} \left(\frac{\partial \log f[Q(u)]}{\partial y} E[W^2 | Y = Q(u)] + \frac{\partial E[W^2 | Y = Q(u)]}{\partial y} \right). \qquad (6.11)$$

In the granularity framework, we have $\varepsilon_n = 1/\sqrt{n}$ and $E[W | Y = Q(u)] = 0$ (see Sections 6.3 and 6.4). Thus, only the second component of the right-hand side of (6.11) matters and is of order $1/n$, as already noted.

6.2.3 Local Analysis of a Distortion Risk Measure

This local analysis is immediately deduced from the definition of a DRM. Indeed, we have

$$\pi(Q_n, H) - \pi(Q, H) = - \int_0^1 [Q_n(u) - Q(u)] dH(u)$$

$$\simeq \int_0^1 \frac{F_n[Q(u)] - F[Q(u)]}{f[Q(u)]} dH(u),$$

if we consider the expression of Bahadur's expansion in Proposition 6.1.

6.3 Granularity Adjustment in the Static Model

In this section, we consider a large portfolio of homogeneous risks $y_{1,t+1}, \ldots, y_{n,t+1}$, which satisfy the assumption of exchangeability. Conditionally on the factor f_{t+1}, the risks are i.i.d. with density $h(y_{i,t+1}|f_{t+1})$. The future portfolio value is $W_{t+1} = \sum_{i=1}^{n} y_{i,t+1}$. Let us assume that the underlying factor values f_t, with t varying, are i.i.d. with density g, which corresponds to a static framework. The P&L density of W_{t+1} is

$$\int h^{*n}(w|f_{t+1})g(f_{t+1})df_{t+1}, \tag{6.12}$$

where h^{*n} denotes the n-th convoluate[1] of density $h(.|f_{t+1})$. It is difficult to compute the n-th convoluate, which involves a $(n-1)$-dimensional integral. The aim of this section is to derive an approximation of the P&L distribution valid up to order $1/n$ and to deduce the corresponding approximation of the risk measures by applying the results of Section 6.2.

We first consider the static Gaussian linear factor model and then extend the results to the general static framework. In this section, we consider the level of reserve by individual asset; that is, the total reserve divided by n. Equivalently, we focus on the quantile of $W_{t+1}/n = \bar{y}_{n,t+1}$.

6.3.1 Static Gaussian Linear Factor Model

The individual risks are

$$y_{i,t+1} = F_{t+1} + u_{i,t+1}, \quad i = 1, \ldots, n,$$

where $F_{t+1} \sim N(\mu, \eta^2)$, $u_{i,t+1} \sim IIN(0, \sigma^2)$, and F_{t+1} and $u_{i,t+1}$ for $i = 1, \ldots, n$ are serially and cross-sectionally independent. In this simple Gaussian framework, the P&L distribution (6.12) is known in closed form

$$W_{t+1} \sim N[n\mu, n^2\eta^2 + n\sigma^2],$$

and

$$W_{t+1}/n \sim N(\mu, \eta^2 + \sigma^2/n).$$

The quantile function for W_{t+1}/n is (see Example 6.1)

$$Q_n(u) = \mu + (\eta^2 + \sigma^2/n)^{1/2}\Phi^{-1}(u).$$

Its first-order expansion in $1/n$ is

$$Q_n(u) = \mu + \eta\Phi^{-1}(u) + \frac{1}{2n}\frac{\sigma^2}{\eta}\Phi^{-1}(u) + o(1/n)$$

$$= Q(u) + \frac{1}{2n}\frac{\sigma^2}{\eta}\Phi^{-1}(u) + o(1/n). \tag{6.13}$$

---

[1] That is the density of the sum of independent random variables with an identical distribution.

The quantile function $Q(u)$ corresponds to a limit portfolio of infinite size with Gaussian P&L distribution $N(\mu, \eta^2)$. Then, the second term in the right-hand side of (6.13) gives the GA for the quantile at order $1/n$. This GA depends on the loss probability u and on the ratio of the common risk variance and the idiosyncratic risk volatility.

The GA for the quantile can also be derived by considering Bahadur's expansion. We have

$$W_{t+1}/n = F_{t+1} + \frac{1}{n}\sum_{i=1}^{n} u_{i,t+1} = F_{t+1} + \bar{u}_{n,t+1},$$

where $\bar{u}_{n,t+1}|F_{t+1} \sim N(0, \sigma^2/n)$. In particular we have

$$E(\bar{u}_{n,t+1}|F_{t+1}) = 0, \quad E(\bar{u}_{n,t+1}^2|F_{t+1}) = \sigma^2/n, \quad \frac{d}{df}E(\bar{u}_{n,t+1}^2|F_{t+1} = f) = 0.$$

By using Proposition 6.2 with $Y = F_{t+1}$ and $W_n = \bar{u}_{n,t+1}$, we get

$$Q_n(u) \simeq Q(u) - \frac{1}{2}\frac{d \log f[Q(u)]}{dy}\frac{\sigma^2}{n},$$

where f and Q are the pdf and the quantile function of F_{t+1}, respectively. Now, we know that

$$\log f(y) = -\frac{1}{2}\log 2\pi - \frac{1}{2}\log \eta^2 - \frac{1}{2}\frac{(y-\mu)^2}{\eta^2}$$

and $Q(u) = \mu + \eta\Phi^{-1}(u)$. We deduce that

$$\frac{d \log f[Q(u)]}{dy} = -\frac{Q(u)-\mu}{\eta^2} = -\frac{\Phi^{-1}(u)}{\eta}.$$

By substitution, we recover formula (6.13).

6.3.2 The General Static Framework

Let us now consider the general static framework of i.i.d. factor values. The factor is not necessarily Gaussian and can be multivariate, and the relation between factor and individual risks can be nonlinear. The standardized P&L is the distribution of $W_{t+1}/n = \frac{1}{n}\sum_{i=1}^{n} y_{i,t+1}$. Because the individual risks are independent and identically distributed given the future factor value, we have at order $1/n$

$$(W_{t+1}/n)|F_{t+1} \approx N[m(F_{t+1}), \sigma^2(F_{t+1})/n], \qquad (6.14)$$

where

$$m(F_{t+1}) = E[y_{i,t+1}|F_{t+1}] \quad \text{and} \quad \sigma^2(F_{t+1}) = V[y_{i,t+1}|F_{t+1}]. \quad (6.15)$$

The approximation (6.14) is derived by applying the CLT in the cross-section at date $t + 1$ **conditional on the factor value** F_{t+1}.

Equivalently, we can write

$$W_{t+1}/n \simeq m(F_{t+1}) + \frac{\sigma(F_{t+1})}{\sqrt{n}} Z, \qquad (6.16)$$

where $Z \sim N(0, 1)$ is independent of F_{t+1}. Then, by applying Proposition 6.2 with $Y = m(F_{t+1})$ and $W_n = \dfrac{\sigma(F_{t+1})}{\sqrt{n}} Z$, we have

$$E\left(\frac{\sigma(F_{t+1})Z}{\sqrt{n}}|m(F_{t+1})\right) = \frac{1}{\sqrt{n}} E[\sigma(F_{t+1})|m(F_{t+1})]E(Z) = 0$$

and

$$E\left(\frac{\sigma^2(F_{t+1})Z^2}{n}|m(F_{t+1})\right) = E\left[\frac{\sigma^2(F_{t+1})}{n}|m(F_{t+1})\right] E(Z^2)$$

$$= \frac{1}{n} E[\sigma^2(F_{t+1})|m(F_{t+1})],$$

where we have used the independence between Z and F_{t+1}. We deduce the GA for the VaR.

Proposition 6.3. *In a static factor model we have*

$$Q_n(u) - Q(u) \simeq -\frac{1}{2n}\left(\frac{\partial \log f[Q(u)]}{\partial y} E[\sigma^2(F_{t+1})|m(F_{t+1}) = Q(u)]\right.$$

$$\left. + \frac{\partial E\left[\sigma^2(F_{t+1})|m(F_{t+1}) = Q(u)\right]}{\partial y}\right),$$

where f (resp. Q) is the pdf (resp. the quantile function) of $m(F_{t+1})$.

The quantile $Q(u)$ is the CSA approximation, is computed for the limit (virtual) portfolio of infinite size, and corresponds to the quantile of the distribution of $m(F_{t+1})$. Indeed, by the LLN applied in the cross-section at date $t + 1$

conditional on F_{t+1}, the standardized portfolio value $W_{n,t+1}$ converges to the conditional mean $m(F_{t+1})$. The CSA approximation of the portfolio quantile by means of function $Q(u)$ corresponds to the Vasicek (1991) approach. The GA $Q_n(u) - Q(u)$ in Proposition 6.3 is the adjustment at order $1/n$ for the finite portfolio size. This GA involves the density of $m(F_{t+1})$, the conditional mean of volatility $\sigma^2(F_{t+1})$ given $m(F_{t+1})$, and their first-order derivatives, evaluated at the loss level $Q(u)$.

Example 6.4.
Let us consider a portfolio of zero-coupon corporate bonds with time-to-maturity 1 and the same nominal equal to \$1. The risk variables $y_{i,t+1}$ are dichotomous and correspond to the individual default events. Then, W_{t+1}/n corresponds to the portfolio loss per bond (assuming a zero recovery rate). The risk variables $y_{i,t+1}$ are conditionally i.i.d. with Bernoulli distribution $\mathcal{B}(1, F_{t+1})$ given F_{t+1}. The factor F_{t+1} admits values in (0, 1) and corresponds to the stochastic default probability at date $t + 1$. We have $m(F_{t+1}) = F_{t+1}$ and $\sigma^2(F_{t+1}) = F_{t+1}(1 - F_{t+1})$. From Proposition 6.3 we deduce

$$Q_n(u) - Q(u)$$

$$\simeq -\frac{1}{2n}\left\{\frac{\partial \log f[Q(u)]}{\partial y}E[\sigma^2(F_{t+1})|F_{t+1} = Q(u)]\right.$$

$$\left. + \frac{\partial E[\sigma^2(F_{t+1})|F_{t+1} = Q(u)]}{\partial y}\right\}$$

$$= -\frac{1}{2n}\left[\frac{\partial \log f[Q(u)]}{\partial y}Q(u)[1 - Q(u)] + 1 - 2Q(u)\right],$$

where f (resp. Q) is the density of F_{t+1} (resp. the quantile function). When $\Phi^{-1}(F_t)$ follows a Gaussian distribution $N(\mu, \eta^2)$, we get $f(y) = \frac{1}{\eta}\phi\left[\frac{\Phi^{-1}(y)-\mu}{\eta}\right]/\phi[\Phi^{-1}(y)]$ and $Q(u) = \Phi[\mu + \eta\Phi^{-1}(u)]$, for $y, u \in (0, 1)$. For instance, in the SRF model for default based on the Merton (1974) and Vasicek (1991) structural models, we have $F_t = \Phi\left(\frac{\Phi^{-1}(PD)-\sqrt{\rho}F_t^*}{\sqrt{1-\rho}}\right)$, where PD is the unconditional default probability, ρ is the asset correlation, and $F_t^* \sim N(0, 1)$ is the systematic risk factor in the structural model of the log asset/liability ratios [see Section 3.1; in particular equation (3.6)]. Thus, we obtain

$$\mu = \frac{\Phi^{-1}(PD)}{\sqrt{1-\rho}}, \quad \eta^2 = \frac{\rho}{1-\rho}.$$

Then, we get the CSA quantile function [see Gagliardini and Gouriéroux (2013)]:

$$Q(u) = \Phi \left[\frac{\Phi^{-1}(PD) + \sqrt{\rho}\,\Phi^{-1}(u)}{\sqrt{1-\rho}} \right], \tag{6.17}$$

and the GA:

$$GA = \frac{1}{2n} \left\{ \frac{Q(u)[1 - Q(u)]}{\phi(\Phi^{-1}[Q(u)])} \left(\sqrt{\frac{1-\rho}{\rho}}\,\Phi^{-1}(u) - \Phi^{-1}[Q(u)] \right) + 2Q(u) - 1 \right\}. \tag{6.18}$$

Although in this example we focus on the VaR for an actuarial loss, we refer to Gordy and Marrone (2012) for an extension to mark-to-market credit risk models.

6.3.3 A Discussion of the GA Order

As for estimation (Chapters 2–4) and prediction (Chapter 5), the GA for the quantile is of order $1/n$. This is due to the unobservable factor. To clarify this point, let us consider the Gaussian model without factor; that is, set $\eta^2 = 0$ in Section 6.3.1. The distribution of the standardized portfolio value becomes

$$W_{t+1}/n \sim N(\mu, \sigma^2/n).$$

The c.d.f. of this distribution is $\Phi(\frac{y-\mu}{\sigma/\sqrt{n}})$. Its quantile function is $Q_n(u) = \mu + \frac{\sigma}{\sqrt{n}}\Phi^{-1}(u)$, and its Laplace transform is

$$\psi(u) = E[\exp(uW/n)] = \exp\left(u\mu + \frac{u^2\sigma^2}{n}\right).$$

The first terms in the expansions of these functions with respect to $1/n$ have different orders. This order is $1/\sqrt{n}$ for the quantile function and $1/n$ for the Laplace transform. The convergence is very fast, and the order depends on argument y for the c.d.f., whereas we would expect a uniform order to deduce a uniform order for the quantile function from Bahadur's expansion.

To understand why the order is $1/n$ uniformly when an unobservable factor is introduced, whereas the order can be varying without this unobservable factor, let us consider the expectation of a twice continuously differentiable function

a of W_{t+1}/n. We have

$$E[a(W_{t+1}/n)]$$

$$= E[a(\mu + \frac{\sigma}{\sqrt{n}}Z)], \text{ where } Z \sim N(0, 1),$$

$$\simeq a(\mu) + \frac{da(\mu)}{d\mu} \frac{\sigma}{\sqrt{n}} E(Z) + \frac{1}{2} \frac{d^2 a(\mu)}{d\mu^2} \frac{\sigma^2}{n} E(Z^2) + o(1/n)$$

$$= a(\mu) + \frac{\sigma^2}{2n} \frac{d^2 a(\mu)}{d\mu^2} + o(1/n). \tag{6.19}$$

The different rates of convergence for the c.d.f and quantile function encountered in a model without an unobservable factor occurs because the c.d.f. is interpreted as an expectation of an indicator function:

$$F_n(y) = E[\mathbf{1}_{W_{t+1}/n < y}] = E[\mathbf{1}_{\mu + \frac{\sigma}{\sqrt{n}}Z < y}].$$

Because the indicator function is not differentiable, the expansion (6.19) does not apply. Let us now consider the model with factor $F_{t+1} \sim N(\mu, \eta^2)$. We have

$$F_n(y) = E[\mathbf{1}_{W_{t+1}/n < y}] = E[\mathbf{1}_{F_{t+1} + \frac{\sigma}{\sqrt{n}}Z < y}] = E[a(Z)]$$

where

$$a(Z) = P\left[F_{t+1} + \frac{\sigma}{\sqrt{n}}Z < y | Z\right] = \Phi\left(\frac{y - \mu - \frac{\sigma}{\sqrt{n}}Z}{\eta}\right).$$

This intermediate integration with respect to the factor transforms the discontinuous indicator function into the smooth conditional probability function. This smoothing explains why the GA order $1/n$ is uniform in a factor model.

6.3.4 Illustration: CSA and GA VaR in the Static SRF Model for Default

In this subsection we study the CSA and GA approximations in a numerical illustration for the static SRF model for corporate default (see Example 6.4 and Section 3.1). Let us first consider these values for the annual unconditional default probability PD and unconditional asset correlation: $PD = 0.01$ and $\rho = 0.12$. They correspond to the annual unconditional default probability of a firm with about a BB rating, and to the smallest value of asset correlation suggested in Basel 2 [see BCBS (2001, 2003)]. The CSA and GA approximations for the portfolio VaR in equations (6.17) and (6.18) are displayed in Figure 6.5 as functions of the confidence level u, for u close to 1. The GA approximations are for portfolio sizes $n = 25, 100$, and $1,000$.

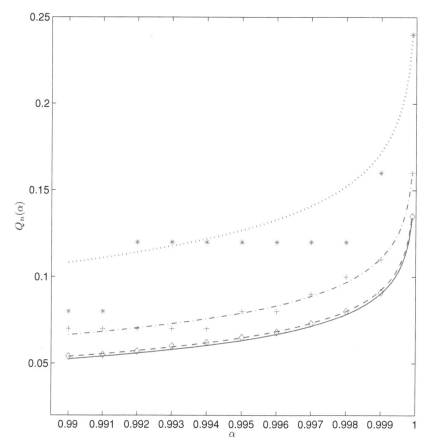

Figure 6.5. CSA and GA VaR in the Static SRF Model. The figure displays the CSA approximation (solid line) and the GA approximations for the portfolio VaR in a static SRF model, as functions of the confidence level α. The GA approximations are for portfolio sizes $n = 25$ (dotted line), $n = 100$ (dashed-dotted line), and $n = 1,000$ (dashed line). Stars, crosses, and diamonds correspond to quantiles computed with Monte Carlo simulation based on $500,000$ replications of the portfolio loss for portfolio sizes $n = 25$, $n = 100$, and $n = 1,000$, respectively. The unconditional default probability is $PD = 0.01$, and the asset correlation is $\rho = 0.12$.

As expected, the approximated quantiles are increasing with regard to the confidence level. Moreover, the GA quantile curves are above the CSA quantile curve, and the granularity adjustment is decreasing with regard to the portfolio size because of the diversification of the unsystematic risk component. For portfolio size $n = 1,000$, the GA approximation is very close to the CSA approximation, whereas for $n = 100$ the granularity adjustment is very important.

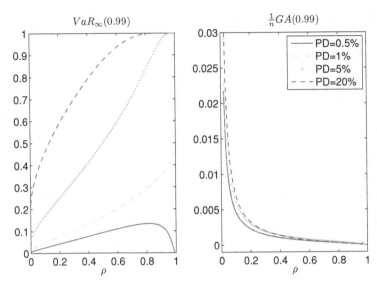

Figure 6.6. CSA VaR and GA in the Static SRF Model as Functions of Asset Correlation. The left panel displays the CSA VaR, and the right panel displays the GA as functions of asset correlation ρ for different values of the unconditional default probability: $PD = 0.005, 0.01, 0.05$, and 0.20, in the static SRF model for default. The portfolio size is $n = 1,000$, and the confidence level is $1 - \alpha = 0.99$.

To assess the accuracy of the GA approximation, we display in Figure 6.5 quantiles computed by Monte Carlo simulation for some confidence levels (see Appendix A, Review Appendix A.1). These quantiles are the empirical quantiles for a simulated sample of $500,000$ replications of the portfolio loss. The discrepancy between the GA approximation and the simulated quantiles decreases with the portfolio size n and is already small for portfolio size $n = 100$. For small values of portfolio size such as $n = 25$, the discontinuity of the portfolio quantile with regard to the confidence level can be clearly seen from the simulated quantile values.

The GA approximation can be used to study the behavior of the portfolio risk measure as a function of the model parameters: the unconditional probability of default PD and the asset correlation ρ. Such a study would be very time consuming if performed using Monte Carlo simulation. In Figure 6.6 we display the CSA approximation and the GA as functions of ρ, for different values of PD. In Figure 6.7 we display the CSA approximation and the GA as functions of PD for different values of ρ. The portfolio size is $n = 1,000$, and the confidence level is $1 - \alpha = 0.99$.

Figure 6.6 shows that the CSA VaR is monotone increasing with regard to asset correlation ρ, when the probability of default is such that $PD \geq \alpha$; for $PD < \alpha$, the CSA VaR is not monotone with regard to ρ, and it converges to zero as ρ approaches 1. The granularity adjustment is decreasing with regard

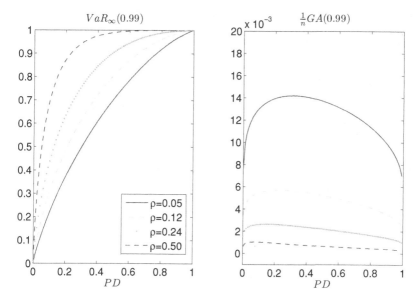

Figure 6.7. CSA VaR and GA in The static SRF Model as Functions of Default Probability. The left panel displays the CSA VaR, and the right panel displays the GA as functions of the probability of default PD for different values of the asset correlation: $\rho = 0.05, 0.12, 0.24$, and 0.50, in the static SRF model for default. The portfolio size is $n = 1,000$, and the confidence level is $1 - \alpha = 0.99$.

to asset correlation ρ, when ρ is not close to 1. Figure 6.7 shows that the CSA VaR is monotone increasing with regard to the probability of default PD. The granularity adjustment features instead an inverse-U shape. The maximum GA occurs for values of PD corresponding to speculative grade ratings when ρ is between 0.12 and 0.24.

6.4 Granularity Adjustment in the Dynamic Model

Let us now consider the dynamic framework, with a factor transition density given by $g(f_t|f_{t-1})$. In this extended framework, two granularity adjustments are required. The first one concerns the theoretical risk measure itself and is the analog of the adjustment derived in the static framework. The second granularity adjustment is a consequence of the unobservability of the factor values and is derived by using the approximate filtering formula of Chapter 5.

6.4.1 Granularity Adjustment for the Distribution of the Portfolio Value

We have

$$W_{t+1}/n = m(F_{t+1}) + \frac{\sigma(F_{t+1})}{\sqrt{n}} Z + O(1/n), \qquad (6.20)$$

where functions $m(F_{t+1})$ and $\sigma(F_{t+1})$ are defined as in (6.15), and $Z \sim N(0, 1)$ is independent of the factor path. Term $O(1/n)$ is conditionally zero-mean because the normalized portfolio value is an unbiased estimator of $m(F_{t+1})$, conditionally on F_{t+1}. Let us denote

$$a(y, f_t, \varepsilon) = P[m(F_{t+1}) + \sigma(F_{t+1})\varepsilon \le y | F_t = f_t]$$

$$= \int \mathbf{1}_{m(f_{t+1})+\sigma(f_{t+1})\varepsilon \le y} \, g(f_{t+1}|f_t) df_{t+1}.$$

The c.d.f. of the standardized portfolio value given the observable information $I_t^* = (y_{1,t}, \ldots, y_{n,t})$ only is

$$F_n(y) = P[W_{t+1}/n \le y | I_t^*]$$

$$= E(P[W_{t+1}/n \le y | F_t, Z, I_t^*] | I_t^*)$$

$$= E\left[a(y, F_t, \frac{Z}{\sqrt{n}}) | I_t^*\right] + o(1/n).$$

Then, by applying the GA for the filtering distribution of F_t given in Corollary 5.2, we obtain

$$F_n(y) = E\left[a(y, \hat{f}_{n,t} + \frac{1}{n}\mu_{n,t} + \frac{1}{\sqrt{n}}I_{n,t}^{-1/2}Z^*, \frac{Z}{\sqrt{n}}) | I_t^*\right] + o(1/n),$$

where Z^* is a standard normal variable, $\hat{f}_{n,t}$ is the cross-sectional approximation of the factor value, $\mu_{n,t} = I_{n,t}^{-1}\frac{\partial \log g}{\partial f_t}(\hat{f}_{n,t}|\hat{f}_{n,t-1}) + \frac{1}{2}I_{n,t}^{-2}K_{n,t}$ is the mean adjustment in the filtering distribution, and the term $I_{n,t}^{-1/2}Z^*$ is the adjustment for the variance. Moreover, the Gaussian variables Z and Z^* are independent, because the first one is due to the Central Limit Theorem, whereas the second one corresponds to the numerical approximation of the filtering distribution, which involves no stochastic argument. The expression of the c.d.f. can be expanded at order $1/n$. Because $E[Z] = 0$, $E[Z^*] = 0$, and $E[ZZ^*] = 0$, $E[Z^2] = E[(Z^*)^2] = 1$, we obtain

$$F_n(y) = a(y, \hat{f}_{n,t}, 0) + \frac{1}{n}\frac{\partial a(y, \hat{f}_{n,t}, 0)}{\partial f_t}\mu_{n,t}$$

$$+ \frac{1}{2n}\left[I_{n,t}^{-1}\frac{\partial^2 a(y, \hat{f}_{n,t}, 0)}{\partial f_t^2} + \frac{\partial^2 a(y, \hat{f}_{n,t}, 0)}{\partial \varepsilon^2}\right] + o(1/n). \quad (6.21)$$

The CSA approximation of the c.d.f. is $a(y, \hat{f}_{n,t}, 0) = P[m(F_{t+1}) \le y | F_t = \hat{f}_{n,t}]$. The GA is the sum of two components corresponding to the granularity adjustment for filtering; that is,

$$\frac{\partial a(y, \hat{f}_{n,t}, 0)}{\partial f_t} \mu_{n,t} + \frac{1}{2} I_{n,t}^{-1} \frac{\partial^2 a(y, \hat{f}_{n,t}, 0)}{\partial f_t^2};$$

and the granularity adjustment for the theoretical c.d.f.; that is,

$$\frac{1}{2} \frac{\partial^2 a(y, \hat{f}_{n,t}, 0)}{\partial \varepsilon^2}.$$

Due to the independence between Z and Z^*, there is no cross GA.

6.4.2 Granularity Adjustment for the Value-at-Risk

The GA for the VaR is directly deduced from the GA of the c.d.f. by applying Bahadur's expansion (see Proposition 6.1). Let us consider the conditional mean $m(F_{t+1})$. Its c.d.f., conditional to $F_t = f_t$, is $a(y, f_t, 0)$, which is the leading term in the expansion (6.21). The associated quantile function (resp. density function) is denoted by $Q(u; f_t)$ [resp. $f(y; f_t)$]. We obtain

$$Q_n(u) \simeq Q(u; \hat{f}_{n,t}) + GA_{risk} + GA_{filter},$$

and the GA for the VaR at risk level u is the sum of two components:

(1)   The granularity adjustment for filtering is

$$GA_{filter} = -\frac{1}{n} \frac{1}{f[Q(u; \hat{f}_{n,t})]} \left[\frac{\partial a[Q(u; \hat{f}_{n,t}), \hat{f}_{n,t}, 0]}{\partial f_t} \mu_{n,t} \right.$$

$$\left. + \frac{1}{2} I_{n,t}^{-1} \frac{\partial^2 a[Q(u, \hat{f}_{n,t}), \hat{f}_{n,t}, 0)}{\partial f_t^2} \right].$$

(2)   The granularity adjustment for the theoretical risk measure is

$$GA_{risk} = -\frac{1}{2n} \frac{1}{f[Q(u, \hat{f}_{n,t})]} \frac{\partial^2 a[Q(u, \hat{f}_{n,t}), \hat{f}_{n,t}, 0)}{\partial \varepsilon^2}.$$

The second GA [see Gagliardini, Gouriéroux, and Monfort (2012)] can also be written as

$$GA_{risk} = -\frac{1}{2n} \left\{ \frac{\partial \log f[y; \hat{f}_{n,t}]}{\partial y} E[\sigma^2(F_{t+1})|m(F_{t+1}) = y, F_t = \hat{f}_{n,t}] \right.$$

$$\left. + \frac{\partial}{\partial y} E[\sigma^2(F_{t+1})|m(F_{t+1}) = y, F_t = \hat{f}_{n,t}] \right\}_{y = Q(u; \hat{f}_{n,t})}.$$

This expression is the analog of the GA in the static factor model of Section 6.3. The distribution of F_{t+1} is now conditional on the current factor value F_t, and this unobservable value is finally replaced by the cross-sectional approximation $\hat{f}_{n,t}$.

It is interesting to note that most studies have proposed the GA_{risk} component as the total adjustment to be applied to the VaR. In a dynamic model, the computations in this subsection show that the other component, GA_{filter}, which is due to the factor unobservability has the same magnitude and also has to be taken into account, as shown in the following illustration.

6.4.3 Illustration: Dynamic Model with Stochastic Default and Recovery

In this illustration we consider an extension of the static SRF model for corporate default presented in Section 6.3.4 to account for the dynamics of the systematic factor and a nonzero recovery rate [see Gagliardini, Gouriéroux, and Monfort (2012)]. The percentage loss on the loan to firm i at the maturity date $t + 1$ is

$$y_{i,t+1} = \mathbf{1}_{A_{i,t+1} < L_{i,t+1}} \left(1 - \frac{A_{i,t+1}}{L_{i,t+1}}\right) = \left(1 - \frac{A_{i,t+1}}{L_{i,t+1}}\right)^+ \qquad (6.22)$$

where $A_{i,t+1}$ and $L_{i,t+1}$ are the stochastic asset value and liability of the firm, respectively, and $x^+ = \max\{x, 0\}$ denotes the positive part of x. The loss variable $y_{i,t+1}$ is the product of the default indicator $\mathbf{1}_{A_{i,t+1} < L_{i,t+1}}$ – which is equal to 1 when the asset value is below the liability and is 0 otherwise – and the percentage **loss given default** (LGD); that is, $1 - \frac{A_{i,t+1}}{L_{i,t+1}}$. The dynamics of the log asset/liability ratios of the firms follow a linear single risk factor model

$$\log\left(\frac{A_{i,t}}{L_{i,t}}\right) = F_t + \sigma u_{i,t}, \qquad (6.23)$$

where the idiosyncratic shocks $(u_{i,t})$ are $IIN(0, 1)$ across time and firms. The single systematic factor F_t follows an autoregressive Gaussian process

$$F_t = \mu + \gamma (F_{t-1} - \mu) + \eta\sqrt{1 - \gamma^2}\varepsilon_t, \qquad (6.24)$$

where the innovations $\varepsilon_t \sim IIN(0, 1)$ are independent of $(u_{i,t})$. The model parameters are the volatility of the idiosyncratic shocks $\sigma > 0$, the unconditional mean μ and volatility $\eta > 0$ of the systematic factor, and its autocorrelation coefficient γ. That coefficient is assumed such that $|\gamma| < 1$ to ensure stationarity. The stationary distribution of the systematic risk factor is $F_t \sim N(\mu, \eta^2)$. When $\gamma \neq 0$, the systematic risk factor features serial dependence.

As in the static model for corporate default (see Remark 3.1 in Section 3.1), there exists alternative parameterizations of model (6.22)–(6.24) that admit a more direct financial interpretation. More precisely, let us consider the

Table 6.1. *Reduced-form and structural parameters*

Reduced-form parameters			Structural parameters		
$ELGD$	PD	ρ	μ	η	σ
		0.12	4.799	0.766	2.074
0.45	1.5%	0.24	4.799	1.083	1.928
		0.50	4.799	1.564	1.564
		0.12	3.050	0.642	1.739
0.45	5%	0.24	3.050	0.908	1.616
		0.50	3.050	1.311	1.311
		0.12	16.993	2.713	7.346
0.75	1.5%	0.24	16.993	3.836	6.827
		0.50	16.993	5.537	5.537
		0.12	10.669	2.247	6.085
0.75	5%	0.24	10.669	3.178	5.655
		0.50	10.669	4.587	4.587

unconditional probability of default

$$PD = P\left[\log\left(A_{i,t}/L_{i,t}\right) < 0\right] = \Phi\left(-\frac{\mu}{\sqrt{\eta^2 + \sigma^2}}\right), \qquad (6.25)$$

and the unconditional asset correlation

$$\rho = corr\left[\log\left(A_{i,t}/L_{i,t}\right), \log\left(A_{j,t}/L_{j,t}\right)\right] = \frac{\eta^2}{\eta^2 + \sigma^2} \qquad (6.26)$$

for $i \neq j$. Furthermore, let us introduce the unconditional **expected (percentage) loss given default** (ELGD):

$$ELGD = E\left[1 - \frac{A_{i,t}}{L_{i,t}} \Big| \frac{A_{i,t}}{L_{i,t}} < 1\right]. \qquad (6.27)$$

Gagliardini, Gouriéroux, and Monfort (2012) derive an expression for $ELGD$ in terms of the structural parameters σ, μ, and η [see also Geske (1977)]. Then, the probability of default PD, the asset correlation ρ, the $ELGD$, and the factor autocorrelation γ provide an equivalent parameterization of the model. In Table 6.1 we display the values of the structural parameters σ, μ, and η corresponding to some choices of the reduced-form parameters PD, ρ, and $ELGD$. In particular, the values 0.45 and 0.75 of $ELGD$ in Table 6.1 are the values of expected loss given default suggested by the Basel 2 accord [see BCBS (2001, 2003)] for senior debt classes on corporate, sovereigns, and banks not secured, and for subordinated classes on corporate, sovereigns, and banks, respectively.

The CSA and GA quantile approximations are derived from the general results in Section 6.4.2. We present here some steps of the analysis and invite readers to refer to Gagliardini, Gouriéroux, and Monfort (2012) for the detailed derivation.

(*) The cross-sectional factor approximation at date t is

$$\hat{f}_{n,t} = \arg\max_{f_t} \left\{ -\frac{1}{2\sigma^2} \sum_{i:y_{i,t}>0} \left[\log(1 - y_{i,t}) - f_t\right]^2 + (n - n_t) \log \Phi(f_t/\sigma) \right\},$$

(6.28)

where $n_t = \sum_{i=1}^{n} \mathbf{1}_{y_{i,t}>0}$ denotes the number of defaults at date t. The factor approximation corresponds to the maximum likelihood estimator of the mean parameter in a Gaussian Tobit regression model with endogenous variable $\log(1 - y_{i,t})$, mean f_t, and variance σ^2. The Gaussian approximation at order $1/n$ of the filtering distribution of the unobservable factor f_t in Corollary 5.2 involves statistics $\hat{f}_{n,t}$, $\hat{f}_{n,t-1}$, and n_t.

(**) Functions $m(f_{t+1})$ and $\sigma(f_{t+1})$ can be derived from the Black-Scholes pricing formula by exploiting the put option structure of the loss variable $(1 - A_{i,t+1}/L_{i,t+1})^+$ and the conditional log-normality of $A_{i,t+1}/L_{i,t+1}$ given $F_{t+1} = f_{t+1}$. We obtain

$$m(f_{t+1}) = \Phi(-f_{t+1}/\sigma) - \exp\left(f_{t+1} + \frac{\sigma^2}{2}\right) \Phi(-f_{t+1}/\sigma - \sigma) \quad (6.29)$$

and

$$\sigma^2(f_{t+1}) = m(f_{t+1})[1 - m(f_{t+1})] - \exp\left(f_{t+1} + \frac{\sigma^2}{2}\right) \Phi(-f_{t+1}/\sigma - \sigma)$$

$$+ \exp(2f_{t+1} + 2\sigma^2)\Phi(-f_{t+1}/\sigma - 2\sigma). \quad (6.30)$$

Function m is monotone decreasing, because the loss $y_{i,t+1}$ is decreasing with regard to the factor value F_{t+1}.

(***) Finally, function $a(w, \hat{f}_{n,t}, 0)$ is given by

$$a(w, \hat{f}_{n,t}, 0) = P[m(F_{t+1}) \leq w | F_t = \hat{f}_{n,t}] = P[F_{t+1} \geq m^{-1}(w) | F_t = \hat{f}_{n,t}]$$

$$= \Phi\left(-\frac{m^{-1}(w) - \mu - \gamma(\hat{f}_{n,t} - \mu)}{\eta\sqrt{1 - \gamma^2}}\right), \quad (6.31)$$

where m^{-1} denotes the inverse of function m.

Figure 6.8 shows the CSA and GA VaR approximations and the GA risk and filtering components as functions of the cross-sectional approximation of the current factor value. The parameters are such that the annual default probability is $PD = 0.05$, the asset correlation is $\rho = 0.12$, the expected loss given default

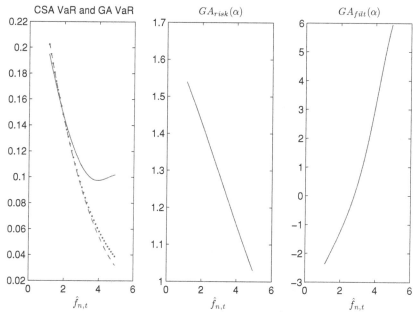

Figure 6.8. CSA and GA VaR as a Function of the Cross-Sectional Factor Approxima-tion. The left panel displays the CSA VaR (dashed line), the GA VaR for $n = 100$ (solid line), and the GA VaR for $n = 1,000$ (dotted line) as functions of the cross-sectional factor approximation $\hat{f}_{n,t}$. The middle and right panels display the GA component for risk and the GA component for filtering, respectively. The information set is such that $n_t/n = PD$ and $\hat{f}_{n,t-1} = \mu$. The confidence level is $1 - \alpha = 0.995$. The struc-tural parameters are such that $ELGD = 0.45$, $PD = 5\%$, $\rho = 0.12$, and $\gamma = 0.5$. In particular, the unconditional factor mean is $\mu = 3.05$ (see Table 6.1).

is $ELGD = 0.45$, and the factor autocorrelation is $\gamma = 0.5$. The corresponding unconditional mean of the factor is $\mu = 3.05$. The information set is such that $n_t/n = PD$ and $\hat{f}_{n,t-1} = \mu$, whereas the confidence level is $1 - \alpha = 0.995$. The CSA VaR is decreasing with regard to the factor approximation, because the systematic factor has a positive impact on the asset/liability ratios of the firms. The granularity adjustment is quite small for portfolio size $n = 1,000$, but is relevant for portfolio size $n = 100$. By comparing the patterns of the GA risk and filtering components, it is seen that the granularity adjustment comes mostly from filtering, at least when the factor approximation is above the factor mean. Indeed, the filtering GA component accounts for the uncertainty of the cross-sectional factor approximation. When this approximation is above the factor mean, the filtering GA component yields an upward correction of the CSA VaR, which reflects a less optimistic belief regarding the unobservable factor value compared to the cross-sectional approximation.

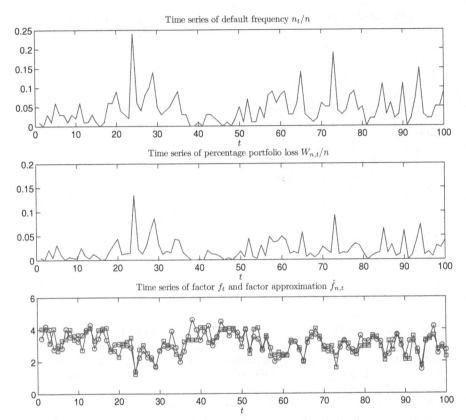

Figure 6.9. Time Series of Simulated Default Frequencies, Portfolio Losses, Systematic Factors, and Cross-Sectional Approximations of the Factor. The upper and middle panels display a simulated time series of default frequencies and percentage portfolio losses, respectively. The lower panel displays the corresponding time series of factor values (circles) and cross-sectional factor approximations (squares). The portfolio size is $n = 100$. The structural parameters are such that $ELGD = 0.45$, $PD = 5\%$, $\rho = 0.12$, and $\gamma = 0.5$. In particular, the unconditional factor mean is $\mu = 3.05$ (see Table 6.1).

In Figure 6.9 we display simulated paths of the default frequency n_t/n, the percentage portfolio loss $W_{n,t}/n$, the factor value f_t and its cross-sectional approximation $\hat{f}_{n,t}$. Figure 6.10 shows the corresponding simulated paths of the CSA and GA VaR and of the GA risk and filtering components. The portfolio size is $n = 100$, the confidence level is $1 - \alpha = 0.995$, and the model parameters are as earlier. The time series of default frequency and portfolio loss have a similar pattern, because they are driven by the same systematic factor. Moreover, at each date the portfolio loss is smaller than the default frequency because of the nonzero recovery rate. The cross-sectional factor approximation

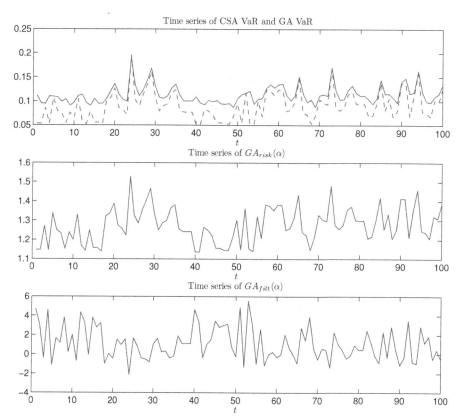

Figure 6.10. Time Series of Simulated CSA VaR, GA VaR, and GA Risk and Filtering Components. The upper panel displays a simulated time series of CSA VaR (dashed line) and GA VaR (solid line) for portfolio size $n = 100$ and confidence level $1 - \alpha = 0.995$. The middle and lower panels display the corresponding time series of GA risk and filtering components, respectively. The structural parameters are such that $ELGD = 0.45$, $PD = 5\%$, $\rho = 0.12$, and $\gamma = 0.5$ (see Table 6.1).

is rather accurate. Figure 6.10 shows that the GA VaR is larger and features a smoother time evolution than the CSA VaR. Moreover, whereas the risk component of the granularity adjustment is always positive and rather stable in time, its filtering component varies quite a lot in time and can eventually take negative values. As already noted in Figure 6.8, the filtering GA component is responsible for most of the granularity adjustment.

Finally, Gagliardini, Gouriéroux, and Monfort (2012) perform a backtesting analysis to compare the GA VaR and CSA VaR in terms of the frequency and dynamic pattern of violations; that is, when the realized portfolio loss exceeds the VaR. They show that the GA VaR is a more accurate approximation of the true portfolio quantile than the CSA VaR.

6.5 Portfolio of Derivatives Written on a Large Portfolio

The VaR and its granularity adjustments also have to be computed for portfolios of derivatives written on a given large portfolio of individual contracts. These derivatives are called collateralized debt obligations (CDOs). Typically, the support for such credit derivatives is a given pool of credits or of credit default swaps (CDSs). Then the derivative payoffs are defined by tranching the (normalized) portfolio value $\bar{W}_{n,t+1} = W_{n,t+1}/n$; that is, by considering payoffs of the type

$$b_j(\bar{W}_{n,t+1}) = \begin{cases} \bar{W}_{n,t+1}, & \text{if } \bar{W}_{n,t+1} \in (a_j, a_{j+1}), \text{ say,} \\ 0, & \text{otherwise,} \end{cases}$$

where a_j and a_{j+1} are the attachment and detachment points, respectively, or by considering straddles defined by combining appropriately European calls with payoffs:

$$b_j(\bar{W}_{n,t+1}) = (\bar{W}_{n,t+1} - a_j)^+,$$

for example. To get a sense of the GA for a portfolio of such derivatives, we consider a portfolio of CDOs with maturity $t + 1$. Their value at $t + 1$ is equal to the payoff, and the future derivative portfolio value is[2]

$$W^D_{n,t+1} = \sum_{j=1}^{J} b_j(\bar{W}_{n,t+1}),$$

where J denotes the number of CDOs in the portfolio. Thus, from (6.20) we deduce the expansion of the derivative portfolio value as

$$W^D_{n,t+1} = \sum_{j=1}^{J} b_j[m(F_{t+1}) + \sigma(F_{t+1})\frac{Z}{\sqrt{n}} + O(1/n)]$$

$$= \sum_{j=1}^{J} b_j[m(F_{t+1})] + \sum_{j=1}^{J} \frac{db_j}{dm}[m(F_{t+1})]\sigma(F_{t+1})\frac{Z}{\sqrt{n}}$$

$$+ \frac{1}{2}\sum_{j=1}^{J} \frac{d^2b_j}{dm^2}[m(F_{t+1})]\sigma^2(F_{t+1})\frac{Z^2}{n} + O(1/n),$$

where the $O(1/n)$ term is zero-mean conditional on the factor.

---

[2] When the maturity of the derivatives is strictly larger than 1, the derivatives' maturity does not correspond to the selected horizon for the VaR and it is necessary to compute the future derivative price. This can be done by the approximate derivative pricing approach introduced in Chapter 5, accounting in particular for the GA of the derivative prices, or by Monte Carlo simulation [see Gordy and Suneja (2010)].

Then, we can apply the GA formula of Proposition 6.2, with $Y = \sum_{j=1}^{J} b_j[m(F_{t+1})]$ as the limiting future derivative portfolio value for infinite n, and the sum W_n, say, of the two other components of the right-hand side to capture the next terms in the expansion. By using the moments $E[Z] = 0$, $E[Z^2] = 1$, we get

$$E(W_n|Y = y)$$

$$= \frac{1}{2n} E \left[\sum_{j=1}^{J} \frac{d^2 b_j[m(F_{t+1})]}{dm^2} \sigma^2(F_{t+1}) | \sum_{j=1}^{J} b_j[m(F_{t+1})] = y \right] + o(1/n),$$

$$E(W_n^2|Y = y)$$

$$= \frac{1}{n} E \left[\left(\sum_{j=1}^{J} \frac{d b_j[m(F_{t+1})]}{dm} \right)^2 \sigma^2(F_{t+1}) | \sum_{j=1}^{J} b_j[m(F_{t+1})] = y \right] + o(1/n).$$

Then, the GA is derived from Proposition 6.2.

6.6 Summary

The recent regulations require the computation of reserves for large portfolios, possibly including derivatives. The required capital is based on risk measures such as the VaR or the expected shortfall. Granularity theory is used to derive closed-form expressions for the reserves at order $1/n$. Such closed-form expressions involve the CSA risk measure, computed for an ideal portfolio of infinite size, and a GA at order $1/n$ that accounts for both the idiosyncratic risks in the portfolio of finite size n and the filtering of the unobservable factor value. The explicit formulas can be introduced in the software for risk management and risk control.

6.7 Appendix: Interpretation of Bahadur's Expansion

Let us prove Proposition 6.2 when Y and W_n admit a joint pdf [see Gagliardini and Gouriéroux (2013) for the general case]. We have

$$-\frac{F_n(y) - F(y)}{f(y)} = \frac{P(Y < y) - P(Y + W_n < y)}{f(y)}$$

$$= \frac{1}{f(y)} \int [\int_{y-w}^{y} f_n(z, w) dz] dw,$$

where $f_n(y, w)$ denotes the joint density of (Y, W_n). Thus, we deduce

$$-\frac{F_n(y) - F(y)}{f(y)}$$

$$= \frac{1}{f(y)} \int [\int_{y-w}^{y} f_n(y, w)dz]dw + \frac{1}{f(y)} \int [\int_{y-w}^{y} [f_n(z, w) - f_n(y, w)]dz]dw$$

$$\simeq \frac{1}{f(y)} \int w f_n(y, w)dw + \frac{1}{f(y)} \int \frac{\partial f_n(y, w)}{\partial y} [\int_{y-w}^{y} (z - y)dz]dw$$

$$= E[W_n|Y = y] - \frac{1}{2} E[W_n^2 \frac{\partial \log f_n(y, W_n)}{\partial y}|Y = y]. \qquad (6.32)$$

Let us now decompose the joint density into the unconditional density of Y and the conditional density of W_n given Y; that is, $f_n(y, w) = f(y)f_n(w|y)$. We obtain

$$-\frac{F_n(y) - F(y)}{f(y)}$$

$$\simeq E[W_n|Y = y] - \frac{1}{2} \frac{\partial \log f(y)}{dy} E[W_n^2|Y = y]$$

$$- \frac{1}{2} \int w^2 \frac{\partial \log f_n(w|y)}{\partial y} f_n(w|y)dw$$

$$= E(W_n|Y = y) - \frac{1}{2} \frac{\partial \log f(y)}{dy} E(W_n^2|Y = y) - \frac{1}{2} \frac{\partial}{\partial y} (\int w^2 f_n(w|y)dw)$$

$$= E(W_n|Y = y) - \frac{1}{2} \frac{\partial \log f(y)}{dy} E(W_n^2|Y = y) - \frac{1}{2} \frac{\partial}{\partial y} E(W_n^2|Y = y).$$

From Proposition 6.1, the result follows.

References

Acerbi, C., and D. Tasche (2002). "On the Coherency of Expected Shortfall," *Journal of Banking and Finance*, 26, 1487–1503.

Bahadur, R. (1966). "A Note on Quantiles in Large Samples," *Annals of Mathematical Statistics*, 37, 577–580.

Basel Committee on Banking Supervision (1995). "An Internal Model Based Approach to Market Risk Capital Requirements," Bank of International Settlements, April, 1995.

Basel Committee on Banking Supervision (2001). "The New Basel Capital Accord," Consultative Document of the Bank for International Settlements, April 2001, Part 2: Pillar 1.

Basel Committee on Banking Supervision (2003). "The New Basel Capital Accord," Consultative Document of the Bank for International Settlements, April 2003, Part 3: Pillar 2.

Fermanian, J.-D. (2014). "The Limits of Granularity Adjustments," *Journal of Banking and Finance*, 45, 9–25.

Gagliardini, P., and C. Gouriéroux (2013). "Granularity Adjustment for Risk Measures: Systematic and Unsystematic Risks," *International Journal of Approximate Reasoning*, 54, 717–747.

Gagliardini, P., C. Gourieroux, and A. Monfort (2012). "Microinformation, Nonlinear Filtering and Granularity," *Journal of Financial Econometrics*, 10, 1–51.

Geske, R. (1977). "The Valuation of Corporate Liabilities as Compound Options," *Journal of Financial and Quantitative Analysis*, 12, 541–552.

Gordy, M. (2003). "A Risk-Factor Model Foundation for Ratings Based Bank Capital Rules," *Journal of Financial Intermediation*, 12, 199–232.

Gordy, M. (2004). "Granularity Adjustment in Portfolio Credit Risk Measurement", in *Risk Measures for the 21st Century*, ed. by G. Szego Wiley.

Gordy, M., and J. Marrone (2012). "Granularity Adjustment for Mark-to-Market Credit Risk Models," *Journal of Banking and Finance*, 36, 1896–1910.

Gordy, M., and S. Suneja (2010). "Nested Simulation in Portfolio Risk Management," *Management Science*, 56, 1833–1848.

Gouriéroux, C. (2010). "Risk Measures: Statistical Estimation," in *Encyclopedia of Quantitative Finance*, Wiley.

Gouriéroux, C., J.-P. Laurent, and O. Scaillet (2000). "Sensitivity Analysis of Value-at-Risk," *Journal of Empirical Finance*, 7, 225–245.

Koenker, R. (2005). *Quantile Regression*, Cambridge University Press.

Martin, R., and T. Wilde (2003). "Unsystematic Credit Risk," *Risk Magazine*, 15, 123–128.

Merton, R. (1974). "On the Pricing of Corporate Debt: The Risk Structure of Interest Rates," *Journal of Finance*, 29, 449–470.

Pykhtin, M., and A. Dev (2002). "Analytical Approach to Credit Risk Modelling," *Risk*, 15, 26–32.

Tasche, D. (2000). "Conditional Expectation as Quantile Derivative," DP Bundesbank.

Vasicek, O. (1991). "Limiting Loan Loss Probability Distribution," DP KMV Corporation.

Wang, S. (1996). "Premium Calculation by Transforming the Layer Premium Density," *ASTIN Bulletin*, 26, 71–92.

Wang, S. (2000). "A Class of Distortion Operators for Pricing Financial and Insurance Risks," *Journal of Risk and Insurance*, 67, 15–36.

Wilde, T. (2001). "Probing Granularity," *Risk*, 14, 103–106.

Appendix A: Review of Econometrics

A.1 Simulation

Simulations are artificial data randomly drawn by the econometrician. Simulation-based approaches are used to compute numerically complicated integrals (Monte Carlo integration) and, in particular, derivative prices, to derive the finite sample properties of an estimator (e.g., bootstrap) or even to define new estimation methods (simulation based method of moments and indirect inference).

A.1.1 The Principle

All simulation techniques are based on the following lemma:

Lemma A.1. *Let X be a one-dimensional random variable with continuous distribution and a strictly increasing cumulative distribution function (c.d.f.) F. Then the variable $U = F(X)$ follows a uniform distribution on $[0, 1]$.*

Proof. Indeed, we have

$$P[U \leq u] = P[F(X) \leq u]$$

$$= P[X \leq F^{-1}(u)] \text{ (because a continuous increasing function is invertible)}$$

$$= F[F^{-1}(u)] = u,$$

which is the c.d.f. of the uniform distribution on $[0, 1]$.

QED

Lemma A.1 implies the following corollary:

Corollary A.1. *Let X be a continuous variable with increasing c.d.f. and Φ the c.d.f. of the standard normal distribution; then the variable $\varepsilon = \Phi^{-1}[F(X)]$ is standard normal.*

The previous results can be directly used for simulating an artificial independent sample from distribution F, by using software to produce i.i.d. standard normal observations (rndn software) or i.i.d uniform observations (rndu software). An example of such an approach follows.

(1) Draw at random S artificial data $\varepsilon_1, \ldots, \varepsilon_S$ from the standard normal distribution by the software rndn.
(2) Then compute the simulated values $X_1, \ldots, X_S$ by $X_s = F^{-1}[\Phi(\varepsilon_s)]$.

This approach is easily extended to multivariate random variables. As an illustration, let us consider a bivariate vector (X, Y) with known distribution. This distribution is characterized by the marginal distribution of X with c.d.f. $F_X(x)$ and the conditional distribution of Y given $X = x$, with conditional c.d.f. $F_{Y|X}(y|x)$.

The simulation approach is as follows:

(1) Draw at random two independent samples of size S from the standard normal distribution by software rndn. These samples are ε_s, η_s, for $s = 1, \ldots, S$.
(2) The simulated values $X_1, \ldots, X_S$ are computed as

$$X_s = F_X^{-1}[\Phi(\varepsilon_s)], \quad s = 1, \ldots, S.$$

(3) Then the simulated values $Y_1, \ldots, Y_S$ are deduced by

$$Y_s = F_{Y|X}^{-1}[\Phi(\eta_s)|X_s], \quad s = 1, \ldots, S,$$

where $F_{Y|X}^{-1}(.|x)$ is the inverse of the conditional c.d.f. with respect to argument y.

The simulation scheme is determined by the analyst, who has to choose not only the form of the distribution but also the number of replications.

A.1.2 Monte Carlo Integration

Integrals or, equivalently, expectations can be computed by simulation. Let us consider an expectation

$$E_0(Y) = \int y p_0(y) dy, \tag{A.1.1}$$

where p_0 is a known probability density function. Then, we can draw S independent observations $Y_1, \ldots, Y_S$ from distribution p_0. By the Law of Large Numbers (LLN), the sample mean of these simulated values $\bar{Y}_S = \frac{1}{S} \sum_{s=1}^{S} Y_s$ is a consistent approximation of the true unknown expectation as $S \to \infty$; that is, $\bar{Y}_S \simeq E_0(Y)$ for large S.

This approach can be extended to improve the accuracy of the approximation. Let us introduce another given probability density function (pdf) $q_0(y)$, called the **importance function**. Then, we have

$$E_0(Y) = \int y \frac{p_0(y)}{q_0(y)} q_0(y) dy. \tag{A.1.2}$$

An approximation of the expectation can be derived as follows:

(1) Draw at random S observations $Y_1^*, \ldots, Y_S^*$ from the distribution q_0.
(2) Then approximate the expectation by

$$\frac{1}{S} \sum_{s=1}^{S} [Y_s^* p_0(Y_s^*)/q_0(Y_s^*)].$$

This approximation is very accurate when $q_0(y)$ is almost proportional to $y p_0(y)$.

A.1.3 Bootstrap

We can now explain how to derive the properties of an estimator for a large but finite number of observations. As an illustration, let us consider a parametric dynamic model

$$y_t = a(y_{t-1}, \varepsilon_t, \theta), \quad t = 1, \ldots, T,$$

where ε_t are i.i.d. standard Gaussian variables and a is a known function. Let us denote $\hat{\theta}_T = \hat{\theta}(y_1, \ldots, y_T)$ as a consistent estimator of parameter θ. Estimator $\hat{\theta}_T$ is a good approximation of θ, which can be used to simulate several artificial paths for Y. More precisely, we can do the following:

(1) Draw a sequence of size T from the standard normal distribution. This sequence is denoted by $\varepsilon_1^s, \ldots, \varepsilon_T^s$.
(2) Deduce the simulated path by recursion:

$$y_t^s = a(y_{t-1}^s, \varepsilon_t^s, \hat{\theta}_T), \quad t = 1, \ldots, T \text{ (with } y_0^s = y_0).$$

(3) Compute the simulated estimate from this path, as

$$\hat{\theta}_T^s = \hat{\theta}(y_1^s, \ldots, y_T^s).$$

(4) Replicate the approach for $s = 1, \ldots, S$.
(5) Then, for large S, the sample distribution of $(\hat{\theta}_T^1, \ldots, \hat{\theta}_T^S)$ is a good approximation of the unknown distribution of the estimator.

Further Reading

Caflish, R. (1998). "Monte-Carlo and Quasi Monte-Carlo Methods," *Acta Numerica*, 7, 1–49.

Efron, B., and R. Tibshirani (1994). *An Introduction to the Bootstrap*, Chapman & Hall.

A.2 Efficiency Bounds

The accuracy of an estimator $\hat{\theta}$ of a (multidimensional) parameter θ depends on its bias – that is, the difference between the expectation of $\hat{\theta}$ and the true parameter value – and on its variance-covariance matrix.

For a consistent estimator, the bias is asymptotically equal to zero, and its accuracy is entirely captured by its asymptotic variance-covariance matrix. It is often possible to find a lower bound for the asymptotic variance-covariance matrix of the consistent estimators of θ. This bound, when it exists, is called an (asymptotic) **efficiency bound**.

A consistent estimator whose variance-covariance matrix coincides asymptotically with the efficiency bound is preferable to any other consistent estimator. It is called an (asymptotically) **efficient estimator**.

A.2.1 Parametric Model Parametrized by θ

Let us first consider a parametric model with likelihood function $l_n(y;\theta)$, where y denotes the vector of observations and n their number. An efficiency bound is given by

$$B(\theta) = [I(\theta)]^{-1}, \tag{A.2.1}$$

where the information matrix $I(\theta)$ can be approximated by

$$I(\theta) \simeq E_\theta \left[-\frac{\partial^2 \log l_n(Y;\theta)}{\partial\theta\partial\theta'} \right], \tag{A.2.2}$$

and E_θ denotes the expectation computed with the value θ of the parameter. In this framework $B(\theta)$ is called the **parametric efficiency bound**.

Under standard regularity conditions, the maximum likelihood estimator

$$\hat{\theta} = \arg\max_\theta \log l_n(y;\theta)$$

has an (asymptotic) variance-covariance matrix equivalent to the (asymptotic) efficiency bound. Thus, the maximum likelihood estimator is (asymptotically) parametrically efficient.

A.2.2 Parametric Model Partly Parametrized by θ

Let us now consider a parametric model including nuisance parameters β, say. The likelihood function is $l_n(y;\theta,\beta)$, and the parametric efficiency bound for the whole parameter $(\theta',\beta')'$ is

$$B(\theta,\beta) = [I(\theta,\beta)]^{-1}, \tag{A.2.3}$$

where

$$I(\theta, \beta) = E_{\theta, \beta} \left[-\frac{\partial^2 \log l_n(Y; \theta, \beta)}{\partial(\theta', \beta')' \partial(\theta', \beta')} \right]. \tag{A.2.4}$$

This information matrix can be decomposed into blocks as

$$I(\theta, \beta) = \begin{pmatrix} I_{\theta\theta} & I_{\theta\beta} \\ I_{\beta\theta} & I_{\beta\beta} \end{pmatrix}, \quad \text{say,}$$

where

$$I_{\theta\theta} = E_{\theta, \beta} \left[-\frac{\partial^2 \log l_n(Y; \theta, \beta)}{\partial\theta \partial\theta'} \right],$$

$$I_{\theta\beta} = E_{\theta, \beta} \left[-\frac{\partial^2 \log l_n(Y; \theta, \beta)}{\partial\theta \partial\beta'} \right] = I'_{\beta, \theta},$$

$$I_{\beta\beta} = E_{\theta, \beta} \left[-\frac{\partial^2 \log l_n(Y; \theta, \beta)}{\partial\beta \partial\beta'} \right].$$

By block inversion, we deduce the northwest block of the efficiency bound, which provides the parametric efficiency bound for θ in presence of a nuisance parameter β. It is given by

$$B_{\theta\theta}(\theta, \beta) = [I_{\theta\theta} - I_{\theta\beta}(I_{\beta\beta})^{-1} I_{\beta\theta}]^{-1}. \tag{A.2.5}$$

A.2.3 Semi-Parametric Efficiency Bound

Let us now consider a semi-parametric model in which the likelihood function is parametrized by a parameter of interest θ and by a functional nuisance parameter $g \in G$. Whereas the parameter of interest is a standard (finite-dimensional) vector, the nuisance parameter can be an infinite-dimensional object (e.g., the unknown density function of the error in a regression model). This semi-parametric model nests all parametric models in which function g has been parametrized $g = g_\beta$, say. The parametric efficiency bound for such a nested parametric model $B_{\theta\theta}(g_\beta)$ can be computed by equation (A.2.5), and depends on the chosen parametrization of function g. The **semi-parametric efficiency bound** is defined as the maximal (i.e., the least favorable) bound corresponding to all admissible nested parametric models:

$$B_{\theta\theta}(\theta, g) = \max_{g_\beta} B_{\theta\theta}(g_\beta). \tag{A.2.6}$$

A consistent estimator of parameter θ is **semi-parametrically efficient** if its variance-covariance matrix is asymptotically equivalent to the semi-parametric efficiency bound. An example of a semi-parametrically efficient estimator is the ordinary least squares (OLS) estimator in a linear regression model under the standard regularity assumptions on the errors.

Further Reading

Chamberlain, G. (1992). "Efficiency Bounds for Semiparametric Regressions," *Econometrica*, 60, 567–596.
Cramer, H. (1946). *Mathematical Methods of Statistics*, Princeton University Press.
Rao, R. (1945). "Information and the Accuracy Attainable in the Estimation of Statistical Parameters," *Bulletin of the Calcutta Mathematical Society*, 37, 81–89.

A.3 Panel Data Models

Panel data models are explanatory models for panel data, which are observations $y_{i,t}$, $i = 1, \ldots, n$, $t = 1, \ldots, T$, doubly indexed by individual and time. The basic Gaussian linear model for panel data is

$$ y_{i,t} = \alpha + x'_{i,t}b + \omega_{i,t}, \quad i = 1, \ldots, n, \quad t = 1, \ldots, T, \qquad (A.3.1) $$

where $x_{i,t}$ are the observations of the explanatory variables and $\omega_{i,t}$ are independent, Gaussian error terms with common distribution $N(0, \sigma_\omega^2)$. The basic model (A.3.1) is usually extended to highlight possible individual or time effects. These effects can be assumed to be either fixed or random.

A.3.1 Panel Data Model with Fixed Effects

The introduction of fixed effects leads to the model

$$ y_{i,t} = \alpha + \beta_i + \gamma_t + x'_{it}b + \omega_{it}, \quad i = 1, \ldots, n, \ t = 1, \ldots, T, \quad (A.3.2) $$

where β_i and γ_t are additional parameters satisfying the constraints

$$ \beta. = \sum_{i=1}^{n} \beta_i = 0, \quad \gamma. = \sum_{t=1}^{T} \gamma_t = 0, $$

to avoid collinearity problems. Parameters β_i (resp. γ_t) are the fixed individual effects (resp. time effects). Model (A.3.2) is a special case of a linear model, and the parameters α, β_i, for $i = 1, \ldots, n$, and γ_t, for $t = 1, \ldots, T$, can be estimated by ordinary least squares (OLS). However, the panel framework does not match the standard regularity assumptions for the asymptotic analysis of the OLS estimator. The reason is that the total number of parameters, equal to $n + T - 1$, is not fixed, but increases with the number of observations; that is, with n and T. This is the **incidental parameter problem**.

The OLS estimators have closed form expressions, which are easily interpreted for a fixed effects model without explanatory variable x; that is,

$$y_{i,t} = \alpha + \beta_i + \gamma_t + \omega_{i,t}, \tag{A.3.3}$$

with $\omega_{i,t} \sim IIN(0, \sigma_\omega^2)$. Let us define the following sample means:

$$\bar{\bar{y}} = \frac{1}{nT} \sum_{i=1}^{n} \sum_{t=1}^{T} y_{i,t}, \quad \bar{y}_{i\cdot} = \frac{1}{T} \sum_{t=1}^{T} y_{i,t}, \quad \bar{y}_{\cdot t} = \frac{1}{n} \sum_{i=1}^{n} y_{i,t}. \tag{A.3.4}$$

The OLS estimators of the parameters are

$$\hat{\alpha} = \bar{\bar{y}}, \quad \hat{\beta}_i = \bar{y}_{i\cdot} - \bar{\bar{y}}, \quad \hat{\gamma}_t = \bar{y}_{\cdot t} - \bar{\bar{y}}, \tag{A.3.5}$$

whereas the residuals are given by

$$\hat{\omega}_{i,t} = y_{i,t} - \bar{y}_{i\cdot} - \bar{y}_{\cdot t} + \bar{\bar{y}}. \tag{A.3.6}$$

Hence, the estimate of the constant is the full sample average of the observations across individuals and time, whereas the estimates of the individual (resp. time) effects are the differences between the time (resp. individual) averages and the full sample average.

A.3.2 Panel Data Model with Random Effects

In this extension, the individual and time effects are assumed to be stochastic. The model becomes

$$y_{i,t} = \alpha + x_{i,t}'b + u_i + v_t + \omega_{i,t}, \quad i = 1, \ldots, n, \quad t = 1, \ldots, T, \tag{A.3.7}$$

where $u_i, v_t, \omega_{i,t}$ are independent Gaussian variables, independent of the explanatory variables, with distributions

$$u_i \sim N(0, \sigma_u^2), \quad v_t \sim N(0, \sigma_v^2), \quad \omega_{i,t} \sim N(0, \sigma_\omega^2),$$

respectively.

In this extension, the number of parameters is fixed, which solves the incidental parameter problem. However, this linear model has a nonscalar variance-covariance matrix function of the three parameters $\sigma_u^2, \sigma_v^2, \sigma_\omega^2$. Except in very special cases (see Chapter 2), the maximum likelihood estimators of the parameters do not admit closed-form expressions. Moreover, the large sample properties of the estimators depend on the considered asymptotic scheme: either $n \to \infty$ and T fixed, or n fixed and $T \to \infty$, or $n \to \infty$ and $T \to \infty$.

A.3.3 Panel Data Model with Both Fixed and Random Effects

In a panel data model it is not possible to introduce a fixed and a random effect of a same type, because the fixed effect will systematically capture the random

Table A.1. *Panel data models with both*
individual and time effects

	Time effect	
Individual effect	Fixed	Random
fixed	X	X
random	X	X

effect. Thus, there exist only four possibilities for a panel data model with both individual and time effects, as seen in Table A.1.

A.3.4 Fixed or Random Effects

There exist testing procedures for choosing between fixed and random effects in panel data models. However, it is often preferable to base this choice on the problem of interest. This choice is well illustrated by applications to credit risk analysis. Let us assume that y_{it} is a quantitative measure of individual risk. The models with fixed individual effect,

$$y_{it} = \alpha + \beta_i + x'_{it}b + w_{it},$$

are used in a first step to divide the set of contracts into homogeneous segments. This segmentation is done as follows. First, estimate the individual fixed effects $\hat{\beta}_i$, $i = 1, \ldots, n$. Second, define the segments from these values $\hat{\beta}_i$ by an appropriate discretization. Segment k, with $k = 1, \ldots, K$, includes the individuals i such that $a_{k-1} < \hat{\beta}_i \le a_k$, where a_k, $k = 0, \ldots, K$, is a given set of thresholds.

In the current Basel regulations such a segmentation has to be defined before analyzing more precisely the risks within and between segments. This second step of the risk analysis has to account for the possible dependencies between two individual risks at a same time or for the successive risks of a same individual at two different dates. This is done by introducing in each segment a random time effect (resp. a random individual effect), because by definition fixed effects are deterministic and thus nonrisky.

Further Reading

Arellano, M., and B. Honore (2001). "Panel Data Models: Some Recent Developments," In *Handbook of Econometrics*, ed. by J. Heckman and E. Leamer, 3231–3296, North Holland.

Baltagi, B. (1995). *Econometric Analysis of Panel Data*, Wiley.

Hsiao, C. (2003). *Analysis of Panel Data*, Econometric Society Monographs, Cambridge University Press.

A.4 Singular Value Decomposition and Principal Component Analysis

Principal component analysis (PCA) is based on the analysis of eigenvalues and eigenvectors of well-chosen symmetric matrices. We first review basic decompositions of matrices in linear algebra.

A.4.1 Singular Value Decomposition (SVD)

Spectral Decomposition of a Symmetric Matrix. Any symmetric matrix Ω of dimension (n, n) can be diagonalized. This matrix admits real eigenvalues λ_i, $i = 1, \ldots, n$, and real eigenvectors u_i, $i = 1, \ldots, n$. These eigenvectors form an orthonormal basis of $I\!R^n$. They can always be chosen such that $\langle u_i, u_j \rangle \equiv u_i' u_j = 0$ if $i \neq j$, and $\|u_i\|^2 \equiv u_i' u_i = 1$, $\forall i$. Let us denote by Q the matrix whose columns are these eigenvectors. The orthonormality restrictions imply $Q^{-1} = Q'$, and the matrix Ω can be written as

$$\Omega = Q \Lambda Q', \tag{A.4.1}$$

where Λ is the diagonal matrix with the eigenvalues of Ω as diagonal elements. Equivalently, the equality (A.4.1) can be written as

$$\Omega = \sum_{i=1}^{n} \lambda_i u_i u_i', \tag{A.4.2}$$

which gives the spectral decomposition of matrix Ω.

SVD of a Rectangular Matrix. Let us now consider a rectangular matrix X with dimension (n, T). Typically, X can be a matrix of observations doubly indexed by individuals and time. This matrix can be used to construct two symmetric matrices by considering the squared matrices XX' and $X'X$. These matrices are symmetric positive semi-definite with sizes (n, n) and (T, T), respectively.
    Then, we can consider their spectral decompositions:

$$XX' = \sum_{i=1}^{n} \lambda_i u_i u_i', \quad \lambda_i \geq 0, \tag{A.4.3}$$

$$X'X = \sum_{t=1}^{T} \mu_t v_t v_t', \quad \mu_t \geq 0. \tag{A.4.4}$$

The following lemma explains that these spectral decompositions can be strongly linked.

Lemma A.2. *Let us denote* $K = \min(n, T)$.

(i) *We can order the eigenvalues such that* $\lambda_1 = \mu_1 \geq \lambda_2 = \mu_2 \geq \cdots \geq \lambda_K = \mu_K$, *with the remaining eigenvalues being equal to zero.*

(ii) *The two orthonormal bases can be chosen such that*

$$\langle v_k, u_k \rangle = 1, \quad k = 1, \ldots, K, \quad \langle v_k, u_j \rangle = 0, \quad \forall k \neq j = 1, \ldots K.$$

(iii) *Matrix X can be decomposed as*

$$X = \sum_{k=1}^{K} \sqrt{\lambda_k} u_k v_k'.$$

Thus, we have the following decompositions:

$$\begin{cases} X = U \Lambda^{1/2} V', \\ XX' = U \Lambda U', \\ X'X = V \Lambda V', \end{cases} \tag{A.4.5}$$

where Λ is the diagonal matrix with elements λ_k, $k = 1, \ldots, K$, U (resp. V) is the matrix with columns u_k, $k = 1, \ldots, K$ (resp. v_k, $k = 1, \ldots, K$), and $\Lambda^{1/2} V = X'U$.

This decomposition of matrix X is the **singular value decomposition** of X; the vectors u_k (resp. v_k) are its **left singular vectors** (resp. **right singular vectors**), and $\lambda_k^{1/2}$ are its **the singular values**.

A.4.2 Principal Component Analysis

When the eigenvalues $\lambda_k = \mu_k$, $k = 1, \ldots, K$, differ, they can be ranked in decreasing order: $\lambda_1 > \lambda_2 \ldots > \lambda_K$. Principal component analysis (PCA) proposes interpretations of these eigenvalues and of the associated eigenvectors.

To understand the PCA interpretation, let us consider the constrained optimization problem

$$\begin{cases} \max_{a \in R^n} a' XX' a \\ s.t. \ a'a = 1, \end{cases} \tag{A.4.6}$$

and introduce a Lagrange multiplier v. The corresponding Lagrangean function $a'XX'a - 2v(a'a - 1)$ can be optimized with respect to vector a. The first-order condition is

$$XX'a^* - va^* = 0 \Leftrightarrow XX'a^* = va^*, \tag{A.4.7}$$

and the optimal value of the objective function in (A.4.6) is

$$a^{*'} XX' a^* = a^{*'}(va^*) = v. \tag{A.4.8}$$

Equation (A.4.7) means that the solution a^* is an eigenvector of matrix XX'. From equation (A.4.8), the associated eigenvalue ν is equal to the value of the objective function, which has to be maximized. Thus, the Lagrange multiplier is equal to the largest eigenvalue $\nu^* = \lambda_1 = \mu_1$, and the solution of the optimization problem (A.4.6) is the normalized eigenvector u_1. By using the orthogonality between the eigenvectors $u_1, u_2, \ldots, u_K$, such optimization can be performed in a recursive way as described in the following property:

Property A.1.

(i) *Eigenvector u_1 is the solution to the optimization problem*

$$\max_a a'XX'a, \; s.t. \; a'a = 1,$$

whereas λ_1 is the associated value of the objective function.

(ii) *Eigenvector u_2 is the solution of the optimization problem*

$$\max_a a'XX'a, \; s.t. \; a'a = 1, \, and \, a'u_1 = 0,$$

whereas λ_2 is the associated value of the objective function, and so on.

Property A.1 is usually applied to a square matrix XX' interpretable as a variance-covariance matrix. Let us consider panel data y_{it}, $i = 1, \ldots, n$, $t = 1, \ldots, T$, and let X be the (n, T) matrix with elements $x_{i,t} = y_{it} - \bar{y}_{i\cdot}$. Then, the matrix $\frac{1}{T}XX'$ is simply the sample variance-covariance matrix of variables y_i with observations $y_{i1}, \ldots, y_{iT}$. The associated eigenvectors $u_1, u_2 \ldots$, called principal components, provide the directions, which are the most variable, the second most variable, and so on. For instance, if $y_{it} = r_{it}$ has the interpretation of an asset return, $u_1 = (u_{11}, \ldots, u_{1n})'$ can be interpreted as a portfolio allocation corresponding to the most risky portfolio return (under the constraint $a'a = 1$). The demeaned values of the return of this portfolio are equal to $\sum_{i=1}^{n} u_{1i}(y_{it} - \bar{y}_{i\cdot})$, $t = 1, \ldots, T$. Because $\sqrt{\lambda_1}v_1 = X'u_1$, these portfolio returns are equal to the components of the first eigenvector of $X'X$ scaled by $\sqrt{\lambda_1}$.

Further Reading

Gantmacher, F. (1959). *Theory of Matrices*, Vol. 1 and 2, American Mathematical Society, Chelsea Publishing.

Jolliffe, I. (2002). *Principal Component Analysis*, 2nd ed., Springer.

Pearson, K. (1901). "On Lines and Planes of Closest Fit to Systems of Points in Space," *Philosophical Magazine*, 2, 559–572.

A.5 Prediction and Kalman Filter

A.5.1 Linear Prediction

Let us consider two random vectors X and Y with dimensions K and n, respectively, with means $E(X) = m_X$, $E(Y) = m_Y$, variances $V(X) = \Sigma_{XX}$, $V(Y) = \Sigma_{YY}$, and cross-covariances $Cov(X, Y) = \Sigma_{XY}$, $Cov(Y, X) = \Sigma_{YX}$. The mean vectors m_X, m_Y have dimensions $(K, 1)$ and $(n, 1)$, respectively. Matrix Σ_{XX} (resp. Σ_{YY}) is the variance-covariance matrix of X with dimension (K, K) [resp. of Y with dimension (n, n)]. The cross-covariances are such that $\Sigma_{XY} = \Sigma'_{YX}$ has dimension (K, n).

The linear predictor of vector Y based on X is a vector $\hat{Y} = \hat{A}X + \hat{b}$ such that

$$(\hat{A}, \hat{b}) = \arg \min_{A,b} E \left[\| Y - AX - b \|^2 \right].$$

Thus, each component $\hat{Y}_i$ provides the best linear approximation of Y_i based on $X_1, \ldots, X_K$ with possibly an intercept. The expression of the linear predictor and of the prediction error is given next.

Property A.2. (i) *Let us assume Σ_{XX} is invertible. The best linear predictor of Y based on X is*

$$\hat{Y} = m_Y + \Sigma_{YX}(\Sigma_{XX})^{-1}(X - m_X).$$

(ii) *The prediction error $\hat{u} = Y - \hat{Y}$ is zero-mean: $E(\hat{u}) = 0$, with a variance-covariance matrix:*

$$V(\hat{u}) = \Sigma_{YY} - \Sigma_{YX}\Sigma_{XX}^{-1}\Sigma_{XY}.$$

When X, Y are jointly Gaussian, the linear predictor $\hat{Y}$ coincides with the conditional expectation of Y given X, which is denoted $E(Y|X)$, and the residual variance $V(\hat{u})$ coincides with the conditional variance-covariance matrix $V(Y|X)$.

A.5.2 Kalman Filter

The standard Gaussian linear state space model assumes

State equation: $F_t = \Phi F_{t-1} + \eta_t$,

Measurement equation: $y_t = B F_t + \varepsilon_t$,

where y_t (resp. F_t) has dimension n (resp. K), and the errors η_t, ε_t are independent Gaussian white noises $\eta_t \sim N(0, \Omega_\eta)$, $\varepsilon_t \sim N(0, \Omega_\varepsilon)$. The matrices Φ, B, Ω_ε, Ω_η are assumed to be given.

The Kalman filter is a set of algorithms to compute recursively (linear) predictors of F_t and y_t and their accuracy. These linear predictors can be either of the type $E(F_t|y_t, \ldots, y_0)$, $E(y_t|y_{t-1}, \ldots, y_0)$, or $E(F_t|y_T, \ldots, y_0)$. When factor F_t is approximated by current and lagged observed values, the algorithm is called a filter. When the information includes also future values, it is called a smoother.

The filter and smoother algorithms were derived by Kalman, using previous results by Thiele and Swerling. They are based on a recursive use of the linear prediction formula in Property A.2. Let us denote

$$\hat{F}_{t|t} = E(F_t|\underline{y_t}), \text{ where } \underline{y_t} = (y_t, y_{t-1}, \ldots),$$

$$\hat{F}_{t|t-1} = E(F_t|\underline{y_{t-1}}),$$

$$\Sigma_{t|t} = V(F_t|\underline{y_t}), \quad \Sigma_{t|t-1} = V(F_t|\underline{y_{t-1}}).$$

The filter involves the following recursions:

Prediction:

Predicted factor: $\hat{F}_{t|t-1} = \Phi \hat{F}_{t-1|t-1}$,

Accuracy of the predicted factor: $\Sigma_{t|t-1} = \Phi \Sigma_{t-1|t-1} \Phi' + \Omega_\eta$.

Updating:

Measurement residual: $\hat{u}_{t|t} = y_t - B \hat{F}_{t|t-1}$,

Residual variance: $H_{t|t} = B \Sigma_{t|t-1} B' + \Omega_\varepsilon$,

Kalman gain: $K_{t|t} = \Sigma_{t|t-1} B' (H_{t|t})^{-1}$,

Updated predicted factor: $\hat{F}_{t|t} = \hat{F}_{t|t-1} + K_{t|t} \hat{u}_{t,t}$,

Updated accuracy of the predicted factor: $\Sigma_{t|t} = (Id - K_{t|t} B) \Sigma_{t|t-1}$.

Further Reading

Harvey, A. (1989). *Forecasting, Structural Time Series Models and the Kalman Filter*, Cambridge University Press.

Kalman, R. (1960). "A New Approach to Linear Filtering and Prediction Problems," *Journal of Basic Engineering*, 82, 35–45.

Lauritzen, S. (2002). *Thiele: Pioneer in Statistics*, Oxford University Press.

A.6 The Newton-Raphson Algorithm

A.6.1 The Basic Algorithm

This is the best known method to find numerically the solutions to a nonlinear system of equations. The modern presentation of the algorithm is due to T. Simpson (1740), based on earlier works by the Persian mathematician Sharaf al-Din al-Tusi (1135–1213), I. Newton (1669), and J. Raphson (1690).

Let us consider a differentiable function g from $I\!R^P$ to $I\!R^P : \theta \rightarrow g(\theta)$, say, and denote $\frac{\partial g}{\partial \theta'}(\theta)$ its gradient, with the different partial derivatives as elements. The idea of the algorithm is to replace the initial nonlinear system

$$g(\theta) = 0, \tag{A.6.1}$$

by its linear expansion (first-order Taylor approximation) around some value θ_0:

$$g(\theta_0) + \frac{\partial g}{\partial \theta'}(\theta_0)(\theta - \theta_0) = 0, \tag{A.6.2}$$

whose solution has the explicit form

$$\theta = \theta_0 - \left[\frac{\partial g}{\partial \theta'}(\theta_0)\right]^{-1} g(\theta_0). \tag{A.6.3}$$

The solution in (A.6.3) is well defined if matrix $\frac{\partial g}{\partial \theta'}(\theta_0)$ is nonsingular; that is, function g is one-to-one locally around θ_0.

The Newton-Raphson algorithm applies this approach iteratively, using the following steps:

Step 1. Choose a starting value $\theta^{(0)}$.
Step 2. Then apply recursively formula (A.6.3)

$$\theta^{(p+1)} = \theta^{(p)} - \left[\frac{\partial g}{\partial \theta'}(\theta^{(p)})\right]^{-1} g(\theta^{(p)}).$$

Step 3. Stop when numerical convergence is reached.

A.6.2 Application to Maximum Likelihood

In the standard cases, the maximum likelihood estimate is a solution to the first-order conditions:

$$\frac{\partial \log l(y; \hat{\theta})}{\partial \theta} = 0, \tag{A.6.4}$$

where l is the joint likelihood function of observations y, vector θ is the parameter, and $\hat{\theta}$ its maximum likelihood estimate.

Then, the recursive equation of the Newton-Raphson algorithm becomes

$$\theta^{(p+1)} = \theta^{(p)} + \left(-\frac{\partial^2 \log l(y; \theta^{(p)})}{\partial\theta\partial\theta'} \right)^{-1} \frac{\partial \log l(y; \theta^{(p)})}{\partial\theta}. \qquad \text{(A.6.5)}$$

When the numerical convergence is reached, we obtain a solution $\hat{\theta}$ of the likelihood equations, which may be the ML estimate. If it is the case, the quantity

$$\left[-\frac{\partial^2 \log l(y; \hat{\theta})}{\partial\theta\partial\theta'} \right]^{-1}$$

involved in the recursive equation provides the estimated variance-covariance matrix of the maximum likelihood estimator.

The choice of the starting value can accelerate the algorithm significantly. In particular, we have the following result:

Property A.3. *Let us consider a consistent estimator $\tilde{\theta}$ of parameter θ. Then*

$$\tilde{\theta}^{(1)} = \tilde{\theta} + \left[-\frac{\partial^2 \log l(y; \tilde{\theta})}{\partial\theta\partial\theta'} \right]^{-1} \frac{\partial \log l(y, \tilde{\theta})}{\partial\theta},$$

is consistent and asymptotically efficient.

Therefore, with this choice, a single iteration is enough.

Further Reading

Ypma, J. (1995). "Historical Development of the Newton-Raphson Method," *SIAM Review*, 37, 531–551.

Appendix B: Review of Financial Theory

B.1 Portfolio Management

B.1.1 Portfolio Characteristics

We consider n risky assets and one risk-free asset. Their unitary prices at date t are $p_{i,t}, i = 1, \ldots, n$ and 1, and their values at $t + 1$ are $p_{i,t}(1 + r_{i,t+1}), i = 1, \ldots, n$, and $1 + r_{f,t}$, respectively, where $r_{i,t+1}$ is the return on asset i, and $r_{f,t}$ the risk-free return.

A portfolio allocation defines the quantity of each asset included in the portfolio. These quantities are denoted $a_{i,t}, i = 1, \ldots, n$, and $a_{0,t}$ at date t, where $a_{0,t}$ is the quantity in the risk-free asset. The portfolio value at date t is

$$W_t(\tilde{a}_t) = \sum_{i=1}^{n} a_{i,t} p_{i,t} + a_{0,t} = a_t' p_t + a_{0,t}, \tag{B.1.1}$$

with $a_t = (a_{1,t}, \ldots, a_{n,t})'$, $\tilde{a}_t = (a_t', a_{0,t})'$, $p_t = (p_{1,t}, \ldots, p_{n,t})'$.

The portfolio value at date $t + 1$ is

$$W_{t+1}(\tilde{a}_t) = \sum_{i=1}^{n} a_{i,t} p_{i,t}(1 + r_{i,t+1}) + a_{0,t}(1 + r_{f,t})$$

$$= W_t(\tilde{a}_t)(1 + r_{f,t}) + \sum_{i=1}^{n} a_{i,t} p_{i,t} r_{i,t+1}^*, \tag{B.1.2}$$

where $r_{i,t+1}^* = r_{i,t+1} - r_{f,t}$ denotes the excess return of asset i. At date t, the allocation, the current prices, and the risk-free rate are known, but the excess returns are unknown. Let us denote $y_{i,t+1} = p_{i,t} r_{i,t+1}^*, i = 1, \ldots, n$ the excess gains in the different risky assets. These excess gains are random at date t, with mean and variance given by

$$\mu_t = E_t(y_{t+1}), \quad \Sigma_t = V_t(y_{t+1}), \tag{B.1.3}$$

where E_t and V_t denote the conditional expectation and variance-covariance matrix given the information available at date t.

The first- and second-order conditional moments of the future portfolio value are

$$E_t[W_{t+1}(\tilde{a}_t)] = W_t(\tilde{a}_t)(1 + r_{f,t}) + a_t'\mu_t, \tag{B.1.4}$$

$$V_t[W_{t+1}(\tilde{a}_t)] = a_t'\Sigma_t a_t, \tag{B.1.5}$$

by using equation (B.1.2).

B.1.2 Mean-Variance Portfolio Management

In the mean-variance approach, the allocation is chosen to maximize a criterion, taking into account the expected gain and the risk, under a budget constraint. More precisely, the optimization problem is

$$\begin{cases} \max_{\tilde{a}_t} E_t[W_{t+1}(\tilde{a}_t)] - \dfrac{A}{2} V_t[W_{t+1}(\tilde{a}_t)] \\ \text{s.t. } W_t(\tilde{a}_t) = W_{0,t}, \end{cases} \tag{B.1.6}$$

where $A > 0$ is a measure of absolute risk aversion. The criterion is increasing in the expected portfolio value and decreasing in its variance, which creates a tradeoff between expected gain and risk.

The budget constraint and equations (B.1.4)–(B.1.5) can be used to deduce an unconstrained optimization problem in the allocation a_t in risky assets:

$$\max_{a_t} a_t'\mu_t - \frac{A}{2}a_t'\Sigma_t a_t. \tag{B.1.7}$$

The first-order condition of problem (B.1.7) is

$$\mu_t - A\Sigma_t a_t = 0. \tag{B.1.8}$$

This provides the optimal allocation:

$$a_t^* = \frac{1}{A}\Sigma_t^{-1}\mu_t, \tag{B.1.9}$$

called the **mean-variance efficient allocation**. The quantity invested in the risk-free asset is then deduced from the budget constraint. We have

$$a_{0,t}^* = W_{0,t} - a_t^{*'} p_t = W_{0,t} - \frac{1}{A}\mu_t'\Sigma_t^{-1}p_t. \tag{B.1.10}$$

B.1.3 The Sharpe Performance

At the optimum, the criterion becomes

$$W_{0,t}(1 + r_{f,t}) + a_t^{*'}\mu_t - \frac{A}{2}a_t^{*'}\Sigma_t a_t^* = W_{0,t}(1 + r_{f,t}) + \frac{1}{2A}\mu_t'\Sigma_t^{-1}\mu_t.$$

It depends on the stochastic properties of risky excess returns by means of the quantity

$$S_t = \mu_t'\Sigma_t^{-1}\mu_t, \tag{B.1.11}$$

called the **Sharpe performance** of the set of risky assets. This quantity is equal to

$$S_t = \frac{[E_t(W_{t+1}^*) - W_{0,t}(1 + r_{f,t})]^2}{V_t(W_{t+1}^*)}, \tag{B.1.12}$$

where W_{t+1}^* is the future value of the efficient portfolio. Thus, $S_t^{1/2}$ provides a measure of the maximal risk-adjusted expected gain for a portfolio based on these n risky assets and the risk-free asset.

Further Reading

Lintner, J. (1965). "The Valuation of Risky Assets and the Selection of Risky Investments in Stock Portfolio and Capital Budgets," *Review of Economic and Statistics*, 47, 13–37.
Markowitz, H. (1952). "Portfolio Selection," *Journal of Finance*, 7, 77–91.

B.2 Arbitrage

B.2.1 How to Normalize Prices

Let us first discuss alternative ways to normalize prices. For expository purposes, we consider the case of three goods with respective prices p_1, p_2, p_3. The economic decisions of the agents, who can be either consumers, firms, or investors, depend on these prices up to a positive multiplicative factor. It is interesting to introduce a normalization to avoid this price multiplicity.

The most frequently used normalization consists in choosing one of the goods – good number 1, say – as a numeraire. Thus, the initial set of prices is replaced by 1, p_2/p_1, p_3/p_1. In economic reality, money is generally used as the numeraire.

However, this normalization is not the most appropriate in finance, because it introduces an asymmetry between goods. Another possible normalization replaces the initial prices by

$$q_1 = \frac{p_1}{p_1 + p_2 + p_3}, \quad q_2 = \frac{p_2}{p_1 + p_2 + p_3}, \quad q_3 = \frac{p_3}{p_1 + p_2 + p_3}. \quad \text{(B.2.1)}$$

This corresponds to the choice of a basket including one unit of each good as the numeraire. An advantage of the second normalization approach is that it provides a possible interpretation of the new prices q_1, q_2, q_3 as a probability distribution, because $q_l \geq 0, \forall l$, and $\sum_{l=1}^{3} q_l = 1$.

The second normalization can also be applied to contingent assets. Let us consider an uncertain future with three states of nature w_1, w_2, w_3. An **Arrow-Debreu security** (or digital option) for state w is an asset providing 1 money unit if state w is realized, and 0 money units otherwise. In our example there exist three Arrow-Debreu securities, with prices denoted by p_1, p_2, p_3, respectively. The basket including one unit of each Arrow-Debreu security provides one money unit with certainty. This is the zero-coupon bond, whose price is $B = \frac{1}{1+r_f}$, with r_f the risk-free interest rate. Thus, the prices of Arrow-Debreu securities can be normalized such that $p_j = Bq_j$, $j = 1, 2, 3$, where B is the price of the zero-coupon bond and q_j is the elementary risk-neutral probability.

B.2.2 Absence of Arbitrage Opportunity (AAO)

The absence of arbitrage opportunity assumes the impossibility of obtaining a positive future portfolio value for an initial nonpositive investment. It is also called the assumption of no arbitrage or of no free lunch. The AAO condition is automatically satisfied in an equilibrium model. Indeed, if a specified positive future value can be obtained from zero investment say, the investors will increase infinitely their investment size (the **leverage effect**) implying an infinite demand for some assets, which is not compatible with the existence of an equilibrium.

There exist static and dynamic AAO conditions. In the static case, the portfolio is crystallized at its initial allocation. In the dynamic case, the portfolio can be regularly updated without introducing or withdrawing cash at each updating (self-financing condition).

B.2.3 Pricing under Dynamic AAO Assumption

The no-arbitrage condition implies strong restrictions between the asset prices. More precisely, let us consider a discrete time framework and assume information I_t available to the investor when updating her portfolio at date t. Then Property B.1 provides a pricing formula.

Property B.1. *Let us consider a financial asset paying cash flows* g_{t+h} *at time* $t + h$, *where* g_{t+h} *depends on the state variables in information* I_{t+h}. *Then, under the dynamic AAO condition, the price of this asset at time* t *can be written as*

$$P(t, g) = \sum_{h=0}^{\infty} E_t[M_{t,t+h} g_{t+h}], \tag{B.2.2}$$

where $M_{t,t+h} = M_{t,t+1} M_{t+1,t+2} \ldots M_{t+h-1,t+h}$, *with* $M_{t,t+1} > 0$ *depending on information* I_{t+1}.

The random variable $M_{t,t+1}$ is called the short-term stochastic discount factor (SDF) and $M_{t,t+h}$ is the SDF for term h. Thus, all asset prices are defined whenever the sequence of short-term SDFs is given. In general, the observed asset prices are not enough to characterize the underlying SDF. This is the incompleteness characteristic of the financial market.

The pricing formula (B.2.2) can be written in an alternative way. Let us first consider a zero-coupon bond with time-to-maturity h. This bond provides a certain cash flow equal to 1 at time $t + h$. Its price is equal to

$$B(t, h) = E_t(M_{t,t+h}).$$

In particular $B(t, 1) = E_t(M_{t,t+1}) \equiv \exp[-r(t, 1)]$, where $r(t, 1)$ is the **continuously compounded risk-free short-term rate.**

Then, we obtain

$$E_t(M_{t,t+h} g_{t+h})$$

$$= E_t \left\{ \exp[-r(t, 1) \ldots - r(t + h - 1, 1)] \right.$$

$$\left. \times \frac{M_{t,t+1}}{E_t(M_{t,t+1})} \cdots \frac{M_{t+h-1,t+h}}{E_{t+h-1}(M_{t+h-1,t+h})} g_{t+h} \right\}$$

$$= E_t^Q \left\{ \exp[-r(t, 1) \ldots - r(t + h - 1, 1)] g_{t+h} \right\},$$

where the **risk-neutral probability** Q admits (for time-to-maturity h) the density $\dfrac{M_{t,t+1}}{E_t(M_{t,t+1})} \cdots \dfrac{M_{t+h-1,t+h}}{E_{t+h-1}(M_{t+h-1,t+h})}$ with respect to the initial probability distribution, called the historical distribution or physical distribution.

Corollary B.1. *Under the (dynamic) AAO condition, the asset price can be written as*

$$P(t, g) = E_t^Q \left\{ \exp[-r(t, 1) \ldots - r(t + h - 1, 1)] g_{t+h} \right\},$$

where $r(t, 1)$ *is the short-term risk-free rate at time* t *and* Q *is a risk-neutral distribution.*

The expression in Corollary B.1 corresponds to the second normalization discussed in Section B.2.1. The risk-neutral probability Q simply defines the normalized prices of appropriate Arrow-Debreu securities and is not unique in an incomplete market.

Further Reading

Chamberlain, G., and M. Rothschild (1983). "Arbitrage, Factor Structure and Mean-Variance Analysis in Large Asset Markets," *Econometrica*, 52, 1281–1304.

Hansen, L., and S. Richard (1987): "The Role of Conditioning Information in Deducing Testable Restrictions Implied by Dynamic Asset Pricing Models," *Econometrica*, 55, 587–613.

Harrison, M., and D. Kreps (1979). "Martingales and Arbitrage in Multiperiod Securities Markets," *Journal of Economic Theory*, 20, 381–408.

Ross, S. (1976). "The Arbitrage Theory of Capital Asset Pricing," *Journal of Economic Theory*, 13, 341–360.

B.3 Risk Measures

The analysis of risky investments is based on quantities summarizing the risk, called risk measures. They can be used not only for descriptive purposes, but also for portfolio management, pricing, or definition of the required capital in a regulatory perspective.

The variance has long been the most successful measure of risk in finance [see, however, Roy (1952)]. It is the basis of mean-variance portfolio management (see Review B.1) and of the idea that the price of a risky asset is equal to its expected value plus a risk premium function of this variance. However, as a measure of risk the variance (or the standard deviation) has some drawbacks. Surveys among professionals have shown that this risk measure was not so well understood. Moreover, it does not correctly capture the extreme risks or the possible skew in the risk distribution. This has led regulatory authorities to suggest the **Value-at-Risk** (VaR) as the new measure of risk in Basel 1 and 2 for banks, as well as in Solvency 1 and 2 for insurance companies. The aim of this review is to discuss some properties of the VaR and of its extensions – the distortion risk measures (DRMs).

Let us consider a random variable X, typically a loss and profit (L&P) variable (i.e., the opposite of a portfolio value) or the total liabilities in a balance. This variable has a distribution with a quantile function $q_\alpha(X)$ defined by

$$P[X \leq q_\alpha(X)] = \alpha,$$

for level $\alpha \in (0, 1)$. Such a quantile function, called VaR in the regulation, characterizes the distribution of $L\&P$ variable X.

Definition B.1. *A risk measure $R(X)$ is a scalar function of the distribution of X, used to measure the risk.*

Of course, not every function of this distribution is appropriate for measuring risk. Different conditions or axioms have been introduced in the literature to restrict the set of appropriate risk measures. We discuss next several of these axioms.

B.3.1 The Unit of a Risk Measure

Unit Axiom: *The risk measure has the same unit as variable X.*

This condition is important if we want to use directly the risk measure as a level of reserve to hedge the risk or as the cost (price) of this risk. For instance, the VaR and standard deviation satisfy the unit axiom, but not the variance. This axiom also shows the importance of defining ex ante the currency, (e.g., dollars or Euros) in which the risk measures are computed.

B.3.2 Deterministic Risk

Certainty Axiom: *If $X = c$ is known, then $R(X) = c$.*

This axiom shows that the search for a measure interpretable as a level of reserve or as a price has to account not only for the uncertainty of the value but also for its "expected value." This condition is satisfied by the VaR, but not by the standard deviation.

B.3.3 The Homogeneity

Homogeneity Axiom: *We have $R(\lambda X) = \lambda R(X)$, $\forall \lambda > 0$.*

This condition is satisfied by both the VaR and the standard deviation. If $R(X)$ is seen as a price, the homogeneity axiom implies that the unitary price of an asset does not depend on the demanded quantity.

B.3.4 Risk Ordering

There exist two main notions of risk ordering in the literature, both based on expected utility.

Definition B.2. *Let us consider two L&P variables X and Y. Variable X stochastically dominates variable Y at order 1 (resp. 2) if and only if*

$$E[U(-X)] \geq E[U(-Y)],$$

for any increasing (resp. increasing concave) function U.

The stochastic dominance at order j, for $j = 1, 2$, defines a preference ordering on the $L\&P$ variable X or, equivalently, on the $P\&L$ variable $-X$.

Risk Ordering Axiom: *We have $R(X) \leq R(Y)$ if X stochastically dominates Y.*

This condition on the risk measure is stronger with dominance at order 2 than with dominance at order 1.

B.3.5 Comonotonic Risks

Two risks X and Y are comonotonous if they are increasing functions of a same underlying risk Z: $X = a(Z)$, $Y = b(Z)$, say. Intuitively, they are increasing functions of a common risk factor.

Axiom of Comonotonic Risks: $R(X + Y) = R(X) + R(Y)$, *if X and Y are comonotonous.*

This axiom has been introduced to define reserve levels (or prices) in a way compatible with no arbitrage (see Review B.2). We have

$$X - K = (X - K)^+ - (K - X)^+,$$

with $(X - K)^+ = \max(X - K, 0)$. Thus, the payoff is decomposed into the payoff of a European call with strike K and the payoff of a short European put with the same strike. We expect to obtain

$$R(X - K) = R[(X - K)^+] + R[-(K - X)^+]$$

to avoid a perfect arbitrage by means of reserves, whereas no arbitrage exists on the market.

The axiom on comonotonic risks is important and implies a first characterization of risk measures.

Property B.2. *The risk measures satisfying the axiom of comonotonic risks, the certainty axiom, and the compatibility with first-order stochastic dominance can be written as*

$$R(X) = \int_0^1 q_\alpha(X) dH(\alpha),$$

where H is the cumulative distribution function of a probability distribution on $[0, 1]$.

Measure H is called a distortion measure and R a **distortion risk measure** (DRM). A distortion risk measure is simply a weighted combination of VaR at several quantile levels. The VaR at level α is itself a DRM that chooses the point mass at α as distortion measure.

When the distortion measure is the uniform distribution on $(\alpha, 1)$, the DRM reduces to the expected shortfall (ES) at level α, given by

$$ES_\alpha(X) = E[X|X > q_\alpha(X)] = \frac{1}{1-\alpha} \int_\alpha^1 q_u(X)du. \qquad (1.1)$$

Corollary B.2. *A DRM is compatible with second-order stochastic dominance if and only if the distortion c.d.f. H is convex.*
The expected shortfall satisfies this condition, but not the VaR.

B.3.6 Subadditivity

Subadditivity Axiom: *For any risks X and Y, we have*

$$R(X + Y) \leq R(X) + R(Y).$$

The DRMs with a convex distortion measure satisfy this axiom, but not the VaR, even if we observe $VaR(X + Y) \leq VaR(X) + VaR(Y)$ for the portfolios risks encountered in practice.

The subadditivity condition is a source of debate among academics and practitioners, especially when it is used as a crude tool for fixing regulatory reserves. Let us assume that a regulator demands that each bank $i = 1, \ldots, n$ fixes its required capital at $R(X_i)$, where R is a subadditive risk measure (for instance, the expected shortfall at 95%). Then

$$\sum_{i=1}^n R(X_i) \geq R(\sum_{i=1}^n X_i).$$

At a first glance, the regulator oversizes the capital required to hedge the global risk $X = \sum_{i=1}^n X_i$; that is, the regulator seems to follows a prudential approach. However, with such a principle, we also have

$$R(X_1 + X_2) \leq R(X_1) + R(X_2),$$

which is a strong incentive for banks 1 and 2 to merge to diminish the level of required capital. Thus, this a priori prudential approach can have negative consequences.

The risk measures satisfying the certainty axiom, the homogeneity axiom, and the subadditivity axiom and that are compatible with second-order stochastic dominance are called **coherent risk measures**. The coherent risk measures can be written as

$$R(X) = \sup_{H \in \mathcal{H}} DRM_H(X),$$

that is, as the supremum of a set of convex DRM risk measures.

Further Reading

Acerbi, C., and D. Tasche (2002). "Expected Shortfall: A Natural Coherent Alternative to Value-at-Risk," *Economic Notes*, 31, 379–388.

Artzner, P., F. Delbaen, J. Eber, and D. Heath (1997). "Thinking Coherently," *Risk*, 10, 68–71.

Gourieroux, C., and A. Monfort (2013). "Allocating Systematic and Unsystematic Risks in a Regulatory Perspective," International Journal of Theoretical and Applied Finance, 16, 1350041 (20 pages).

Kusuoka, S. (2001). "On Law Invariant Coherent Risk Measures," *Advances in Mathematical Economics*, 3, 83–95.

Roy, A. (1952). "Safety First and the Holding of Assets," *Econometrica*, 20, 431–449.

Wang, S. (1996). "Premium Calculation by Transforming the Layer Premium Density," *ASTIN Bulletin*, 26, 71–92.

Wang, S., V. Young, and H. Panjer (1997). "Axiomatic Characterization of Insurance Prices," *Insurance: Mathematics and Economics*, 21, 173–183.

Index

Printed in the United States
by Baker & Taylor Publisher Services